HEART OF A FAN

The Life & Career of
Bob Powel

By

Tom Baker

ISBN-13: 978-1514303474

ISBN-10: 1514303477

Dedicated to all FANS, *that group of worthy, neglected individuals who, by their blind faith and devotion, enable the stars to stay on top.*

CONTENTS

HEART OF A FAN

50 Years In & Out of Country Music

The life and career of Bob Powel, by latter-day friend
and companion, Tom Baker.

Foreword

When I proposed writing Bob Powel's life story in February, 2013, I was unsure how the esteemed country music DJ and journalist would react, but he agreed readily, and, throughout the interviewing process, remained, with a few exceptions, good-humoured and co-operative. He seemed to truly enjoy recounting his rich experiences, both within and without country music – from tentative beginnings in journalism in 1965 to the last radio broadcast in 1990. From idyllic childhood in rural Canada, to the somewhat isolated final days in Sidcup, Kent. As he said to me many times, "I'm fortunate in that I've enjoyed everything I've ever done in life." I, too, relished the challenge of trying to reproduce in print the life of someone I'd admired from afar. Being a novice, I'd allowed myself a generous two and a quarter years to complete the project, and, halfway into this, was well on target to meet the proposed publishing date.

Then came the tragic events of 8 May, 2014, shocking his friends and associates, many of whom had been out of touch with him for a long time. His action shocked me, too, for he did not have a gloomy or melancholy disposition, something reflected in the general tenor of the book. It also hardly gave the project his seal of approval. My immediate reaction, understandable, in the circumstances, was to scrap the whole thing. To continue seemed not only irrelevant, but almost in poor taste. Feeling obliged to at least produce something, I flirted with the idea of going through the interview tapes again and presenting them in pure 'Question & Answer' form. Another option was to start an entirely new book, focussing more on our three and a half year friendship, but neither proved viable.

And so the situation remained, until my eventual realisation that, by not proceeding, friends and fans' genuine interest and empathy was not being addressed and there could never be proper closure. For these reasons, and because I want Bob to be remembered positively, I decided to press on and hope that the final result would have earned his blessing and approval.

Obviously, there are amendments and additions to the original as it stood at the time of his death. Not having looked at the book since that date, when finally doing so, in March this year, I was able to view it from a clearer perspective, and make appropriate changes.

In tackling this project, you could argue that I've been handicapped, compared to, say, Faron Young biographer, Diane Diekman, who, although similarly inexperienced, enjoyed the advantage of introductions to many stars and industry 'insiders'. But apart from the fact that I don't move in those circles, Bob, judging by the silent response from Nashville (ironic, considering the vociferous support he gave to so many artistes in his day), seemed largely forgotten by the country music fraternity.

So, just as only a small percentage (7%) of *London Country* shows are known to survive on tape, despite my best efforts, I may have barely scratched the surface of Bob's life – his reputation spread far and wide and I know for a fact there are many stories out there that did not make their way to me. However, we can only work with what we have, and I've tried to paint the fullest picture possible with the tools at my disposal. Having sat listening to him for many hours, I believe that still represents a considerable amount.

Furthermore, this is not merely a ghost-written autobiography, and I was privileged to be granted telephone and/or email interviews with many of Bob's closest friends and work associates, as well as family members. In alphabetical order, these are:-

David Allan, Craig Baguley, Irvine Brookes, Tony Byworth, Bryan Chalker, Neil Coppendale, John Cowling, Arie den Dulk, Alan & Jean Earle, Shaun Greenfield, Goff Greenwood, Frank Jennings, Stan Laundon, Dave McAleer, Nancy McDougal, Jim Marshall, Marie O'Connell, Terence Pettigrew, Jon Philibert, Ernie Reed, Dave Travis and Dave Turner.

I thank them all for their input, whether large or small. I extend particular gratitude to Tony Byworth for agreeing to cast a professional eye over my work – no routine task, given his close involvement in the subject's life – but just the sort of boost I needed, having toiled blindly for so long. Also, appreciation to Alan and Jean Earle, who helped in a variety of ways, not least by supplying *Four-On-The-Floor*'s magazine, containing the all-important Don Ford interview. Without a home computer, I depend on public ones, so grateful thanks are due to the staff at Sidcup, Blackfen, Eltham and New Eltham libraries – especially Martin Stone – for technical advice and assistance, imparted with unfailing patience and courtesy throughout my many visits.

Heart of a Fan was chosen as the title of this book because when Bob put his enthusiasm to something, he did so wholeheartedly, and a key motivation in its writing was the fact that when we met, that wonderful enthusiasm, as real and alive in him as ever, was being applied to things like online solitaire. It seemed a waste when the wealth of experience and depth of knowledge accumulated in him through the years might be shared more widely.

The target publication date of May, 2015 is also significant, as it represents the 50th anniversary of his first ever trip to Nashville, the details of which, when submitted by him to an obscure English country music publication, led to his distinguished career in journalism, which, in turn, led to his much-cherished radio show.

Bob once told me that many guests, recalling their *London Country* experience, described it as a "unique experience." Well, as a newcomer, I'll settle for less, and if the general consensus is that this tome is faithful not only to the facts but also to his unique spirit, then I'll be satisfied. He undoubtedly had within him the truth that lies at the heart of country music and my aim has been to capture and convey that truth. Whether he emerges as victim or villain is for the reader to decide. From my viewpoint, I found him to be perfectly open, honest and accessible at all times.

Tom Baker, June, 2015.

Introduction

Fire Down Below

Monday, 14 August, 1950: the day began like any other in the tiny Canadian village of Tadoussac, 120mi/193km north east of Quebec City. Situated at the confluence of the Saguenay and mighty St. Lawrence rivers, with a population of less than one thousand, the area's main claim to fame is that, being France's first and – especially in the 17th century – most important trading post on the mainland of New France, it is the oldest continuously inhabited European settlement in Quebec, the oldest surviving French settlement in the Americas, and the site of the oldest Christian mission in Canada.

Its name, deriving from the two round and sandy hills bordering the west side of the village, is attributed to the indigenous Montagnais tribe whose original word, *Totouskak*, means (depending on the translation) "udders" or "breasts". According to other interpretations, it could also mean "place of lobsters" or "place where the ice is broken" (from the Montagnais *shashuko*). A further description is provided by the Mi'kmaq people who frequented the territory in the second half of the 16th century, their own name for the area being *Gtatosag* ("among the rocks").

Despite its history as an important settlement and fur-trading centre (the site was chosen to profit from its location at the mouth of the St. Lawrence), by the 1950s, little evidence of its illustrious past remained, and then, as now, it was chiefly known as a tourist destination, owing to the rugged beauty of the Saguenay fjord and its facilities for marine mammal and whale watching. The entire area is, in fact, rural, or still in a wilderness state, with several federal and provincial natural parks and preserves competing for prestigious spots. (Tadoussac encompasses the first marine national park of Canada, the nearest urban agglomeration being Saguenay, 62mi/100km west). The area has two further claims to fame: it boasts one of the oldest wooden chapels in North America (*St. Anne's* – built with birch bark by French Recollet missionaries in 1617, destroyed by an Iroquois raid in 1661 and rebuilt 1747) and, in the Saguenay, one of the deepest rivers.

This, then, was the environment in which a cute, tussle-haired youngster with freckled features spent the majority of his summers, and, on the day in question, witnessed an event that, as well as being the most famous – or infamous – in the town's history, remained engrained in his memory for life. The drama was slow to unfold…

1730hrs: as usual, a sizeable crowd had gathered wharf-side to view the docking of the *S.S. Quebec*, one of four steamships operated by Canadian Steamship Lines (the others being the identical *Tadoussac* and *St. Lawrence* and the slightly smaller *Richelieu*). Known as the 'Great White Fleet', they had been built in 1928 and, from the 1930s, had offered throughout the summer luxury cruises along the St. Lawrence and Saguenay rivers, departing from Montreal and stopping at Quebec City, Murray Bay and Tadoussac, where CSL owned the local hotel.

The docking procedure, although generally smooth, could vary in length. On this particular day, it was completed in record time – a miracle, which almost certainly saved lives, as a fire had been raging below decks since erupting in a linen room with the liner still four miles from shore. The first clue townspeople had of the tragedy was a dense plume of smoke streaming from the ship's upper deck, followed by the sight of a seaman desperately attempting to extinguish a fire on deck with a hose. It soon became obvious they had a full-scale disaster on their hands, as crew members, emergency workers and anyone brave enough to volunteer struggled to deal with the task of rescuing and comforting dazed, injured and dying passengers.

Unable to offer much in the way of assistance, our befreckled young friend, aged just seven, stood among the crowd, transfixed at the scene of devastation before him. Of the 462 people aboard that day, seven perished, many more were injured and the *S.S. Quebec* never sailed again. (It later transpired that the fire had been deliberately started and the sprinkler system sabotaged.)

Although obviously not realising it at the time, this event was to be a defining moment of the youngster's life, the fire representing the furnace that burned fiercely within him, eager and aching to blaze a trail away from the cosy, protected Tadoussac existence – and, from the very beginning, plain and simple country music was to be his vehicle of choice, in whatever capacity it took.

Chapter 1

From Bickley to Sillery: 1943-55

Hey, Good Lookin' ("I'm free and ready…")[1]

Robert Harcourt Powel ("one L of a Powel,"[2] as he liked to describe himself) was born in Beckenham Hospital, Kent, England, on 16 January, 1943; the second child – and only son – of Harcourt ('Harky') Powel and wife, Bessie Mae Davidson[3] (nee Sharpe), who, because

---

[1] *Hey, Good Lookin'* – Written and originally recorded by Hank Williams, although – supposedly – based on an obscure, similarly titled Cole Porter composition, this became a No.1 country hit for Hank in 1951. Others who have recorded the song include Jo Stafford & Frankie Laine (No.21 pop, the same year), Ray Charles (1962), the Mavericks (No.73, 1992) and Jimmy Buffet (No.8, 2004).

[2] "One L of a Powel" – Samuel Powel, the ancestor referred to in para. 4, was a master carpenter as well as Mayor. His wife knocked off the second L of his surname after discovering another local man with the same name.

[3] Bessie Mae Davidson – The surname 'Davidson' was included among Betty's forenames in honour of a local wealthy family, who, it was hoped, might bestow financial favours in return (they didn't!).

the only other 'Bessie' she knew was a cow(!), preferred to be called Betty.

Parenthood came relatively late to the household, Betty having given birth to daughter, Marylee, just 18 months earlier at the advanced age of 41 (four years younger than her husband). Now, the addition of a son made the family complete. Although living at *Lauriston House* [4] in nearby Bickley, both parents had, in fact, been born in the Americas – Harcourt in Philadelphia, Pennsylvania, on 6 March 1896 and Betty in Hawkesbury, Ontario (50mi/80km west of Montreal), on 3 May 1900, the former a descendant of 17th century Welsh settlers.

The surname Powel, usually spelt with two 'L's, is, in fact, one of the most ancient in that country. Sometimes said to mean, "Son of the servant of St. Paul", it is more likely to be a patronymic of the first name, Howell (from Hywell – *"Lordly"*), the Old Celtic term "ap" meaning "son of", hence ap Howell, which then converted to Powell. The county with the highest frequency of this surname is Breconshire, although the name is spread liberally throughout Wales (some even migrating to Ireland).

Tracing back the Powel lineage to its furthest and most prestigious American point, we find one Samuel Powel (1738-1793), Bob's great-great-great-grandfather, who has the distinction of being the last Mayor of Philadelphia under British rule and the first under American. He was a next-door neighbour of Benjamin Franklin and near-

---

[4] Built around 1868 as *Sunnyside*, this sizeable house was part of the first phase of George Wythes' Bickley Park estate. Divided into flats in the 1930s when it gained the name *Lauriston*, its most famous resident was the spy, George Blake, who had a flat here for a short while prior to his arrest in 1961. Bob's friend and fellow Thailand visitor, Dave Travis, also lived here for a time. In 1989, it was replaced by a large, purpose-built private nursing home, retaining the name *Lauriston*.

neighbour and close personal friend of George Washington, with whom his wife, Elizabeth (nee Willing), was rumoured to have had an affair; unsubstantiated then and unlikely to be proved now! What is certain is that this formidable lady exerted considerable influence over America's first President, to the extent of convincing him to run for a second term of office, arguing that only his stature and integrity could hold the fledgling nation together (he ran and easily won a second term). When the Washingtons moved, the Powels purchased the majority of their furniture, which is on permanent display at *Powel House*[5] in Philadelphia. After Samuel Powel died of yellow fever in September, 1793, his descendants subsequently made a fortune in the iron industry, before promptly losing it again with the advent of steel.

As for Harcourt, he was the youngest of four children. Brothers Herbert and Robert were both victims of warfare, the former dying (as part of the Canadian Army) at the *Battle of Ypres* in World War I, the latter never recovering from the effects of gassing in the same conflict, seeing out his days at a home in California. Sister Banney, who later lived in Newark, New Jersey, completed the quartet.

Betty Sharpe was also one of four: two boys and two girls born to James Peter Sharpe (1864-1939) and wife, Anne Jane, nee Abernethy (1861-1938). The Sharpe surname (with variant spellings, all meaning "quick, smart") can be traced back to the Scottish border region immediately south of Edinburgh, although James was actually born and brought up in Hawkesbury. His wife, however, grew up in Stonehaven, 14mi/22km south of

---

[5] *Powel House* – Situated in the Society Hill neighbourhood of Philadelphia, Pennsylvania, this elegant Georgian brick mansion, built in 1765 by merchant and shipmaster, Charles Stedman, and sold to Samuel Powel four years later for £3,150, is reputed to be America's finest existing Georgian colonial townhouse.

Aberdeen, on the icy north east coast of Scotland. Immigrating to Canada in 1890, the Abernethy family, headed by father, Archibald, soon settled in Hawkesbury, where Anne met her future husband, the pair marrying on 22 November, 1894. The Scottish connection possibly explains why, as a baby, Bob was rocked to sleep to the soothing strains of *Flow Gently, Sweet Afton*,[6] sung by his mother.

Betty, elder sister Georgena, and brothers Archibald and James McDonald (known as 'Donnie'), have all long since passed on, the latter being last to do so, in 1991. However, his daughter – Bob's cousin – Nancy, who grew up in Westmount, London, Ontario, and who now resides at North Bay, 260mi/418km due north, in the same province, remembers her childhood fondly: describing herself as "a typical teenager," one "oblivious to world events," the situation "all changed in 1963," the year of the first FLQ (Front de Liberation du Quebec) bombings. As an affluent and predominantly Anglophone region of the city, Westmount suffered more than its share of devastation, mail boxes being particular targets. Nancy recalls:-

"I was in High School and we had a number of evacuations. I remember walking home and crossing the street to avoid passing a mailbox. I could hear the explosions as the army purposely detonated the bombs."

Continuing throughout the 1960s, the atrocities reached a climax in October, 1970, leading to Canada's

---

[6] *Flow Gently, Sweet Afton* – 1837 musical adaptation by Jonathan E. Spilman of a lyrical poem describing the Afton Water in Ayrshire, Scotland, written by Robert Burns in 1791.

only peacetime use of the *War Measures Act* (at the direction of Prime Minister Pierre Trudeau). This resulted in 3,000 searches and 497 detentions, the long-term effects being loss of support for the violent wing of the Quebec separatist movement and increased support for political means of attaining independence.

One interesting piece of historical data from this side of the family concerns Betty's great grandfather, James Thomson (1795-1885), who, as well as being related to renowned Scottish poet, Robert Burns, served on the British Royal Navy frigate, *Undaunted*, which, under Admiral Thomas Usher, accompanied Napoleon Bonaparte to Elba in 1814. A newspaper clipping of the day describes how, "at Portoferraio, he (Thomson) stood sentry over the fallen conqueror of Europe and shared in the reward he gave to the men of the Royal Marines serving on board the *Undaunted* frigate."

Returning to Harcourt and Betty: they met in the small town of Grand-Mere, situated on the St-Maurice River, 75mi/120km west of Quebec City, where the young man was employed as a salesman for Price Bros., the third largest pulp merchants in Canada (later taken over by Gulf Oil and currently trading as Price Paper). Harcourt had originally worked for rival firm St-Maurice Paper Co. – possibly to avoid accusations of nepotism, since there were family connections to Price Bros., his mother's sister, Amelia Blanche, being married to company president Sir William Price. In fact, Mrs. Powel (nee Smith) – plus children, including Harcourt – lived with the Prices for many years, which caused considerable friction, owing to her unfortunate habit of interfering. Later, this same lady put a strain on Harcourt's own marriage, insisting that she be addressed by her daughter-in-law as Mrs. Powel (although Harcourt apparently worshipped her throughout).

On Sir William's death by an avalanche of mud and clay

at the company sawmill in Arvida in 1924, son Arthur Clifford (always called, for unknown reasons, 'Coosie') took over presidency of the company and immediately set about bringing cousin 'Harky' into the family business. Perhaps the offer was too good to refuse, or Coosie's powers of persuasion too strong to resist. Whatever the reason – nepotism or no nepotism – Harcourt made the move and never looked back, remaining on the best of terms with his cousin for life. It's unclear exactly when Betty appeared on the scene, but it seems likely to have been shortly before her 'beau' received the call to be Price Bros.' 'Man in Europe.' If she expected him to marry and take her with him, she was disappointed – he was young, attractive and sophisticated, and enjoyed his freewheeling lifestyle a little too much for that.

So, around the mid-1930s, newly installed as vice-president of the Sales Division, Harcourt Powel departed for England – *Lamorbey House*,[7] Sidcup, to be precise, on the London-Kent border, where, far from home, his thoughts soon began turning to romance; he was rarely seen without a pretty girl on his arm. Yet, beneath the frivolity, he seems to have nurtured a serious side, one that yearned for the deeper commitment of marriage. Why else would he have maintained a lengthy correspondence with the girl he left behind in Grand-Mere?

By Bob's own admission, Betty was no beauty – nevertheless, she must have possessed an innate charm or some endearing personality trait, for, over subsequent months – and years – Harky bombarded her with reams of

---

[7] *Lamorbey House* – Grade II listed building said to have been built c.1750 but presumably re-cased c.1840 in Elizabethan style. In Harcourt's time, a long-stay hotel, today it is used as an adult education centre by *Rose Bruford College* drama students whose alumni include Freddie Jones, Gary Oldman and Tom Baker (no relation!)

verse pledging undying devotion. But the young lady was in no hurry. Aware of her husband-to-be's philandering reputation and convinced he would never settle down, she kept him waiting. And waiting. And waiting. If it was a game, it was a dangerous one. Eventually, however, love triumphed: arriving in London in June, 1939 without prior notice, she so surprised and delighted her smitten suitor, they became man and wife within 24 hours – which caused problems later on, as one of the conditions for granting a licence was that both parties needed to have been resident in the country for at least 48 hours (prompting Bob's latter-day acknowledgment that, "on those occasions in life when I've been called a 'no-good b******,' my accusers may have been at least half right!")

But to return to his infanthood: young 'Bobby', as he was affectionately addressed by all (except Uncle Coosie's wife, the part-Native American, Ray, to whom he was always 'Robert'), although a bright, bonny baby, failed to make an immediate impact on his Kentish environs for the simple reason that, before reaching the age of three and upon cessation of wartime hostilities in 1945, he and the rest of the Powel clan headed back to Canada[8] and another dwelling at the heart of the logging industry. On this occasion, the large, imposing 'Rectory', at No. 2058 St. Louis Road, Sillery, a city (as opposed to town, its population exceeding 10,000) then just west of Quebec City, now officially amalgamated into it. Named after a wealthy 17th century French diplomat who renounced his worldly goods to become a Catholic priest, the port, not much larger than Grand-Mere, served as the Powels' base for the next 10 years.

---

[8] The family travelled on *The Thanet Head*, which has a couple of distinctions. It was: a) the first ship sunk in WWII, and b) the first to take passengers after the war. Bob recalled there being exactly twelve people aboard that day, the maximum number allowed without the necessity of a doctor.

For Bobby, it provided the first real home he'd had, or remembers having; the place where he formed his first friendships and where he received his initial education. Not that master Powel distinguished himself academically at tiny Bishop Mountain School, situated just at the bottom of his road (and now a schools administration centre). In fact, failing his Grade 6 examination at the age of 12, he was scheduled to be kept back a year until a return to England spared him the humiliation – and, unfortunately, his class behaviour was no better. As teacher Mrs. Langellet reminded him during a caning: she had needed to do this only once before in her career and the recipient then had been none other than himself – a pity, really, as she was quite fond of the boy, and he of her. Still, at least he had not suffered the indignity of bending over, the punishment being administered to the hand.

It seems that, while in many respects a typical child – one who, according to cousin Nancy McDougal, "liked to play with his little cars" – there was, from the outset, a dual aspect to his personality: firstly, the cute, freckle-faced youngster, a favourite of everyone in town, someone considered so attractive he was chosen to model outfits for the local tailor at the tender age of ten; and, then, the slightly brattish individual who insisted on having his own way, causing havoc and stress to those around him, especially his loving – and not-so-young – parents. Bob even went so far as to say that, had he the charge of his formative self, there might well have been a strangulation in this most civilised and peaceful of places, but he was surely exaggerating – or was he...?

A typical example of his obnoxious behaviour – and uncanny knack of emerging as wronged victim – occurred the day Dad was driving family and friends out to their holiday home in Tadoussac. From the moment of departure, the group's most boisterous member began causing trouble – and the further they went the worse it got. Eventually, two miles from the ferry crossing at Bay-Saint-Catherine, Mr. Powel, unable to take any more, braked hard and ordered the youngster out, with instructions to walk the rest of the way. The tearful lad had progressed barely 20 yards when a Catholic priest who happened to be travelling the same road stopped to investigate and, hearing the boy's sorry tale, motioned him aboard. Reaching the ferry first, this dutiful cleric, upon the parents' arrival, delivered to the father a stern ticking off, much to the pleasure of young Bobby, who, needless to say, acted like the cat who got the cream for the remainder of the journey!

Another family outing provided an illustration of the youngster's tenacity (or stubbornness), the setting on this occasion being a ski resort just outside Quebec City. Nearing the end of a long, enjoyable, but exhausting day on the slopes, the Powels were ready to leave – all except one… This individual seemed hell-bent on conquering a particular run that had frustrated him throughout the afternoon, owing to a nasty bump halfway down that sent him flying each time. Finally, with the family's patience wearing thin, he, on his twentieth (or thereabouts) attempt, managed to clear the offending ridge and land safely on the other side, prompting the triumphant cry, "Dad, I did it!" Whereupon, through sheer delirium or whatever, he lost his balance and fell flat on his face!

Bob: "We gave up after that, but at least I got over the bump, which was the main idea!" It's not known whether, on the homeward journey, he was hero, villain – or clown.

Joker or not, his presence was certainly appreciated the day, during the family's annual Tadoussac vacation, Dad and work colleague Ted Collister, were attempting to remove a door from its hinges. Having disconnected all relevant joints and screws, the object, despite their heaving, would just not fall free. Up stepped the precocious onlooker, and, prodding a solitary finger at an –

obviously highly strategic – point, condemned the offending article to the floor. This was simply too much for Mr. Powel, who, although a man not normally given to overt displays of emotion, instantly – rather like the door – fell to the ground in hysterics. Such is the effect his son seemed to produce on occasion. However, no one was laughing the day this unwitting hero became a real-life one…

It happened when a friend got stuck in what appeared to be stable mudflats. Without hesitation, citizen Powel, junior, did what any right-thinking individual would, wading in to pull the victim to safety, earning the cheers of all concerned. Only later, when it was pointed out to him he had entered highly dangerous quicksand, did the full implications of his action hit home, prompting the thought that in future perhaps it might be wiser to curb his more heroic impulses.

Sillery may not have offered much in the way of entertainment for youngsters, but, being a natural optimist, Bob wasn't complaining – besides, you created your own fun back then. A good day out was considered to be a visit to the Maple Syrup Shack, whose patrons were invited to collect sap in buckets from taps connected to maple trees before emptying the contents into a large barrel tied to a horse's back. Once full, the barrel was heated in a furnace to produce syrup, which in turn was poured onto the snow outside to create a delicious sweet dessert, although, for convenience, Bob preferred the more readily available (albeit illicit), liquid alternative on offer at the nuns' convent across the road.

Then there was the improvised skating-rink: Dad's wooden boards (obtained through his work) laid out in the front garden, scraped, hosed down and polished to create the perfect surface for dozens of neighbourhood kids to display their roller-skating – and other – skills. Hockey was Bob's favourite, making up in enthusiasm what he lacked in talent. One can only imagine the bruised ankles of the poor kids, as they limped away from the Powel residence, probably ruing the day they ever set foot in the place! This exhilarating pastime led to one of the most alarming incidents of his childhood, when, on an icy winter's day, following a particularly energetic performance at Bishop Mountain School, Bob, perspiring heavily, suddenly became unable to move: his sweat had frozen solid on him! All he could do was lie still on the spot, which happened to be a main road, until, seen by a passing motorist, he was taken home where a hot bath thawed him out.

Such incidents, along with others – like warm hands stuck solidly to metal railings and feet lacerated by tiny slivers of ice – were commonplace then, possibly less so today, with improved clothing. Nevertheless, he would not swap his childhood environmental experiences for anything – especially those of the wintertime, a seasonal preference that also prevailed among his pals, as a snap poll on the eve of his departure for England proved. Something about the snow obviously created a magical appeal to young minds and hearts,[9] and this was never truer than at Christmas time, usually spent by the Powels at cousin Susan Smith's grandmother's home – followed by a visit to Uncle Coosie's scenically situated residence, beside the St. Lawrence River, at Wolfesfield, on the far side of Quebec.[10]

---

[9] An event Bob would have enjoyed just once as a youngster (owing to his return to England) was the *Quebec Winter Carnival*, held each February from 1955 to the present day. With attractions that include skiing, snow rafting, ice sculptures, snow slides and outdoor shows, it remains a hugely popular event, traditionally timed to end on the feast of *Mardi Gras* ('Shrove' Tuesday), immediately before the 40-day fasting observance of Lent.

[10] At one stage, Coosie moved away temporarily from this house to Brockville, Ontario. Upon discovering the Council was

Bob remembers these family get-togethers as lavish affairs overflowing with fine cuisine and festive fun. In particular, he recalls the deluxe Christmas crackers Coosie would order from London's Fortnum & Mason store, containing watches and other items well in excess of the standard plastic nick-nacks! He and Marylee also did very nicely, present-wise, even if Mr and Mrs. Powel were once accused of not loving their only son, because "Santa brings me lots of gifts but you give me none!" (The fact that his birthday fell shortly after the festive season, when funds – and gifts – tended to be sparser, increased the boy's sense of injustice.)

The outdoor life brought with it additional dangers, unassociated with snow. One day, walking home from school, and just yards from his front door, Bob somehow managed to put his hand into a wasp's nest, incurring sixty stings, and, for once, his parents were not around to deal with the emergency. Luckily, neighbour Mrs. Billings came to the rescue with a hot bath, on this occasion one containing plenty of disinfectant. Unsurprisingly, the boy was more than wary of wasps for a considerable time afterwards. Another disinfectant bath followed his only childhood encounter with a skunk. He never discovered exactly what he'd done wrong, but its retribution – the direct spraying of a foul-smelling vapour ("an unbelievable odour") delivered in customary fashion with upturned tail – was something he would not forget in a hurry, the venom being so potent that his clothes had to be burnt immediately.

Fires of a different nature were occasionally created in Tadoussac for social reasons. Invariably, these took place in front of Uncle Coosie's holiday home, *Pilot House*, overlooking the dark blue waters of the Saguenay River, at

---

imposing taxes on his old (empty) property, he razed it to the ground.

a point famous for attracting minke whales. Built on solid rock and acquired from his mother in 1949, the property later, in 1967, passed to his son, Harold. Back in the 1950s, however, participants young and old, having spent an afternoon gathering driftwood from the beach and arranging it in a large pile, would light the concoction as dusk fell, its warm glow providing a magical centrepiece to many a family get-together. Beloved French nanny Ylonde rather charmingly christened these conflagrations "fire bons" – but to everyone else they were bonfires.

Being a lively, inquisitive boy-about-town, Bobby sought out the company, not just of his peers, but of older, possibly more interesting residents, which is how he came to meet local wood-carver, Harry Doyle. Thrilled to observe a skilled craftsman at work, the lad gradually developed a keen appreciation of his art, so that, when the family decided they needed a new set of salad bowls, he had no hesitation in nominating his new-found friend for the job of moulding them. Ignoring the youngster's recommendation, Mrs. Powel instead opted for the high-quality service offered by prestigious Montreal merchants, T. Eaton. Back home, having made a satisfactory purchase, the good lady, at her son's urging, turned over one of the ornate items to discover, clearly engraved on the base, the maker's name: 'H. Doyle of Sillery.' Learning a lesson, she never again overlooked her neighbour's talents – nor her son's instincts.

Young Bobby's admiration for Harry Doyle was matched only by his love for the elderly French-Canadian buggy driver known to all as 'Sac de Papier' (paper bag), this representing his one and only 'swear' word. Their encounters followed a familiar routine: 'Sac' (an appropriate nickname since he was Tadous*sac*-based) parked his horse-driven buggy outside the Powel holiday home in anticipation of help from its young inhabitant, who, gladly offering, would subsequently hail disembarking boat passengers in their native – invariably English – tongue, inviting them aboard and generally playing the cheerful host/interpreter, thus earning his place 'up-front' for the duration of the journey, a pleasure no doubt enjoyed equally by both parties. Contemporary Benny Beattie, in his book, *Tadoussac: The Sands of Summer*, describes a typical dockside scene of this era:-

"The wharf was always congested at boat time (5.30pm). Most prominent were the buggies lined up in two rows, ready to take the tourists for a ride around the village to see the sights. First, they were taken along in front of the [Tadoussac] Hotel to the Indian Chapel. Then up past the Protestant Chapel, down to the fish hatchery at the ferry wharf, which for more than a century has been used for stocking lakes and streams with trout and salmon fingerlings. Turning round at the ferry wharf, the buggy would then retrace its way through the village and go up the golf course, where it would turn around and return to the boat. The drivers spoke only French and their passengers usually only English, so there was little conversation between them."

'Sac' gained further fame as the only local inhabitant to have been struck by lightning twice. In later years, Bob met up again with Harry. However, of his other, special friend, he learned only that, after the boats and buggies disappeared, he had invested successfully in a trucking business, leaving those carefree days spent traversing Tadoussac's rich landscape as just one more enduring memory of a quainter, gentler age.

Pets were very much a part of Bob's childhood, and, just as in *London Country* days he owned a dog named Casey, so now the politically-incorrectly named Sambo, a pup surplus to Uncle Coosie's requirements, became the first family pet – a canine wonder no less lively than his English counterpart but considerably more aristocratic, being pure Labrador. A favourite trick (which Bob swears no one in the family taught him) involved jumping up on the backs of unsuspecting victims and making off with their bobble-hats, which were then either deposited in some obscure place or chewed to such an extent Mrs. Powel felt she had no option but to offer replacements. Kept in a special tray, these would be presented to callers at regular intervals, along with an appropriate apology (although Bob felt some enterprising folk may have exploited this gesture!).

Sambo, being a much-cherished member of the family, received due loyalty and attention, never more so than on the day, while they were picnicking, he chased after something at the mouth of the Saguenay River, ending up stranded on a tiny strip of land at high tide, resulting in family members taking it in turns to wait with him until the waters subsided. They had owned the pet only a year when, with a return to England imminent, next-door neighbours the Rourkes agreed to take possession of him, subsequently having him neutered and sold to a farm, after which, sadly, nothing further was heard.

Another fun activity centred on the 'Chateau Frontenac' Hotel (the most illustrious in town, and still operating), which boasted an impressive toboggan run – purely for the use of paying customers, of course. However, there were ways around this. The procedure was that clients, having bought a ticket entitling them to a day's worth of rides, had, by mid-afternoon, usually grown a little bored with it – which is the moment Bob and his pals struck, or, rather, turned the situation to clever advantage. In their favour was the fact that they spoke English, guaranteeing speedy acquisition of the prized ticket from the (overwhelmingly American) tourists, while their French counterparts' more animated pleas merely produced puzzled looks. For the lucky few, hours of happy tobogganing ensued.

Perhaps, at this point, it's worth referring to some of the traditional French/English prejudices that exist at the heart of everyday life in Quebec. Basically, it's a case of: "no French, no progress" – which is why so many English speakers feel driven to depart, usually for Montreal, whose French-speaking inhabitants reverse the process (Bob himself was a non-French speaker). The previously mentioned Bishop Mountain School, for instance, closed for no reason other than that there were insufficient English-speaking pupils. And Bob talked of a visit to a local 'Marie Antoinette' 24-hour restaurant where, politely requesting an English menu, he was informed that no such thing was available, provoking the immediate – and justifiably indignant – response: "That's funny, you had one yesterday!" (When a different waitress had served him).

Then there was the case of a local radio station which, uniquely among the city's thirty-odd, broadcast in English. On hearing an announcement condemning listeners who objected to French-language music being played on the station, the ex-inhabitant protested strongly 'on-air' that as this was the only English language station in Quebec, listeners were perfectly justified in objecting, adding that he spoke "both as a radio presenter and lover of French-Canadian music."

Why things should be this way is one of life's mysteries, but its origins lie in attitudes going back centuries and so deeply engrained in the local psyche they would take a social upheaval of seismic proportions to shift.[11]

---

[11] The political situation in Quebec is something Bob did not often comment upon. However, in an interview with Don Ford in *Four-On-The-Floor* magazine (4 December 1976), he expressed his views: "It's an extremely complex situation and I've got a lot

Nevertheless, Bob (who, despite being born in England, spending by far the majority of his life there and holding a British passport, regarded himself as Canadian) felt no bitterness towards the area or its people. On the contrary, the province of Quebec was very special to him, and holiday retreat Tadoussac, in particular, a place that held the dearest of memories. He was not alone in his admiration – Laura Benet, writing in the *New York Times* on 31 August, 1930, calls it:-

"One of the loveliest of comparatively untouched Canadian villages, lying at the entrance to the Saguenay. Indian legend has it that this spot was the first in the world to emerge upon the face of the deep. The land has significant terraces of sand called Mamelons that rise a thousand feet above the waters, each representing a dropping away of the sea. The bay was a noted gathering place for numerous Indian tribes, both friendly and hostile."

Set amidst the rolling hills and unspoilt terrain of the Cote-Nord region, the area, a natural beauty spot and popular tourist destination to this day, has none of the hustle and bustle or business distractions found in Quebec City. More to the point, it's the place where the Powel

---

of sympathies for (French-Canadians). They are very honest, they admit that they are one of the best-treated minorities in the world and I suppose it is very frustrating for them to be a minority. But the great majority of them do not want separation, which, of course, would mean Quebec being a separate country. It is always the people who have the bombs and paint slogans on walls that get the publicity. The great majority want to be recognised as a known force but they certainly do not want separation. It is not as serious a situation as people make out and there has not been any violence for the past ten or fifteen years."

family – minus Dad, who, unless on vacation himself, managed to attend only at weekends – holidayed for 3-4 months each summer between 1948 and 1955, just as their forebears had done for close to a century. (Although they would generally drive down, for their first visit, they travelled via the ill-fated *SS Quebec*,[12] Bob's only trip aboard one of the 'Great White Fleet' of ships.)

With a hugely impressive summerhouse, *Fletcher Cottage* (still in use today), which Dad had purchased outright,[13] a

---

[12] During this journey, Bob got chatting to a fellow passenger, who asked him his name. When told, the passenger responded, "I have a son named 'Bobby.'" The man then enquired after Bob's sister's name. Hearing it was 'Marylee', he revealed he had a daughter, Mary. Finally, on being told Bob's surname, he responded, "That's *my* surname!" Bob related all this to his father, who barked back, "Tell him he's a liar!" Eventually, however, the two adults got together and it transpired that although not a relative, the man was a younger brother of one of Harcourt's closest friends, 'Chiney' Powell (no relation). The man also had a reputation for never laughing – but was in stitches over this incident!

[13] *Fletcher Cottage*. Mr. Powel announced – to everyone's delight – the purchase of this summerhouse (situated at *La Rue du Bord de L'Eau*) one evening early in 1948 at the family dinner table. Bob, in *CMP*'s 'Canadian' issue (October 1972), described it as looking "more prosperous than it is, as the century-old house is showing its years and is liable to be lopsided in places (and lovely mushrooms are grown in the dining room) but it's home." The property, which proved useful for sheltering casualties during the *SS Quebec* disaster, was eventually sold by Betty and Marylee to Montreal theatre director – and Sir William Price grandson – William ("Bill") Glassco, who converted it to the *Glassco Playwrights Residence*, with the aim of "facilitating the exchange of ideas, revealing our cultural uniqueness to each other and, in turn, to worldwide audiences" (i.e. they translate plays). Although Glassco passed on in 2004, his legacy continues. Bob's response to the sale: "It was the right decision, but I was really upset."

boathouse (now sadly defunct), and surrounded by assorted distant relatives, including Uncle Coosie and family, the resort offered everything a child with a love of the great outdoors could desire – a 1950s child, at least. Today's generation of activity-obsessed children would no doubt have found much to be desired – there were few amenities or entertainments (a tennis club served as the main focal point for social activities) and no TV or cinema, while bicycles provided the main mode of transport – and source of fun. A dip in the bay was out of the question, owing to the permanently ice-cold water, though there was a freshwater lake nearby. Alternatively, a season ticket entitled its holder to free use of the open-air swimming pool at the then-CSL-owned 'Tadoussac Hotel', which also incorporated a nine-hole golf course. Boat rides provided a welcome, regular treat, the Powels owning their own craft: adorned with name-plates appropriated from Uncle Lex (whose much grander yacht they had once graced) and fitted with a 10hb engine, *The Empress of Tadoussac* soon became the youngster's pride and joy, bringing endless hours of amusement – even if "the name-plates were longer than the boat itself!"

Other fun activities included haycart rides, berry-picking, picnicking (both usually at nearby Moulin Baude), collecting shells on the beach, or just messing around on the sand dunes. "We were never bored," says Bob. Backing this up, Benny Beattie, in his aforementioned book, devotes a full eight pages to the various amusements on offer, in spite of which, most modern-day tourists stay only long enough to undertake a whale watching safari before returning home again, usually within 48 hours, thus missing out on the resort's more subtle delights. Beattie, writing in the 1990s, reflects sadly on the changes time has wrought:-

"Gone are the sandy streets and the buggies, the

wooden goelettes [durable schooners that carried lumber from sawmills to Quebec City] and the CSL steamers, the salt-water swimming pool and the hotel dances. Gone is the slow, peaceful pace of a rural village, where time seemed to stand still for so long. Tadoussac has been modernised…"

Nevertheless, to earlier generations, the principal attraction remained that of being young, free and vitally alive in a beautiful location without fear of danger (one reason why the SS *Quebec* disaster of 1950 had such a dramatic and lasting impact on the young Powel). Tadoussac must also have served as a haven for Harcourt, suffering a stress-related illness at this time (subsequently diagnosed as a mild form of epilepsy). In later years, his son, having downloaded dozens of photographs of the area and arranged them so they ran in sequence on his computer screen, was able to revisit this special place at leisure, accompanied by acute pangs of nostalgia, and who can fail to comprehend his delight in doing so? After all, he knew it was the closest he was likely to get to his holiday home again.[14]

So far, we've skipped through our subject's formative years with no mention of the two words around which his whole life was destined to revolve. So, how did the fascination with country music first seep into the Powel consciousness – or, when and where did he encounter and fall in love with a minority musical genre more generally associated with the people of the area in which it originated: the Southern States of America?

---

[14] For accompaniment, Bob might have listened to English folk/country musician Brian Golbey's recording of *Tadoussac, You're Calling*, co-composed by himself and Golbey, whose career he managed at the time. (They also wrote the equally personal *Uncle Coosie*).

Well, for a start, a boy of his tender years and 'non-country' background had little opportunity to attend 'live' country music shows, which anyway were a rarity in those days (especially in Canada). TV had yet to catch on, while, unlike many performers who went on to become country stars, no friends, neighbours or relatives played or sang, even for fun. As for the family gramophone record collection,[15] apart from the odd Sons of the Pioneers album – his father's one concession to country music – this tended to reflect Mr. Powel's operatic tastes, any 'hillbilly' records that might have slipped through being supplied by Bobby himself, usually after hearing them on the only remaining medium, the one that enabled a child as young as nine to escape his limiting (and perhaps over-expansive) surroundings and enter a world of magic, wonder – and intimacy. It was also the one that was to make his name…

Strange that so much pleasure could be had from so plain-looking a device. Not that Bob remembered the first radio he set eyes – or ears – on. The first *station* is another matter. That was CFCF[16] in Montreal (no longer in existence), one of whose disc jockeys, 'Gordie' Sinclair, introduced in 1952 a new daytime show – *Western Swing* – that immediately grabbed his attention,[17] hooking him on

---

[15] Marylee also owned several records in the collection, notably the Crewcuts' *Sh'Boom* (originally recorded by the Chords the same year, 1954) and *(My Baby Don't Love Me) No More* by the De John Sisters (1955).

[16] Station CFCF – Despite undergoing several name-changes through the years, this managed to survive until 2010, when it suddenly closed down with just 24 hours' notice. Upon hearing the news, Bob posted a comment that he "owed his career to the station."

[17] *Western Swing*'s signature tune, *Boomerang,* was a self-composed Arthur 'Guitar Boogie' Smith instrumental that provided the

this sad, mournful, yet vibrant sound, one he readily related to – it was a simple case of *Heart to heart*.[18] "*That's* when I became a country fan," said Bob.

Later, he did manage to acquire a radio of his own. This was a 'Zenith',[19] a lightweight, though deceptively powerful, Bakelite effort that had actually been given to his parents, only it somehow found its way into his bedroom. As he recalled, tongue-in-cheek: "No one knows to this day how it got there." Now, with a more powerful set, he was able to tune into Nashville's mighty, legendary WSM station, 1,500 miles away, which broadcast the *Grand Ole Opry*[20] show Saturday nights. The only obstacle was the

---

guitarist with a No.8 country hit in 1949. Bob, having written into CFCF as a youngster to discover its title (his letter actually being read out on air), promised himself it would introduce his own programme, which it duly did, though a different, 4-minute piece (by an unremembered artiste) performed the closing honours. TRIVIA NOTE 1: Smith also composed, in 1955, the instrumental, *Feudin' Banjos*, which later appeared, without due credit, under the title, *Duellin' Banjos*, in the 1973 movie, *Deliverance*, causing him to take (successful) legal action in order to gain back royalties. TRIVIA NOTE 2: Gordie Sinclair's father, also called Gordon, penned *The Americans (A Canadian's Opinion)*, a No.35 country hit for Tex Ritter (his last) in 1974.

[18] *Heart to Heart* – a No.16 country hit for Roy Clark in 1975 (on ABC/Dot).

[19] 'Zenith' Radio – Founded in 1918, manufacturers of radio and TV receivers, based in Lincolnshire, Illinois – for many years, its slogan was: "The quality goes in before the name goes on." Inventors of modern remote-control, it has been Korean-owned since 1999. Of his own model, Bob once commented on *London Country*: "The tubes used to make a terrible noise for about two or three minutes – you had to turn it off and then put it on again till it started behaving itself."

[20] Broadcasting from 1927 to the present day, this holds the record as the longest-running radio programme in USA. Country fans may be familiar with the story, but it's perhaps worth

ever-present danger of sleep, his mother having a perfectly reasonable habit of peeping in each night during a break in her bridge game (usually when she had a dummy hand) to turn off the radio if she thought young Bobby might be 'out for the count!' Oh, how he tried to stay awake, and mostly succeeded, feeling very cross with himself the next morning on those rare occasions he failed to last out till the 11pm watershed.

One distinct memory of this period is Ferlin Husky's solemn announcement from the *Opry* stage, on the night of 3 January, 1953, that Hank Williams had died two days previously (when Bob would have been just weeks short of his 10th birthday). There followed a rousing rendition from all present at the theatre of Hank's *I Saw The Light*.[21] How many others tuning in that night must have felt as he did, shedding tears at the thought that country music's most famous son, its 'poet laureate', the country boy from

---

repeating how WSM's *Barn Dance* became the *Grand Ole Opry*. When, in 1925, journalist George D. Hay (later nicknamed 'The Solemn Old Judge') was appointed director of the station, he wasted no time in organising the first *Barn Dance*, which, by the following year, had been allocated a 3-hour spot on NBC Radio's Red Network, airing immediately after a 'Music Appreciation Hour.' On December 10th 1927, at the start of his show, Hay announced, "For the past hour, we have been listening to music taken largely from grand opera, but from now on, we will present *Grand Ole Opry*." (By a curious coincidence, the Opera/'Opry' extremes perfectly reflect the opposite tastes of Mr. Powel senior and son.) The name *Grand Ole Opry* stuck – unlike the location, which is currently (after seven changes) part of the Opry Mills mall, twenty miles outside Nashville, though in the winter it returns to its original home, the *Ryman Auditorium*.

[21] *I Saw the Light* – Hank Williams-composed gospel song covered by numerous artistes, including Crystal Gayle (1995), Jerry Lee Lewis, Etta James (2001), Nitty Gritty Dirt Band (No.56 country hit, 1971), Earl Scruggs, Jerry Reed and Willie Nelson (1979).

Alabama who sang of pain, heartache and grief as though he had invented them, was now, at the early age of 29, no more. The words to his composition, *I'll Never Get out of This World Alive* [22] (coincidentally on release as a single at the time) never rang so true nor hit home so hard. Bob unhesitatingly nominated Hank as the all-time No.1 country singer-songwriter and there are few who would disagree with that assessment.

Another popular show was the *Wheeling Jamboree*, also broadcast Saturday nights, from station WWVA[23] in West Virginia – less than half the distance from WSM and a useful back-up in case that signal was weak. The *Jamboree* starred Doc & Chickie Williams, the Clinch Mountain Band, featuring duo Wilma Lee & Stoney Cooper, Wayne Raney and dozens of other acts – most of all, singing DJ, Lee Moore, who additionally hosted a weekdays-only 2am to 6am show, Bob's favourite (although, unbeknown to his parents, he needed to set his alarm especially to hear it).

Commonly referred to as 'the coffee-drinking nighthawk', Mr. Moore, guitar at the ready, would oblige listeners' requests with a 'live' performance on air. At the first sign of daylight, the signal from this station would start dying: Bob's cue to switch off and grab a couple more hours' sleep! He credited the many nights spent following this routine with the fact that throughout his adult life he managed to function on 4-5 hours' sleep a night. It also

---

[22] *I'll Never Get out of This World Alive* – Hank Williams-Fred Rose composition that reached No.1 later that month, January, 1953. Fred Rose died in December of the following year. Covered by Asleep At The Wheel, Jerry Lee Lewis and Hank Williams, Jr., among others.

[23] WWVA and WSM were known as 50,000-watt clear channels, meaning no other radio station could have their call number – in the evening and night time, at least, when the signal was strongest.

explains why, as he put it: "I knew more about country music than Tony Byworth, Bryan Chalker or any of those for the simple reason that I started earlier – they fell in love with it when they were 15 or 16 – I was 9."

The banjo-laden – or more typically, honky tonk-driven – sounds emanating from the radio in the early 50s provided the springboard for his life, triggering something profound within him, something that would not rest until this music was more widely known, loved and accepted – and he would achieve this by presenting his very own show. Excited at the prospect, yet never straying into starry notions of being up there on stage or even behind-the-scenes as producer, he now made a promise to himself that, come the day of his debut, he would open with recordings by two of his favourite country stars, who both happened to be called Hank: Williams and Snow.[24]

In truth, at this early stage (he had yet to reach his teens), the ambition amounted to little more than a crazy dream – no different from those nurtured by a million others his age. Yet it was one he believed in sufficiently to share with his father – perhaps secretly hoping that 'Pop' might share his enthusiasm, though, as a devout opera fan, he would hardly be likely to encourage support for that dreaded 'hillbilly' music! (Actually, Mr. Powel, for some reason, harboured hopes that his son might pursue a career in mechanical engineering, a subject Bob knew as much about in later life as then – precisely nothing!). The response, therefore, when it came – "Don't worry son, you'll grow out of it." – was entirely predictable, but did nothing to deter the youngster, who simply carried on

---

[24] In fact, Bob, via *Powel's Point of View* in *CMP*'s August, 1977 edition (marking the sixth anniversary of the show), lists the following 3 records as the first played on *London Country*: *Howlin' at the Moon* by Hank Williams, *There's a Bluebird on Your Windowsill* by Wilf Carter and *Ninety Miles An Hour* by Hank Snow.

regardless. Time would prove the validity or otherwise of his 'dream'.

Chapter 2

Return to England: 1955-65

I Can't Escape From You ("My memory is chained to you...")[25]

Ironically, just as one love affair – that with country music – was beginning to bud, so another, the great Tadoussac romance, was curtailed, though not entirely ended. The reason? Dad's services were once again required in Europe, and where he went, the family followed. Thus, in 1955, they relocated, partly via the *Franconia* liner, to *South Park Lodge*, a large, if (from the outside, at least) rather unattractive mansion, complete with tennis court and gardener's cottage, situated in the commuter town of Sevenoaks, Kent. Slightly further out than Sidcup, but still on the fringe of the capital (actually 24mi/39km from the centre), its name derives from seven large oak trees planted in Knole Park in 800AD.[26]

---

[25] *I Can't Escape From You* – Hank Williams' sparse demo-recording of this self-composition was issued as a 'B' side single in June, 1953 (6 months after his death), the 'A' side, *Weary Blues From Waiting*, reaching No.7 on the chart.

[26] The original trees long since having died or been uprooted, seven replacement oaks were planted on the Vine Cricket

This historic park happened to provide the setting for yet another childhood accident, when, learning that the normally shy deer were out foraging for food one harsh winter, Mr. Powel and son loaded up with appropriate nourishment and headed for the snowbound pastures. The youngster was having the time of his life feeding a baby deer, until, reaching the end of his feed, a larger stag suddenly appeared and – perhaps angry at missing out on a meal – lunged at him with its antlers, cutting into his cheek like a knife through paper. The startled lad immediately burst into tears, provoking a fierce rebuke from Dad: "You damned cry baby – what's wrong with you, it's just a scratch!" Whereupon the bad-tempered buck, as if offended by this insult to its potency, delivered a repeat performance – on Mr. Powel. Seeing his father wince with pain somehow made the boy feel much better and he soon returned to a more typical demeanour.

Although there were tears that day, there had been none from either child at leaving behind their beautiful Quebec home and idyllic lifestyle – there was little time to indulge such emotions, for, no sooner had they adjusted themselves to their new surroundings than they were shipped off to private boarding schools, Bob's being in the small Buckinghamshire village of North Crawley, close to Newport Pagnell, in neighbouring Berkshire, some 70mi/112km north west of Sevenoaks. Called 'Five Acres' and situated in the High Street, it was actually a converted house run by a Major Jeffries that held just 20 pupils. The building, although still standing, has long since reverted to its former use and only older residents of the town recall its existence. Bob himself had limited memories of his time there, which nevertheless provided him with the

ground in 1902. As well as keeping alive the tradition of seven oaks in the town, these commemorated the coronation of Edward VII the previous year. Unfortunately, six of these were demolished in the Great Storm of 1987.

opportunity to display his vocal talents as a member of the school choir. Whatever the merits or otherwise of his performance, it was an experience never to be repeated, for, after just one year, he transferred to the altogether grander 'Abbotsholme' in Derbyshire, close to the border with Staffordshire,[27] accurately described by him as "the No.1 private boarding school in the country – alphabetically speaking…"

Founded in 1889 by young Scottish academic Dr. Cecil Reddie, it was an attempted "shift away from the rigid conformity of the traditional public school towards spontaneity, leadership and compassion for others based on co-operation rather than competition, a friendly, supportive relationship between staff and pupils and a wholehearted respect for the environment," which sounds more like a modern-day Liberal manifesto than an educational policy statement dating back 125 years! And indeed, Reddie, proud of his forward-thinking theories on education, called his pet project "The New School."

So, did this flagship of the educational *avant garde* live up to its founder's high ideals – at least during Bob's years there? And how did he fit in with this privileged group of his peers (with whom he must have had little in common), while ensconced in an environment far removed – in so many ways – from the one with which he was familiar? Again, it seems his naturally upbeat, resilient attitude served him well, for, while many of his classmates, especially in the early days and weeks, were quiet and withdrawn, or, in extreme cases, reduced to tears, he took

---

[27] The school's official website lists the address as: Rocester, Uttoxeter, Derbyshire, which is confusing, as neither Rocester nor Uttoxeter is in Derbyshire – both are in Staffordshire, but the school, apparently, is in Derbyshire. Just to confuse things further, during his stay, Bob roomed at Mill House – in Rocester! (The moral of this story is: don't ever bet on which county the school is located in, because you can't win.)

everything in his stride, actually relishing being away from home and parents for the first time and having a degree of independence. As he put it, "being away from my parents didn't worry me one iota."

In fact, his fortitude was put to the test early, when, having arrived a few days after his classmates, he met up with a teacher, now recalled only as being Egyptian, the classroom conversation proceeding roughly as follows:-

Sir: "Ah, you're new, aren't you, boy?"

Bob: (Innocently) "Yes, sir."

Sir: "So, you haven't had one of my 'clips?'"

Bob: (Uncertainly) "Er, no, sir…"

Sir: (Whacking him sharply about the ear) "Well, you have, now!"

Welcome to 'Abbotsholme'. Not an uncommon occurrence in those days, and, even if the youngster had felt aggrieved, there was no one with whom to share his sense of injustice, so he simply had to get on with it, which possibly explains something about his subsequent 'no-nonsense' approach to life.

Still, he seems to have made an immediate, if somewhat dubious, impression in one field, at least: that of soccer, the team coach describing him as "both the keenest and worst player in the school!" Bob remembered a particular incident that highlighted his qualities – or lack of – in this department. The procedure on match days was that each player took turns at being captain. When master Powel's turn came, he shrewdly picked the best players available – so skilfully, in fact, that his side soon ran up a rugby-type score-line, prompting his team-mates, each of whom had bagged several goals apiece, to lay on chance after chance in an effort to earn their honourable leader a share of the glory. Sadly, all were somehow squandered – until, eventually, with seconds remaining, Captain Powel hit the back of the net, to the relief of everyone – not least himself!

He recalled one further incident of note, concerning an exercise book kept by pupils in which, if they misbehaved, the teacher would enter an appropriate sentence (usually consisting of 'lines'). In order to get out of this, student Powel adopted the simple expedient of tearing out the offending page, thus destroying the evidence. This worked a treat – for a while. Unfortunately, after repeating the trick a dozen or more times, the book began to look as though it were suffering from the textual equivalent of anorexia nervosa. (Bob: "I wasn't crafty enough to stick in empty pages to compensate!") The game was clearly up, but, luckily for the perpetrator, he got on reasonably well with headmaster 'Fingerless' Hodgkins (so named because he lost several fingers through frostbite while indulging his passion for mountain climbing – rumour has it that, but for this injury, he would have been part of the 1953 Everest expedition team). Perhaps this is why his punishment, consisting of a day's detention to be served after the last day of term, happened to be one on which the following year's batch of prospective students was sitting the entrance exam, resulting in the entire time being spent by him, not cleaning up the school grounds as expected, but sitting at the front of class, acting as supervisor – which, naturally, suited master P. to a T! Feeling rather pleased with himself, he then chanced his arm and cheekily enquired of the head whether he might spend the next day in detention also, as his friend, Hatch, was travelling back to London then and he could join him. "No, you cannot!" came the outraged reply. (Hatch, having struck a teacher, was serving two days in detention).

These episodes, far from spoiling his school days,

served only to add to the fun, as he told me, "I have this knack of enjoying everything I've ever done, and, all things considered, it was OK at 'Abbotsholme' – but bloody cold in the winter!"

If the young student felt settled in Derbyshire, he was in for a shock. After just two years, he was transferred again – to a school that had more in common with his first, at North Crawley, except it was 180mi/290km south west of it (and, coincidentally, the same distance from 'Abbotsholme'), in far-flung Devon – the small town of Bradworthy, to be exact. Although similarly owned and presided over by a Major – Fraser, in this case – and with a comparable intake of 20 pupils, it was even more isolated, the only relief coming from free rides around an improvised cycle-track in a nearby wood and Saturday excursions to the nearby town of Bideford, Bob typically stealing a march on his school-pals by cadging early morning lifts from the milk-churn delivery man "to save on bus fares."

These pursuits apart, it was a fairly bleak existence – in a location so remote that electricity was generator-powered. Any simple activity, such as reading by lamplight (depending on how many others were doing likewise) could set the thing off, with all the associated noise and hullabaloo – not to mention punishment for the perpetrator. Reading at night was, of course, forbidden, as was listening to the radio. However, that didn't stop the boy in the third bed from the end, the cute one with the tussled hair and freckled features, slipping under the sheets with a tiny, battery-operated transistor pressed close to his ear... listening in the still of the night, deep into the small hours while all around were wrapped in silent slumber... did he like what he heard? Not really – it was, well, different from the 'down-homey' sounds he was used to hearing back in Quebec. Still, he continued listening, and, as the drowsiness eventually overcame him, he vowed that one day, if the chance came, he'd introduce a dash of sweet 'Americana' to the bland British airwaves. One day...

For now, there was the small matter of completing his full-time education – and it was not to be achieved at barren Bradworthy, but at Littlehampton, a seaside resort 170mi/274km eastwards along the Sussex coast. The story is that a (Naval) Captain Oliver arrived on the scene, bought out the Major and moved the whole operation to this quiet, sedate town, for reasons long since lost in the mists of time. As for Bob, he was just glad to be somewhere that offered scope for youngsters to let off excess energy. Situated beside a golf course, incorporating a (now demolished) windmill and with instant access to the sea, it had the added attraction of a Fun Fair[28] (run by Billy Butlin, more famous for his holiday camps), though rides were not as easily 'cadged' as at the 'Chateau Frontenac'.

Inevitably, these simple days came to an end, and the young student returned home for good, the route between his four educational establishments having created a near-perfect diamond shape, the total area of which amounts to an amazing 1,600 square miles (2,560km). Such an academic passage seems rather unusual – and harsh. Despite the assertion that he held "no bad memories" of his schooldays, it's likely he was very lonely at times – he would have missed greatly the familiar Tadoussac landscape, and, knowing him as someone who valued friendships, it surely would have upset him to be whisked away just as these were developing. Add to this the fact

---

[28] Sunday was 'church' day, when boys were segregated according to their denomination and marched off to the relevant church for morning service. Noticing there were no Methodists, student Powel instantly converted. With supervision considered too much of a luxury for a one-member church, he was now free to spend the time as he wished – in his case, helping out on one of the Fun Fair stalls.

that he clearly had little aptitude for formal learning while at the same time carrying the (apparently) high expectations of his parents and it's easy to see why the radio would provide a big comfort to him, even without his beloved country music.

What were his parents' motives? Undoubtedly loving and caring, they were presumably trying to provide the very best for their only son, whose special qualities they would have noted. How were they to know his talents lay elsewhere? Bob's own theory – at least to explain the 'boarding-school' choices – was that "my parents, both being so much older than us, liked the idea of not having the children for 12 months of the year – and who could blame them?" Whatever the truth, despite the interruptions and upheavals, he emerged relatively unscathed, tougher, in fact, having gained the strong sense of independence he retained throughout life, although – perhaps unsurprisingly – minus any qualifications.

Disappointed at this apparent failure, his parents persuaded the ever-willing teenager to attend a 'cramming' course, in order to gain the necessary pass-marks for a university place. Thus Bob enrolled at the somewhat incongruously named establishment of Davies, Laing & Dick in London. Founded in 1931, this was – and is – the oldest tutorial college in the capital. Here, he managed to gain three 'O' level passes: in English Language, English Literature and History, the award of the first-named prompting a blistering comment from his tutor at the time: "Well, Powel, your essay must have been particularly enthralling because you can't spell and your handwriting is atrocious!"[29] (It would be nice to think this gentleman read

---

[29] Having noted that Mr. Powel senior's spelling was as poor as his son's, the fair-minded tutor added: "At least you inherited it honestly." (By contrast, Mr. P.'s handwriting was immaculate, as indeed might have been his son's, had he not remained a lifelong left-hander.)

some of Bob's subsequent articles, for *Country Music People* and other publications, but I suppose this is unlikely.)

Marylee, meanwhile, fresh out of full-time education and equally keen to comply with her parents' wishes (although generally more opinionated than her brother), had, on her mother's initiative, enrolled as a State Registered Nurse, in which capacity she served with distinction for many years, including midwifery duties and working among eskimos, before going on to run a kennels in Smithers, British Columbia. Following retirement in 2011, she moved to Alberta, where she resides to this day. Having been educated at different boarding schools, and, from the very start, leading pretty much a separate life, Marylee found little to add to this book.

So, what of brother Bob? With university now out of the question, his future did not seem anywhere near so clear-cut or assured, and being naturally amiable and easy-going did not help matters. It was a difficult period, during which he was, to use his own words, "just floundering about." The turning point came the day he asked his mother's help in obtaining some item, only to be refused, "because you're not earning any money," to which the aggrieved response was, "That's the last time you'll be able to say that!" And so it proved, for, within a week, the 18-year-old was living in digs (in Finsbury Park, North London) and engaged in full-time employment as junior member of the small team (consisting of just himself and kindly manageress, Mrs. Fleming) in a greetings card/stationer's suppliers located immediately adjacent to Warren Street tube station in central London.

Hardly a position from which to set the world alight, although he remained typically upbeat, despite which he was soon, in the words of Hank Snow, *Moving On*[30] – in his

---

[30] *I'm Moving On*, written and originally recorded by Hank Snow, provided a No. 1 country hit for him in 1950, subsequently

case, to a larger, more prestigious organisation in Brewer Street, central London: Ryman & Co. (no relation to a certain Nashville auditorium!). Here, encountering the public daily on a face-to-face basis, he soon learned to deal with every type of situation – albeit on his own terms, as in the case of a particularly difficult customer, who seemed to delight in finding fault with everyone and everything. If the aim was to goad staff into retaliation, it worked, but not quite as the disagreeable fellow intended. One day, in full flow, he was surprised by an interjection from the new salesman:-

"Excuse me, sir, may I say something? I must admit, I *admire* you."

"You *do*?"

"Why, yes. You come in here almost every day, and yet you hate the place – and that takes a lot of guts, to force yourself to return somewhere that's so disorganised, with terrible staff, poor service and lousy products. I really admire you for coming back."

No doubt the deflated gent left the store considerably less self-aggrandised – and more confused – than when he entered. As for management, having noted this unusual, innovative approach to customer relations, they knew exactly where to look the next time an outdoor representative position became available, as it shortly did. With his sharp wit and verbal dexterity, the bright newcomer would surely prove a fine choice – or would he…?

Fate dictated (an unfortunate word, in light of what

---

being covered by many artistes, including Don Gibson in 1960 (No.14) and Emmylou Harris in 1983 (No.5).

followed) that his first customer in the sales field should be satirical comedian Peter Cook, then chiefly known for the stage success *Beyond The Fringe* and occasional appearances on ITV's *The Braden Beat* (hosted by another British-based Canadian, Bernard Braden), but shortly to become nationally famous via the TV comedy series, *Not Only But Also*, co-starring Dudley Moore. Bob's assignment this particular day was to demonstrate a Dictaphone machine to Mr. Cook, at his nightclub, *The Establishment*, located in Greek St., Soho, the only problem being that, try as he might, he could not get the thing to work.

Anticipating all sorts of sarcastic comments from the notoriously sharp-tongued comic designed to exploit his embarrassment, the 'rookie rep' was becoming increasingly flustered. To his great relief, however – and Mr. Cook's credit – the potential buyer was kindness itself, even lending a hand in trying to rouse the comatose contraption – to no avail. "Amazingly," recounted Bob, "he didn't buy it!" Eventually, both decided to give up the struggle, one traipsing off, cursing the machine, the other perhaps secretly filing the incident away in his subconscious, for use in some future sketch. And so ended the Ryman employee's first and last venture into the world of outdoor selling.

Bob's next move was to another stationer's, A. Southey & Co., in the City of London, where he happily divided his duties between serving behind the counter and fulfilling orders for clients, the latter enabling him to get out and about and do a spot of sightseeing. Possessing a National Trust ticket, he indulged his interest in historical buildings, the Tower of London holding a particular fascination, but one can imagine that the entire city experience – its narrow, crowded streets, architectural eccentricity and unique customs and traditions – made quite an impression on the youngster more used to the formal structures and wide open landscapes of rural Canada.

Although the future broadcaster appeared to be drifting from job to job during this period, it was not due to any dissatisfaction on the part of his employers, who were invariably pleased with his performance – in particular, he earned a fine reputation for time-keeping, something he strived to maintain all his working life. "It makes for better relations all round," he said. The moves were just logical attempts to improve his lot. There was one further position in the world of stationery to come before other interests took hold: assistant manager with a firm based at Tottenham Court Road. The prospects looked good, but by this stage our country 'ambassador' is surveying wider, more challenging horizons…

It is 1965, he is 22 years of age, and, as yet, showing no sign of greater things ahead. Now living at Inderwick Road, Hornsey, just north of Finsbury Park, and juggling a second job, his working life is hectic, social life obviously less so, although one regular treat is a weekly visit to Highbury soccer stadium to watch local favourites Arsenal, whose reserve team squad at this time included many members who went on to become part of the famous double-winning team of 1971. Through it all, he is quietly listening to country music – not so much from outside sources ("there was nothing at all being played") as from a burgeoning record collection, which will be boosted further in the forthcoming year, a result of his first, never to be forgotten, trip to Nashville – a five-month adventure that will transform his life.

Chapter 3

Nashville & Beyond: 1965-69

I Can't Help It ("My heart fell at your feet…")[31]

It's a bold man who dares to take a large chunk of a year off work to roam freely around foreign parts with little prospect of its leading to gainful employment – or anything worthwhile, for that matter. 18-year-old students with a raft of qualifications behind them and guaranteed university places ahead do so, of course, but, for 22-year-olds with none-too-distinguished academic histories and scrappy, unpromising work records, it might be regarded as bordering on the reckless. That's possibly how his parents viewed it, anyway, but then they failed to understand or appreciate that within their beloved son lurked a deep fascination with American country music – and its larger-than-life personalities – that overrode all other considerations, something he could not shake off –

---

[31] *I Can't Help It (if I'm Still In Love With You).* Written and originally recorded by Hank Williams, this poignant ballad reached No.2 on the country chart in 1951, the same position attained by Linda Ronstadt's revival 24 years later. Other artistes to have recorded the song include Margaret Whiting, Adam Wade, Johnny Tillotson, B.J. Thomas and Al Martino.

nor wished to. He was young, adventurous and keen to follow his dreams, which, as we know, if not indulged, do not bear fruit. And so he joined the exclusive list of brave, hardy souls whom fortune favours…

Wednesday, 5 May, 1965 could now be added to Monday, 14 August, 1950 as one of the most significant days in Bob Powel's life, for it was then that he sailed to America (via Canada) with only vague notions of what to do on arrival. One of these 'notions' was to attend a country music concert, for, amazing as it seems, despite listening to thousands of country records, he had never up to this point actually sampled the real thing, 'live' and 'in person'. In fact, apart from a brief, televised glimpse of Jim Reeves on UK pop show, *Ready, Steady, Go!* and an only slightly less brief cinematic snatch of Ferlin Husky in *Country Music Holiday* (1958), he had never viewed a country performance anywhere.

However, first things first, and, as soon as the boat docked in Quebec, he headed for the home of his parents, who had moved back there from England the year before. Given the efforts they had made to give their only son a suitable educational start in life, it would be understandable if relations were somewhat strained during this 10-day stopover, but Bob maintained that, throughout the venture, his parents offered total support, proud that "I had worked hard to finance the trip independently."

Then it was off to the States, accompanied by a $99 'Greyhound' ticket (bought in England) entitling him to 99 days of travel – by his own admission, "one of the smartest investments I ever made." Arriving in New York on 20 May, he immediately began sniffing out likely sources of product among the renowned and not-so-renowned record stores dotted about the city. Only a fellow devotee – or non-downloader – could understand the feelings of anticipation and excitement, as, heart pounding, he sifted through racks of rare, hitherto unknown recordings, many of which, having saved his pennies over previous months and years, he could afford to buy. Pure joy! By the end of the day, no doubt a good deal lighter in pocket but richer in soul, he had added significantly to his stock, in the process identifying King Karol Record Shop,[32] 111 West 42nd St. as "the only shop in New York with a good selection of discount LPs." That evening, he viewed his first country TV programme, a Jimmy Dean Show originally filmed in Nashville the previous year. (Jimmy is best known in England for the self-penned *Big, Bad John*, a No.2 pop hit for him in 1961).

From New York, Bob took the 'Greyhound' bus to Nashville but was disappointed to discover little that warranted its 'Music City USA' reputation – at least in terms of 'live' entertainment – weekends excepted. TV programmes compensated, especially the *Bobby Lord Show*, which he rated "the best C & W show I saw in the States." This also happened to provide his introduction to the world of celebrity, when, having travelled out to the studios to attend a televised performance, he (as the nearest equivalent in the audience to a living Englishman!) was chosen to be interviewed by the host. (Being broadcast on a small, regional channel, WSM, this early TV appearance is unlikely to ever surface in video or DVD form).

Again playing the 'English' card(!), he managed to obtain a ticket to attend the *Grand Ole Opry*, his main reason for going to Nashville, and the four and a half hour show he witnessed that Saturday night, featuring no fewer than 23 top-line country acts, was one he would "always remember." While in the city, he visited the newly opened

---

[32] King Karol Record Shop – Founded by Ben Karol and Phil King in 1950s, closed in 1980s. This was the main store but there were eight other branches in New York. Firm also operated a mail order business.

Roy Acuff Museum and was thrilled to actually meet the star himself. Having tasted 'live' entertainment, Bob now wanted more, and so, tracking Buck Owens' touring itinerary – not necessarily attending the shows, but purely because it offered a wide sweep of the country – he visited Albuquerque, New Mexico (Buck Owens, Merle Haggard and Little Jimmy Dickens – "all good"), Denver, Colorado[33] (Kitty Wells group, Archie Campbell, Grandpa Jones and Ferlin Husky – "bit of a let-down", "very funny", "the real stuff", and "plastered"[34] respectively!), Salt Lake City ("beautiful and very clean"), San Francisco ("worse weather than England"), Los Angeles ("hot and smog-laden"), Houston ("even hotter"), Mississippi ("hottest of all"), Seattle, the Grand Canyon ("impressive and boring at the same time!"), the Rocky Mountains, Victoria, Cincinnati, Vancouver, Oklahoma City and St. Louis (where he obtained the bargain of the trip – over 100 mid-fifties 45/EPs for £10). Altogether, he visited "hundreds of record shops and bought a great many

---

[33] While in Denver, Bob witnessed the effects of the June 16th South Platte River floods that left 21 people dead, 250,000 acres inundated and caused $540 million worth of damage. Heavy rains on four consecutive days in three different areas of the South Platte basin caused flooding from Plum Creek, south of the city, to the Nebraska state line.

[34] This remark, as quoted in Bob's article for *Country & Western Roundabout* (Issue 15 – June, 1967), provoked the following angry response (Issue 16 – March 1968) from reader, Derek Lea, of Flintshire, Wales:-

"Boy, page 19 latest issue has got me mad. I refuse to believe that Ferlin Husky would act the way Robert Powel says he did, the sun shines out of Ferlin as far as I am concerned. I think I can prove that Ferlin wasn't drunk, too, he's a gentleman in every sense of the word." (Mr. Lea neglects to explain how he might prove his point.)

records." Approaching the end of his trip, he paid an enjoyable visit to the *Calgary Stampede*,[35] which featured 'the Arizona Cowboy', Rex Allen, one of his favourites. Next stop was New York City, where he endured a humid fortnight, before travelling northwards to spend a month with his parents in beloved *Fletcher Cottage*, Tadoussac.

It was at this point that the trip scheduled to launch his career almost brought about the sinking of his hopes – literally. Paying a visit to Uncle Coosie, the pair, sailing downstream from Tadoussac to Quebec on the latter's yacht, *Jamboree I* (the first in a series of four), encountered a small island with a manned lighthouse that seemed worth investigating. Coosie, on reflection, preferred to take a nap, so his more adventurous relative launched the on-board canoe alone and paddled across to meet the folks (which, if his life had developed differently, might have become a regular routine – see end of chapter). Without realising his error, the novice canoeist sat at the back of the craft instead of the middle, causing it to jut up out of the water, at an acute angle, in spite of which he somehow, with the aid of the tide, managed to make it to shore, whereupon, having exchanged pleasantries with the island dwellers, he set about the return journey, again seated at the canoe's rear.

On this occasion, the tide against him, he was not so fortunate, and, after a while, the tiny craft tipped up, depositing him in the icy, turbulent 20-mile wide St. Lawrence waterway and posing an immediate, serious dilemma: hang on to the upturned canoe and be carried by the current to who-knows-where or let go and hope to be

---

[35] *Calgary Stampede* – Annual rodeo, exhibition and festival held every July in Calgary, Alberta – a 10-day event, attracting one million visitors each year. Its origins lie in 1886 Fair, which developed into a rodeo by 1912, finally establishing itself under current name in 1923.

able to swim to the island shore, although he was not the most proficient in that regard. At the critical moment, with the green-grey waters swirling about him, he had sufficient presence of mind to feel for the river bed with his foot. Nothing. Managing to inch a little closer towards the island, he tried again, this time touching what must have seemed like Heaven itself beneath his feet: firm ground. Having just been frantically shouting for help, there now came the almost comical-sounding retraction: "Cancel that!" On reaching safety and assuring the concerned onlookers of his welfare, he set out once more in the canoe – this time, firmly situated in the middle.

Bob concluded his visit by driving south-west alongside the St. Lawrence River to Montreal, where he attended a show starring Ernest Tubb, Carl & Pearl Butler and (again) the Kitty Wells group, of which he enjoyed Mr & Mrs. Butler the most. Finally, after a couple of weeks in Quebec, he sailed for home (on the *Carmania*)[36] on 5 October, five months to the day after setting out, arriving on English soil seven days later.

Returning to normality proved difficult for this incurable enthusiast – the trip had reignited the flame within him recently reduced to a flicker by the wearying demands and routine obligations of everyday life. Thus, although a few days rest took care of any physical exhaustion he may have felt, the inner excitement was not so easily treated. He found himself walking around in a state of permanent euphoria, desperate to share his experience – to shout it from the rooftops, if necessary –

---

[36] During this voyage, Bob, for one of the very few occasions in his life, got drunk – a result of too many glasses of Pimms No.1, a favourite drink of his at the time. In fact, the full effects did not hit home until the following day, when, having imbibed just one glass more, he went out like a light during a game of 'deck-tennis!'

but no one seemed interested. In a way (and somewhat unfairly, he thought), this situation was better suited to performers, who, through sheer artistry and charisma, had the power to hold an entire audience under their spell, controlling its mood and emotions – educating them, in a sense – with a few subtle lines of verse, while exorcising their own demons at the same time. No such avenue existed for him. Considering his options, he decided to contact a country magazine, the only one he knew of being a small quarterly publication entitled *Country & Western Roundabout,* printed in Loughton, Essex by a fellow named Charlie Benson. And so, Mr. Robert Powel, of the poor handwriting and spelling, put pen to paper and produced the first of many articles: the tale of his epic trip to the Promised Land, one flowing with milk, honey and the sweet sounds of the music he loved.

If the article had not been accepted, would Bob have returned to anonymity and the world of *Bic* pens and *Tipp-ex*[37] paper, condemning his 'trip of a lifetime' to the back pages of history, a 'one-off' event never to be repeated except by word of mouth to envious – and possibly disbelieving – friends and acquaintances over cups of coffee in dingy street cafes? I like to think not – some things are just destined to happen, and it's pretty certain he would have persevered until someone sat up and took notice. Luckily for him, Charlie Benson did just that – or perhaps he had nothing better to print that particular month. Certainly, the article, when eventually published, was not exactly given 'star' treatment, being serialised over the course of three different issues, meaning that, because the mag was not produced as regularly as it ought ("he was

---

[37] *Tipp-Ex* paper has a – tenuous – country music connection, the German firm's American equivalent, *Liquid Paper,* having been founded by Bette Graham, the mother of country-rock star (and ex-Monkee) Mike Nesmith in 1955, when he was 13 years of age.

always behind"), a full year had elapsed before it appeared in its entirety. Nevertheless, his name was now out there!

Next came the launch of a new magazine by Larry Adams and Gordon Smith.[38] The former, a lifelong country music fan, was a sales rep for a major catering supplies manufacture, when, along with his fellow country fan (whom he'd met in 1966), he set up $Opry^{39}$ in response to the dearth of information available on the genre at that time. The first issue appeared in July, 1968, and, upon discovering it, Bob, although having no journalistic ambitions as such, was keen to be involved in some way. Introducing himself over the phone as a writer of note – three whole articles to his credit (sort of) – how could they refuse him? Quite easily, as it turned out. However, he impressed the owners sufficiently to be granted an occasional column, commencing in Issue No.5 (November), by which time Bryan Chalker had been

---

[38] Working for a music publishing company when he met Larry, Gordon Smith was, initially at least, just as committed to the country cause as his friend (who, having introduced Gordon to his wife's sister, subsequently became his brother-in-law). After parting company with *CMP*, he pursued various activities within the music business, including working as a Radio 2 staff producer and, later, UK boss of "as-seen-on-TV" company *K-Tel* Records. (Died 2010.)

[39] Owing to difficulties in getting accepted by the printing and distribution trade and in raising finance – the latter not helped by an infamous *London Palladium* concert starring Hank Snow, Willie Nelson, Johnny Darrell and disappearing conman – *Opry* folded after 18 months. Adams' solution was to transfer ownership and subscriptions to Reg Field and start again under the newly named (courtesy of himself) *Country Music People*. Following his departure from *CMP*, Larry went on to host Radio Medway shows, *Kent Country Scene, Gospel Train* and *Whole Lotta Country*, do promotions work with Mervyn Conn and launch his own, short-lived rival country mag. Whatever the success or otherwise of his activities, he remains a genuine country music lover.

recruited as editor.

Glancing through this issue, which features a full colour photo of the Hillsiders on the cover and – inside – articles by such as Gordon Smith (Dave Dudley and Jerry Kennedy), David Allan (*Page*), Richard Day (*Country Music at the Movies*), Bryan Chalker (history of country music), David Bussey (Jim Reeves), James Hatfield (Osborne Bros.), and Alan Cackett (Loretta Lynn), one needs to turn to page 22 to locate *the Bob Powel Column*. This occupies the whole page and contains six paragraphs of considered opinion on matters country, displaying just a hint of – if not exactly greater, then certainly more controversial – things to come.

The first paragraph is merely self-introductory, while the second charts the progress made by country music in the last five years, simultaneously lamenting the increased cost of imported records.

It's in paragraph 3 that the newcomer lets his feelings be known – in no uncertain terms – and the recipient is old pal, Wally Whyton. Born in London in 1929 and proficient on multiple instruments, including piano, trombone and guitar, the well-known TV singer/presenter's first foray into the world of entertainment came in the mid-fifties via the Vipers skiffle group, who soon gained a residency at the 2i's coffee bar in London's Soho. Subsequently moving into TV, his credits include *Lucky Dip* and *Five o'Clock Club*, but it was through his then-current radio show, *Country Meets Folk*, that he became most familiar to country fans.

In his article, *Opry*'s newest writer objects to Wally's preference for Hank Williams' 'with strings' recordings, i.e. original studio recordings to which strings were – posthumously – added by the record company. Bob feels this action is "unforgivable" and will be regarded as such by any "real country collector."

The fourth paragraph has him urging country fans to tune into the *Grand Ole Opry*, available on radio's 344 metres band on Saturday evenings, while paragraph 5 sees him drawing on his knowledge of the genre to point out several errors in writer Richard Day's article the previous month entitled, *Country Music at the Movies*, the inaccuracies relating specifically to MGM's Hank Williams' biopic, *Your Cheatin' Heart*.

Finally, paragraph 6 deals with a pet topic: the non-availability of deleted material, about which he later – in the digital age – believed the opposite, i.e. that *too much* product was being issued purely by virtue of its having been originally released on an obscure, 'collectable' label, or recorded at some legendary studio, the musical quality being practically irrelevant. Still, his *Column* seems to have been generally well-received and now his foot is in the (barn) door…

A second article, focussing exclusively on *Folk Voice*'s (see Chapter 4) annual concert at Islington Town Hall, follows in December, and subsequently, with the exception of January, his page – initially entitled *Column*, then, from March, *Viewpoint* – appears monthly. There is even a James Hatfield-written biography, albeit just 288 words long, in April's issue, while June sees the new writer receive his first mention in *Mailbag* – a positive one, from reader Paul Crosbie of Wexford, Eire, who writes: "Your magazine is really wonderful, particularly Bob Powel." Just to keep him on his toes, however, the very next issue, in July, includes a letter from Norma Hughes of Chippenham, Wilts., who objects to his criticism (in May's issue) of Larry Cunningham's *Wembley Festival* appearance. (Bob had written that, with his backing group, they came across as a "showband, and therefore seemed out of place at Wembley" – something, he later told me, "they never subsequently repeated.")

This issue – July, 1969 – is notable for being first in a

new, larger size (remaining so up to the final issue) and for featuring on its cover *Ode to Billie Jo* star, Bobbie Gentry, clad in nothing but a skimpy, yellow polka dot bikini. It also contains an interesting interview with Wally Whyton (who has obviously forgiven his friend for the Hank Williams comments). In the interview, Wally, referring to *Country Meets Folk*, reveals the shocking fact that 75% of mail received from country – as opposed to folk – fans is abusive, much of it violently so, like the listener who threatened to bring 200 mates down to do him (Wally) in, just for playing *Danny Boy* by Pete Stanley and Brian Golbey! Bob wonders "why we don't get this at *Opry*?"

WW: "Your medium is different, with a magazine. When I get *Opry*, for instance, I skip through, I'm looking for various things. If I see a page about a country artiste I don't particularly like, I turn over the page, but you don't turn over on Radio 1's *Country Meets Folk*... and if you are a Buck Owens fan and you hate Johnny Cash, then you've got to sit through two minutes 50 seconds of that artiste and sit there fuming because your one hasn't been played."

The interview concludes with the following note from editor, Bryan Chalker:-

"We found this interview to be fascinating in every respect, and as we have now received a large quantity of mail pleading for the return of David Allan to *Country Style* – because of the 'mushy' sentimentality employed by Pat Campbell – we would ask you to send us your views, for and against. The writer of the most constructive letter will receive £1 1s 0d."

The invitation produced a huge response, spread over several issues, with opinion divided – some even suggesting the two men host on alternate weeks. Competition winner – Mr. A. Byworth of Herts. (a regular, enthusiastic correspondent in these early days) – argued that there should be greater emphasis on current releases, and less "annoying sentimentality," which showed clearly where his loyalties lay.

At this stage, *Opry*'s future seemed bright. The readership certainly approved of the content, one writer (B. Roebuck, Ashton-on-Lyne, Lancs. in July, 1969) describing April's issue as "the most interesting and informative magazine I have ever read on any subject!" Likewise, demand was rising steadily. However, behind the scenes, financial and other factors were conspiring to undermine the team's good work. Owner Larry Adams, in *CMP*'s 200th edition (September, 1986), explains:-

"It took Surridge Dawson & Co., the newspaper wholesalers, eight months to accept national distribution…We couldn't get any further help from the bank. Then Surridge Dawson gave us our initial order, which was four times what we'd printed each month up to then!...Our printer wouldn't increase our print run without some up-front money. We were stuck!"

As for the magazine's bright, young columnist, he had concerns of his own: although a regular contributor to the mag, Bob (now living at 27 Montague Avenue, Brockley, S.E. London) was far from being a full-time employee. In fact, claiming unemployment benefit, the country enthusiast was spending his days rather idly, hanging around a record stall in Rupert Street market, Piccadilly, and drinking endless cups of tea in a nearby café with like-minded fans, including David Allan and stall-holder, John Thorpe. The former was destined to become a close associate in the years ahead. Starting out as a DJ on pirate radio station 390 in 1966, he went on to present BBC Radio 2's *Country Style* from 1968 (until replaced by Pat

Campbell the following year) and the same station's
Country Club from 1976, win the American *CMA* (*Country
Music Association*) 'International Broadcaster of the Year'
Award (2002) and perform regular hosting duties on both
BBC and ITV, including, of course, the *Wembley Festival*. By
this stage, his career had started to take off – unlike that of
his companion, who, to supplement a meagre income,
would sell reel-to-reel tapes compiled from his substantial
record collection for 6d (2½p) each (Dave Peacock, later
of Chas & Dave fame, being among his customers).
However, despite the hardship, he was, thanks to youthful
optimism and a naturally upbeat disposition, as cheery as
ever.[40]

It happened that now, coincidentally or not, Mr. Powel,
senior, appeared on the scene. Aware of his son's situation
– and perhaps fearing an indolent slide into oblivion – he
arranged through a friend (who just happened to be
president of the company) for him to start work in the
boiler spares department of J. Stone & Co., operating from
a disused church in Deptford, South East London. This
must have seemed about as attractive to Bob as a smack in
the face. However, being partly subsidised by 'Pop' at the
time, he was in no position to argue, and, typically, having
accepted the offer, grew to enjoy the work, to the extent
that, 45 years later, he was as keen to elaborate on the
intricacies of boiler maintenance as on any of the joys of
country music! His explanation: "I'm one of these guys
that rolls with the flow."

This job led to another unusual (part-time) occupation:

---

[40] Bob offered another explanation for his 'upbeat' outlook.
Attending Bishop Mountain School in Sillery along with him was
a sweet-natured girl named Barbara Ross, who happened to
share his date of birth, 16 January, 1943. Tragically, she died
aged just 8, of liver disease and, if ever he felt down or upset
because things were not going his way, he reflected on the cruel
twist of fate that denied her the life he enjoyed.

starter's assistant at West Ham's Speedway[41] track, the chance arising when J. Stone 'spares' boss Harry Horton invited him to replace another man. Never having heard of the sport before, it says a lot about Bob's willingness to tackle anything that he accepted such a potentially hazardous position, which involved standing trackside with three similarly minded individuals, holding back an eager bike-rider astride his noisily revving machine. At a given signal, bike and rider, with a little help from their assistants, would roar off into the night at great speed – and danger to those nearby. Goff Greenwood, who accompanied his fellow DJ to one meeting, recalls that "it was probably the only time I saw him engaged in hectic physical activity," summing up the experience as "an interesting evening of dust, sweat and noise!" Despite such discomfort, Bob claimed to have enjoyed the highly charged atmosphere of these occasions – however, his real opportunity was yet to come…

Thanks to *Opry*, the budding journalist had a toehold in the business, but knew that, in order to be taken seriously by his colleagues, he needed to be available should opportunity come knocking ("the industry hates part-timers") and this was not possible while committed to the 9-5 demands of J. Stone. Fate lent a hand when the company relocated to Crawley in Sussex (not related to

---

[41] Motorcycle Speedway, usually referred to as just Speedway, is a motorcycle sport involving four and sometimes up to six riders competing over four anti-clockwise laps of an oval circuit, meetings generally taking place in large stadiums at night. Bikes use only one gear and have no brakes, while tracks consist of dirt or loosely packed shale. On straight sections of track, bikes reach speeds of 70mph. Origins of the sport are not known, although there is evidence of racing being practised in the USA before WWI and in Australia in the late 1910s/early 1920s. Now, it is most popular in central/northern Europe and, to a lesser extent, in Australia and the USA.

North Crawley) and Bob, seizing the chance, followed suit, landing a clerical post at London's famous Smithfield Market[42] – with wholesale butchers, H. S. Emus[43] – the advantage being its early start, 7am, leading (if you managed to reconcile your sales dockets) to an early afternoon finish. This, in turn, ensured availability for any prospective record company and A & R appointments. He was starting to feel more professional, as he gradually moved further into his chosen field.

There then occurred one of those incidents that casts everything into sudden doubt. The same friend of his father who helped secure the J. Stone position telephoned out of the blue with an unusual job offer: supplying orders for lighthouses, the interesting part being that it entailed worldwide travel, which appealed to the intrepid side of Bob's nature. Now, although his own personal performance at *Opry* had been good, he knew that, with ongoing problems of finance and distribution coming to a

---

[42] Established 800 years ago, Smithfield Meat Market is situated in the north-west corner of the City of London and is the last remaining wholesale market in the capital. Dominated by the imposing Grade II listed covered market designed by Victorian architect Sir Horace Jones in the late nineteenth century, it was for centuries, along with Tyburn, the main site for public executions in London.

[43] H.S. Emus – Bob claims, in his Don Ford interview, that "every article I ever wrote for *Opry* was written in Smithfield Market. I even started doing my first broadcasting when I was there. Mr. Emus was very nice about it – he at that time was doing the 6.15am Market Report on Radio 2, so looked on me as a fellow broadcaster." This job also introduced him to the world of cockney rhyming slang, which he found fascinating, if sometimes puzzling, like the occasion he was told "a 'Gregory' is in the post," later discovering 'Gregory' stood for Gregory Peck – cheque! (This particular example came from Chas Hodges' partner in Chas 'n' Dave, Dave Peacock.)

head, the magazine's future was in doubt. Requesting time to consider the offer, he had not long replaced the receiver when the phone rang again. It was Larry Adams, the conversation proceeding roughly along the following lines:-

"Hi Bob, sorry to break the news, but *Opry* magazine is folding. However, we are launching a new magazine, *Country Music People*, with myself as editor. Oh, and would you care to be its chief feature writer?"

To Bob Powel, Canadian-bred and 'country' to the core, lighthouses, wherever situated, had never seemed so remote – or irrelevant… Now, he was really on his way – and yet, despite his new professional status, complete with proper salary, he remained at Smithfield Market – "for the extra income" – although the choice cuts of Irish beef and Suffolk lamb available to staff at huge discount prices each Friday presumably helped in his decision!

The London country music fraternity at this time (1969) was quite small and tightly knit and Bob was as well-known within it as anyone. These ardent enthusiasts, who included Dave Travis and members of popular bands of the day such as the Jonny Young Four,[44] would often

---

[44] Possibly Britain's most talented ever country group, Kent's Jonny Young Four were certainly the unluckiest. Formed in 1965, within days of signing for the RCA label in 1969, the group was involved in an accident which claimed the life of bassist, Bob Gibbs, and injured other members. Jonny was subsequently awarded £1200 damages from the other driver, who happened to be British comedian Charlie Chester. Taking the best part of a year to recover, they went on to produce top quality music, including, in *Country Pride* (1972), that rarity – an original British country classic. One of Bob's fondest memories was of Jonny, after playing a gig at *The Roebuck*, treating him to

meet up at, among other places, the *Roebuck*[45] pub in Lewisham, to listen to 'live' country music and exchange news and views, so, it was no surprise when he was invited one day by Dave Peacock, then a member of up-and-coming outfit, the Tumbleweeds, to join them at a gig they were due to play at the *Ponderosa*, a newly opened country venue close to Portsmouth on the south coast. Situated at Boar's Hunt, just outside Portsmouth and incorporated in the Boar's Head Hotel, *The Ponderosa* opened in March 1969, soon becoming the most popular country location in the South of England. It had the added distinction of being the first UK venue to hire a bona fide Nashville act – Justin Tubb, son of the famous Ernest. Other stars, including Stonewall Jackson, Tex Ritter and Faron Young, soon followed.

Accepting this invitation, Bob, during the evening, got chatting to owner Tom Butler. Hugely impressed with what he saw and heard, Bob enquired how the operation was financed. "With difficulty," came the reply, the disenchanted gent proceeding to list various expenses and overheads that, between them, were threatening its existence – this despite getting regular packed houses. During the course of their conversation, Bob learned that the Tumbleweeds were being paid a fee (excluding agents and managers' cuts) of £85, which did not tally with the £60 he subsequently discovered the group was receiving.

---

an Indian meal at a nearby restaurant, which he claimed was his first ever!

[45] Situated at 25 Rennell Street, Lewisham, South-East London, *The Roebuck* – or *Ye Old Roebuck Hotel*, as it was known in 1905 – featured 'live' country entertainment from 1964 through to the 1980s, whence it became a 'gay' bar. Subsequently, shortly after the turn of the millennium, it underwent a name change, to *Bar Phoenix*, before closing in 2008. Today, nothing remains of the building or anything else that side of Rennell Street, which is subject to road-widening and redevelopment.

And so, when Mr. Butler contacted him just three weeks later to say he was throwing in the towel, Bob revealed what he knew, i.e. that the booking agent was fiddling him, and, upon confirming that the balance between the amount paid and what was actually passed on would be sufficient to keep the business solvent, offered to replace the crooked agent. His offer was gladly accepted, enabling him to enter a new phase of his career, as, from then on, he received a percentage of the business, spent the majority of his weekends at the location and continued straddling the two positions right up until securing editorship of *Country Music People* magazine in December 1970. Bob credited Tom Butler with "getting me full-time into country music" (this position pre-dating *CMP* by several months).

Chapter 4

Convention Bound: 1969-87

Deep in the Heart Of Dixie ("Wishing I could stay forever...")[46]

While Bob, David Allan and company were congregating at venues in and around London to discuss their favourite musical genre, so hundreds, maybe even thousands of like-minded enthusiasts up and down the country – unbeknown to each other – were doing likewise, among them northerners, Stan Laundon and Goff Greenwood (of Hartlepool and Doncaster, respectively) and Jim Marshall from Brighton, on the south coast. Nottingham-born Jim, having moved to Brighton at an early age, initiated several locally based folk/country ventures, including two long-running clubs (one devoted to folk, the other country). He also produced BBC Radio Brighton/Sussex's *South Coast Country*, presented by Neil

---

[46] *Deep in the Heart of Dixie.* First recorded by Ronnie McDowell in 1976 and subsequently covered by Roy Drusky on his 1978 album, *Night Flying.*

Coppendale, which later, with Bob Powel at the helm, became *Country Sounds* (see Chapter 10), and, later still, Jim having been invited to return as presenter, *That's Country*. As a journalist, he co-edited, with Wakefield-based Mike Storey, the tape magazine, *Folk Voice*. Founded in 1958, this, as well as providing relevant news and information, encouraged readers to attend occasional 'get-togethers' (including an annual concert), held mostly in London, where it soon became evident that there existed:-

"...a network of people all over the UK, all doing their bit to further the cause of country music. The trouble was that their efforts were fragmented. What was needed was some sort of central organisation to which these dedicated people could belong. The idea had been mooted by other people earlier on, but it was Goff Greenwood who suggested that he, Mike Storey and I try to get the thing off the ground." (Jim Marshall, 'Ten Years...of *BCMA*,' *Country Music People*, September, 1978).

Thus, on 8 November, 1968, at the Russell Hotel, Russell Square, London, WC1, was born the *British Country Music Association*,[47] which, within a few weeks of its formation, had attracted an impressive 4,000 members to its ranks. The aims and objectives were outlined in an article written three and a half years after its formation:-

"To promote all forms of country music in Britain by liaison with record companies, the press, radio, television, artistes, clubs and promoters. It provides an excellent source of news and information and tries to co-ordinate

---

[47] This organisation has no connection with the *Country Music Association (GB)*, a trade organisation set up to promote country music in the UK.

the many efforts being made to further the acceptance of all forms of country music in this country…the *BCMA* is a non-profit making organisation, all revenue being ploughed back into the *Association* to provide an improved service. The *BCMA* aims to be a truly representative 'voice' of country music in Britain."

The article then proceeds to list its achievements:-

- "Laid secure foundations for future growth,
- Joined forces with *Folk Voice* to produce an annual country music festival of British artistes (in London),
- Established a close working relationship with the American *Country Music Association*,
- Helped to get country shows on BBC network of local radio stations,"

And, finally, benefits of membership (costing just 50p per annum):-

- "Regular bi-monthly bulletin (including details of concerts and record releases),
- Annual Yearbook and Directory (listing clubs, performers, records available, review articles, etc.)
- Eligibility for charter flights to Nashville."

(*CMP*, March, 1972)

This last inducement, which referred specifically to the annual *DJ Convention*, was what persuaded many to subscribe to the *Association*. After all, part of the fascination of country music is its surrounding 'mythology', elements of which might be probed simply by visiting its hallowed shrines: the *Ryman Auditorium*, *Hall of Fame Museum*, Music Valley, etc. Best of all, visitors would have an opportunity to meet some of their heroes. The following is how this initial trip to the heart of American country music was advertised in October 1968's edition of *Opry* magazine:-

"TAKE A JOURNEY OF A LIFETIME TO NASHVILLE, USA, IN 1969

"To coincide with the *Disc Jockey Convention* in Nashville during October, 1969, plans are afoot to organise a 10-15 day visit to 'Music City USA' at a cost far lower than possible if planned on an independent basis. The arrangement will be approximately 10 days (but not more than 15) and the cost will include return flights to New York from London, basic accommodation and bus travel to Nashville. It is hoped to include sight-seeing, *Opry* visits, meetings with entertainers, etc.

"Most meals will not be included, but it is important to note that, under present regulations, there will still be ample personal spending allowed from participants' travel allowance. Businesses taking part will, of course, be able to claim a business travel allowance.

"The visit to Nashville is intended for enthusiasts, collectors, broadcasters and all with a firm interest in American folk and country music. It will appeal to individuals involved in journalism, record production, record retailing, as well as performers, song-writers and all wishing to take advantage of a once-in-a-lifetime chance of a low-price arrangement which will include the cost of a visit to Nashville.

"It is impossible at this stage to determine the cost, as this will depend very greatly on the numbers wishing to participate. You are invited to advise us immediately if you are interested in the arrangement. This does not commit you in any way."

The following paraphrased account of Bob's editorial for October 1974's *CMP* illustrates the nature and importance of the *DJ Convention* within American country music at this time:-

"In Britain – courtesy of the *Wembley Festival* – late March or early April represents country music's 'prime time.' In the States, however, October is traditionally country music month, the *Grand Ole Opry*'s yearly celebration being held then. This involves a big push by record companies, radio stations, record shops and the powerful *CMA* (*Country Music Association*), enabling anyone and everyone connected with the industry to meet in Nashville and get to know one another better. Over the years, it has developed into a huge event, attracting upwards of 6,000 people, in the process becoming an essential date on the calendar for nearly all country artistes, because, in the USA, DJ's are, quite simply, the lifeblood of the industry. Although there are many thousands of radio stations, just one DJ can 'break' a record, so the artiste is well aware they are important people and goes to some lengths to gain their friendship. Thus, the '*Convention*', as it is commonly known, represents a happy reunion of people in country music, which, accounting for 10% of all music sold in America (compared to 1.6% of jazz), means big business."

Ironically, the year this was written, 1974, saw the *BCMA* switch its destination from the *Convention* to the *Fan Fair*, but for now – 1968 – the *DJ Convention* is clearly *the* Nashville event to target, if only because there was little else happening at other times of the year. As for the *Opry* offer, it was more than just an invitation to British fans to sample some of the delights of their favourite musical city: *BCMA*'s core members were acutely aware that, without the support necessary to hire a charter flight, the cost of any trip would be beyond many of their means (Mike Storey, employed by *Lunn-Poly* at this time, would have pointed out the financial realities). Fortunately, 118 people responded, making the 'Journey of a Lifetime' viable.

So, how did Nashville respond to the news that an assortment of British fans, tourists and media people were set to descend on an – essentially trade – event that had been happily operating for close to 20 years with little change or disruption? Surprisingly well, it seems, the group's good relations with *CMA* Chairman (at the time) Jo Walker ensuring they were afforded royal status wherever they went, to the extent of being granted "a motor cycle escort when meeting the Mayor of Nashville – all while enjoying free meals, alcohol and even record albums, courtesy of the record labels!" (Jim Marshall). Whether such grand hospitality would have been lavished had Nashville's hierarchy realised the entourage included quite so many 'non-media' personnel is open to debate. However, it's nice to think that America's renowned 'Southern' hospitality would have won the day, regardless.

As for the lucky participants, naturally, they lapped it up, and, on returning home, extolled the virtues and generosity of their country cousins to all and sundry – to such an extent that, for the next 39 years, the annual trip became a regular, successful event, *CMP*'s March, 1972 article, written after three *Convention* excursions had taken place, providing an insight into its early itinerary:-

"On occasions, the parties flew to New York and then travelled by 'Greyhound' coach to Nashville along a route specially planned by *Lunn-Poly* to include some of the greatest scenic attractions in America. Apart from big cities like New York and Washington, the travellers visited places like Williamsburg, Bristol, Cherokee, Knoxville and the Great Smoky Mountain National Park. (The first group) in 1969, was given the freedom of Nashville by the mayor and a civic reception, (while) the following year, Wheeling, Virginia (home of the famous WWVA *Jamboree*) bestowed a similar honour. All participants were entitled to pay several visits to the *Opry* (then still in its old home at the *Ryman Auditorium*), investigate the *Hall of Fame* and see almost all of the stars of country music at *Convention* shows. During the 1970 trip, the party had the added attraction of a special performance of the *Renfro Valley Barndance*, a real treat for old-time fans. Altogether, nearly 500 people have travelled with *BCMA* to Nashville."

And so, the *BCMA* continued organising trips up to and including 2008, although there were many innovations and alterations along the way, both in the group's itinerary and the format of the event itself, which soon divided in two, as the following summary shows:-

- 1969 – First ever trip (12-24 October), comprising 118 participants.
- 1970 – Bob's first trip.
- 1972 – Owing to congestion at the venue, a separate event designed exclusively for fans, *Fan Fair*, is launched at Nashville's *Municipal Auditorium* on 12 April, attracting 5,000 people. The *DJ Convention* continues to be held at the same venue in October, even if its emphasis is increasingly on two events tied in with it since 1967: the *Grand Ole Opry Birthday Celebration* and *CMA Awards Show*.[48]

---

[48] Nowadays, *Country Radio Seminar* (*CRS*) occupies the position previously held by the *DJ Convention*. This event, held late February at the Nashville Convention Centre, "offers a chance

- 1973 – Month of *Fan Fair* brought forward to June in the hope of more favourable weather conditions (remaining here to present day). Attendance doubles to 10,000.

- 1974 – *BCMA* switch destination from *Convention* to *Fan Fair*.

- 1979 – *BCMA* itinerary is radically overhauled and 16-day trip now includes stopovers at Dallas, Little Rock and Memphis en route, and Meridian (Mississippi), New Orleans and Shreveport, Louisiana on homeward journey.

- 1980 – *BCMA* trip includes stopovers in New York (outward) and Miami (return), with internal flights (rather than coach travel) for first time.

- 1981 – Tony Byworth (*CMP*, December, 1981) describes the week-long *Convention* 'bash' as "representing very little of (its) original intentions, with the Nashville music industry moving into it to push primarily a lot of their own wares, with the DJ's being given a secondary role."

- 1982 – Location of *Fan Fair* moves to the Tennessee State Fairgrounds to accommodate more fans.

- 1983 – *BCMA* itinerary modified again to include visits to San Antonio and Dallas (Texas) and St. Louis (Missouri).

- 1987 – Final *BCMA* trip to *Fan Fair* (though occasional Nashville trips still organised, usually in September).

---

for folks in the radio industry to interact with their peers as well as superstar artistes and country newcomers. It's a chance to network and to hear new music in various settings from intimate acoustic showcases to full band performances in various venues around town. Attendees also have numerous workshops to choose from throughout the 3-day event or they can just hang out at any number of Nashville nightspots."

(theboot.com/country-radio-seminar-2013)

- 1991 – 20th anniversary of *FF* celebrated with an expanded show schedule, more than 65 artistes appearing in more than 34 hours of live stage shows.

- 1992 – Over 600 media representatives present from countries including Switzerland, Japan, Brazil, Sweden, Spain, England, Ireland, Luxembourg and France.

- 1996 – 25th anniversary sees sell-out crowd of 24,000 being entertained by over 100 artistes, including those evergreen country-surfers, the Beach Boys.

- 2001 – Event moved to several sites in Downtown Nashville, also held for first time over long weekend (Thur-Sun) instead of midweek. 175 artistes appear.

- 2002 – Thanks mainly to Downtown move, aggregate attendance over four days soars to 126,500.

- 2004 – Name is changed to *CMA Music Festival.* Also, ABC televise event, attracting 9 million viewers.

- 2006 – No *BCMA* trip, owing to the death of Mike Storey.

- 2007 – Final *BCMA* trip to Nashville – but not the *Music Festival,* which itself sets a new attendance record: 191,154 people participating in more than 100 hours of concerts, 30 hours of organised autograph signings, family activities, celebrity sports competitions, interactive exhibits, giveaways, games and much more, including over 400 celebrities making appearances.

- 2008 – Final *BCMA*-organised trip (itinerary: Fort Worth, Austin, Bandera, San Antonio, Houston).[49]

Quite a breathtaking transformation – and, in some ways, an impressive one. However, behind the fanfare (pun intended) and extravagance, it is felt by many that an essential element has been lost, or, at the very least, diluted, as the event begins to resemble a carnival. Here,

---

[49] The cost of this trip was £1,665 – compared with £115 (+ $10 *DJ Convention* fee) for the first.

Jim Marshall reflects on his long involvement with the *BCMA* and *Convention/Fan Fair:-*

"The forty years from 1969 to 2008, during which the *British Country Music Association* was active, were probably the happiest in my life so far. I reckon I got involved in country music at just the right time, although I would give anything to have been around Nashville back in the 50s.

"The *BCMA*'s first visit to 'Music City' was an extremely exciting experience for someone like me whose only contact with the music had been by way of records. True, we did get to see Mervyn Conn's star-studded first ever *Wembley Festival* in early '69 – and what a thrill that was – but witnessing the 1969 *CMA Awards Show* at the *Ryman Auditorium* when it was still home of the *Grand Ole Opry* was a notable highlight. I even got to interview an idol of mine, Gene Autry, who'd been inducted into the *Country Music Hall of Fame.*

"I tell no lie when I say that on *one* Saturday night *Opry* show alone (in October, 1973), the line-up included Tex Ritter, George Jones, Tammy Wynette, Bill Monroe, the Osborne Bros., Roy Acuff, Dottie West, Porter Wagoner, Dolly Parton, Tom T. Hall, Ernest Tubb, Loretta Lynn, Hank Snow, Hank Locklin, and, to end the evening, the irrepressible Marty Robbins, whose spot regularly over-ran into the early hours.

"Today, the *Opry* is a shadow of its former self – it was only half full when I last visited there in 2007! I'm pretty sure my observations will be echoed by Bob Powel, whose radio shows made fascinating listening at the time but which would probably not be given airtime today. Just imagine a two-hour incisive interview with Taylor Swift! I'd pay good money to hear that!"

These observations certainly were echoed by the subject of this book. However, back in the 1970s, the week-long *Convention* – or *Birthday 'Bash'* – remained the premier event on the calendar for professionals, representing a time when not only was the music less 'sanitised' but DJ's still had some 'clout' within the industry (unlike today, where they operate at the behest of radio stations, which, in turn, are controlled by major record labels). Among the many hundreds of DJs present on these occasions, one of the most familiar was, of course, the same Mr. Powel, who, missing out on the first *BCMA*-organised trip and joining the second excursion in 1970, subsequently preferred to make his own way to the event, bypassing *Fan Fair* and 'sticking to *Convention.*'

Here, typically attired in smart jacket and bow tie, this true country devotee was invariably at the heart of things, ever ready to communicate, build up contacts, conduct interviews and raise awareness of his own activities. In the same way that Britain enjoys a special relationship with America, he enjoyed a special relationship with Nashville. "Right from the start, he had the knack of opening doors in Nashville that other journalists/organisations, even the BBC, couldn't." (David Allan).

Bob explained how: "There was no secret to this. As *CMP* editor, I regularly posted two copies of each month's magazine to all major US record labels, enabling me to reach prominent industry people in a way that BBC networked radio shows *Country Meets Folk* and *Country Style* could not."

Leaving aside the serious business at hand, it often tended to be happenings around and about – or before and after – that provided most interest and amusement on these occasions, especially in the early days, when a natural ease and friendliness existed between artiste, media person and fan that made their encounters very special. It was not unusual then for stars to open their doors to visiting fans, and such was the case in 1970 when old-time musicians Sam and Kirk McGee welcomed Bob and Brian Golbey to their home in Franklin, just south of Nashville.

First appearing at the *Grand Ole Opry* in 1926, the brothers had teamed up with Uncle Dave Macon's band the following year, fiddler Arthur Smith in the 30s and Bill Monroe & his Bluegrass Boys in the 40s, before the folk revival of the 50s/60s brought fresh approval and recognition. Although Sam usually played guitar and Kirk banjo/fiddle, they were, in fact, proficient in multiple stringed instruments, and, on this occasion, the presence of a couple of other musicians (as well as Golbey) ensured an entertaining afternoon, especially when word of the event began to spread, attracting music-loving friends and neighbours. (The brothers had initially earned local recognition for being the earliest owners of a car in their district, subsequently, according to Bob, "spending the first few years using the vehicle for little else but transporting people with shotgun wounds to and from hospital!")

During this particular session, Brian Golbey easily matched the McGees note for note, but looked to ex-manager, Bob Powel, to suggest song titles, one of which happened to be *Faded Coat of Blue,*[50] described by him as "a gorgeous old song." Brian duly performed the tune, at the end of which, instead of the enthusiastic applause that had greeted his previous efforts, there was complete silence. Eventually, Sam turned to his brother and observed drily, "That's a Yankee song, ain't it, Kirk?" Shifting uncomfortably in his seat, the title's proposer feared he might just be lynched, but needn't have worried, for, out of goodwill or whatever, Sam insisted Brian play it again!

---

[50] *Faded Coat Of Blue.* Civil War-era song by little-known writer, J. H. McNaughton, popularised by the Carter Family via their Victor recording.

(In fact, the McGees themselves recorded *Kingdom Coming*,[51] complete with verses describing the cowardly retreat of "Ol' Massa," though later claiming it had been their agent's idea).

Another memorable episode occurred a couple of years later, in 1972, when Bob, accompanying Tex Ritter and band on tour through Cleveland, Mississippi, happened to remark on the snow-like substance covering the surrounding countryside. The star, instructing guitarist/driver Bill Merritt to stop the vehicle, led his curious companion to the centre of a field, where, in front of bemused labourers, he introduced him to cotton in its pure, natural state, before giving a demonstration in the art of picking it! A few days later, at the *Convention*, superstar Charley Pride, having spoken to Tex in the interim, strode over to the British DJ and announced in a booming voice: "Howdy, pal – I hear you and me are fellow Mississippi cotton-pickers!" (Ironically, just two years later, Charley was to enjoy a No.3 country hit with *Mississippi Cotton Picking Delta Town*).

The aforementioned incidents are recalled quite clearly and backed up by written verification (*CMP*'s of December 1970 and February 1974, respectively). The following year, 1973, however, while travelling to the *Convention* with fellow journalist, Tony Byworth, there occurred what subsequently became known as 'the speeding incident' recalled so differently by each that it's necessary to present two versions:-

---

[51] *Kingdom Coming*. Civil War song written by Henry C. Work, ardent abolitionist and Union supporter, in 1862. The song celebrates promised freedom to slaves whose master ("Ol' Massa") has been frightened away by Union military forces.

VERSION A (In Tony Byworth's own words)

"Bob's mother lived in Quebec and this particular year, he said, 'Why don't you come to Quebec and we'll drive down?' (to the *Convention*)

"I said, 'Fine,' so we spent a couple of days at his mother's apartment and then set off.

"Now, it was a bit of a bad beginning because the day we set off, at about 10 or 11 o'clock in the morning, Bob wanted to eat, and I thought, 'Well, I've just had breakfast, I don't want to eat,' but we stopped somewhere – it must have been a shopping mall or something like that. Bob went off to eat and I went off looking around the shops and found a couple of LPs which I bought – to be honest, I cannot remember what they were – then went back to meet Bob, who got very upset. 'Logically,' he said, 'if you hadn't been with me, you wouldn't have found those LPs, so I have a right to those LPs' – I think he was prepared to pay me for them. The next stop was around lunchtime and he wanted to walk around with me everywhere – to make sure I didn't see any more records, I presume. He wouldn't go and eat unless I was coming to eat as well.

"Then, it must have been the next day, the speeding incident happened. It must have been on this trip because I only went once from Quebec to Nashville with him. We must have stopped at least once overnight and I know the incident with the records happened on the first day, so whether it was the next day or the day after that the speeding incident occurred. Anyway, it was Sunday morning, in a place called Painesville, at about quarter to nine, a police car turns up and stops. Bob was driving, nobody around... Bob turns to me and says, 'You're the passenger, you should have spotted them.' I was 'riding shotgun,' was his argument. So, we get dragged off to Painesville Prison, the sheriff's office, pay the fine, which I believe was 30 dollars, which I think we split. The thing I remember most about it is that, when we arrived there, they were letting the drunks out of jail from the night before. The whole thing sounds like a Tom T. Hall song!

"Then, of course, after (the *Convention*), we had to go back to Quebec, and I thought, oh God, I'm not looking forward to the trip back, Bob being a bit 'moody' about the whole thing! But anyway, we did get back and it was fine – he showed me the family house in Tadoussac. Tadoussac is not a place to go if you want a night life – the only thing you can do at six o'clock in the evening is watch a ferry – there's absolutely nothing there – not even a friendly bar to have a drink!"

VERSION B (In Bob Powel's own words)

"We departed Quebec in Marylee's car and drove all the way to Erie, Pennsylvania in one day, choosing that particular stopover point because Tex Ritter was appearing there and we wanted to catch his show. *Google* quotes the distance between Quebec and Erie as 644 miles, with an estimated driving time of 9 hours 41 minutes, meaning that, even with an early morning start, we had little time for eating/rest stops, much less a stroll around a shopping mall. In his version, Tony is, I believe, getting confused with a stop on our homeward journey, which I shall refer to later.

"The next morning, we set off for Nashville and, as my friend and colleague correctly relates, it was during this journey, at Painesville, Ohio, that the speeding incident occurred. Tony told me off for getting nabbed for speeding and I pointed out (jokingly) that on country music buses, the person sitting beside the driver rides 'shotgun' and is in charge of looking out for 'smokeys' (cops). The Highway Patrolman took our driving licences and led us to a police station (not a jail, in the British sense of the word). There, we were met by a desk-sergeant who said to the Patrolman, 'Hey, Joe, so you got yourself a Brit. Is that your first one?'

Joe: 'No, I caught one the other day, and he was most indignant – he said, 'I was only doing 70 and the sign says 90 [Interstate 90 Highway sign].'

To which I remark, 'Oh, that was a good idea – did you let him off?'

Joe: 'No – but anyway, you were on *Highway 20*!'

"I thought we were fined $50 but it could have been $30. Either way, I thought it was fair, though I couldn't resist commenting, when handing over my share of the money: 'I'm sure you've heard this many times before, but this is a very *well-named* town.'

"The sergeant laughed and said, 'Actually, I haven't!'

"The only incident I recall involving records occurred on the homeward journey. Having met at the *Convention* a great character (and musician) by the name of Tex Justice, we called into his Boonville-based radio station, where he allowed us to trawl through two large boxes of unwanted records and to keep any interesting finds. My box happened to contain country material, Tony's pop, but there were plenty left in the country box after I finished.

"I have to admit Tony was not enamoured of my favourite place in the whole world – Tadoussac – though, to be fair, we did go in October, when the season was just about over. But then again, it's not a swinging little village at any time – just one of the most beautiful places in the world, in my biased opinion. However, it's not true that all you can do at 6pm is watch a ferry – you're allowed to *board* one, if you wish – free-of-charge! And where else would you be offered bear steaks at 8 o'clock in the morning, as we were in our hotel! (Not that either of us took advantage)"

Two contrasting interpretations. Boonville, New York, and Erie, Pennsylvania are both en route from Quebec to Nashville, at distances of 350mi/563km and 644mi/1,036km respectively, making a stop at either place in one day feasible. Bob, in February 1974's *CMP*, while paying tribute to Tex Ritter (who died the previous month) sticks fairly faithfully to the above account, one small discrepancy being the amount of the fine, quoted at $25. As for what really happened, *No One Will Ever Know.*[52]

Journalists and photographers, by the nature of their work, are accustomed to enduring all kinds of calamity and disorder, but *Conventions* appear to be in a class of their own in that regard, as the following account of her first visit to Nashville by Marie O'Connell, of Doug McKenzie Photographic Services (suppliers of numerous *CMP* photographs), illustrates:-[53]

"Bob asked if I might be able to go to Nashville, Tennessee, to cover the *CMA Convention* one year. Nashville was a real learning curve for me, in all kinds of ways. I had been trampled on during photocalls before by some of the most notorious bands of photographers both

---

[52] *No One Will Ever Know* – Fred Rose-Mel Foree composition, a No.42 country hit for Frank Ifield in 1966 and No.13 for Gene Watson in 1980. Also recorded by Hank Williams, Marty Robbins, Hank Snow and Roy Orbison.

[53] Marie had cause to be grateful to Bob on this trip. Knowing her fear of flying and aware he needed to learn how to operate the camera she intended loaning him at the end of her visit, he made her go over the directions again and again during the flight – up until the moment of touch down, at which point she realised he was not quite as slow as she was beginning to think he might be!

in the UK and Europe. As a woman photographer, I had learned to stand my ground and give as good as I got in order to get my pictures. I took no prisoners either – it was the only way to survive.

"However, Nashville was the first time I had ever been run over in an audience stampede, with each individual grasping a Kodak Instamatic. In the days before digital photography, practically everyone had one of these simple little rectangular cameras. It happened following Willie Nelson's introduction – suddenly, I found myself pinned to the front lip of the stage by what seemed like a thousand screaming fans! Instamatics were being brandished like weapons! I'd never seen so many of the little cameras in one place before. Somehow, I still managed to get my shots regardless of being pushed, shoved and partially blinded by all the little flashes…well, you can't travel all that way and not get a result, can you?

"Anyway, at the end of the performance, I was putting my gear away and a young man and a woman approached me to see what I had thought of the show. They had heard that Bob and I were from London. Without looking up, I muttered something about: 'Well, it was great, apart from nearly being killed by the 'Instamatic Brigade.' I had not realised that they were reporters and in the next day's paper there was a large photograph of me, dishevelled hair and all, complete with the Instamatic quote.

"Needless to say, Bob was in hysterics about it all, more so my indignation. He kept waving the newspaper at me and showing it to everyone. He reminded me of it repeatedly over the years."

A further *Convention* memory concerns the occasion, while staying with WBAP Radio's Farm Director, Dick

Yaws[54] in Fort Worth, Texas, prior to travelling to Nashville, Bob was invited to appear on the station. Starting with trucker's favourite Bill Mack's late-night programme (10pm-4am) and continuing into the next, he was still on air by the time Yaws' early morning *Farm Report* appeared at 5.45am. Here, much friendly banter ensued, including a reference by the host to the auctioning of 'Hurrford' cattle, prompting an interruption from his guest, keen to provide the correct pronunciation:

"Excuse me, but they're called Herre-fords – it's a county in England."

"Boy," barked the plain-speaking presenter, "It's been 'Hurrfords' as long as I've been alive and it's gonna stay 'Hurrfords!'"

Bob refrained from provoking the situation by repeating a response previously given to Ralph Emery following a disagreement over the word 'Datsun': "*We* invented the language, but *you* changed it!"

There must have been other lively exchanges with all three presenters, for, a couple of days later, at the *Convention*, upon approaching Reba McEntire to supply a short spoken ad for his show (commonly called 'Idents'), the singer, one of country music's most successful ever female performers, asked if he was from England. "Yes," came the answer.

"And were you on the Bill Mack show?" she queried. Again replying in the affirmative, Bob was somewhat flattered at her subsequent announcement: "Well, my

---

[54] Dick Yaws. As a matter of interest, this gentleman happened to be a policeman at the time of J. F. Kennedy's shooting. With regard to a story then doing the rounds that it was not murderer Lee Harvey Oswald's body in the grave, he commented: "Yes it is – I know because my friend put the head in the coffin and I put the feet in."

daddy rang me about you and said I should meet up with you, as you sound like a real interesting person!" In spite of which, they never had any further meetings beyond this brief encounter.

Occasionally, having attended the Convention, Bob would venture further afield, combining his travels with a visit back home. This particular year, he found himself 440mi/708km south west of Quebec – in Toronto, where he received a call from Gary Buck. The Canadian singer-songwriter was due to perform with a new band at Niagara Falls that evening and wondered if his DJ friend might care to accompany him on the journey. With no outstanding engagements, the keen music lover was more than happy to accept and the pair drove the 80mi/129km around the western edge of Lake Ontario to the venue.

Although enjoyable, it was what happened during the interval that made the occasion memorable for Buck's special guest. Deciding to go for a walk – and giving no thought to his geographic location – he crossed Whirlpool Bridge, at which point he felt the call of nature. Managing to restrain himself until reaching the other side(!), he enquired at a duty station if he might use their facilities. The officer, after checking his passport, duly granted permission, adding, "And how long are you staying in the United States of America?"

"Just as long as it takes me to spend a penny," came the instant reply.

Having attended to business, Bob, on the way back to the Club, heard a voice call out after him, "I hope you enjoyed your visit to the United States!"

Chapter 5

Country Music People, 1st Term: 1970-76

Move It On Over ("Move over skinny dog, 'cos the fat dog's moving in...")[55]

Issue No. 1 of *Country Music People* magazine emerged in February, 1970, bang on schedule (something that would not always be the case, especially in the early months of its existence). With a full-colour photo of Johnny Cash on the front cover (an obvious selling-point) and asking price of 3/6d (17½p – less than one twentieth of current cost), the magazine had a positive 'vibe' right from the start, Larry Adams' page 3 editorial setting the tone: "Country music has been on the verge of a big breakthrough for a couple of years now and every sign was there for this to happen in 1969... etc."

Articles were spread liberally throughout its 32 pages, among 13 different contributors, including co-founder

---

[55] *Move It On Over*. Hank Williams composition that provided him with his first country hit – No.4 in 1947. Other artistes to have recorded it include: Bill Haley, Ray Charles and Hank Williams, Jr.

Gordon Smith (his Lucky label's Pye distribution deal), promoter Mervyn Conn (item hailing the arrival of 'modern' country reprinted from *Record Retailer*), David Brassington (bluegrass feature), Chris Comber (piece on obscure 1920s string band), David Bussey (Jim Reeves 'Scene'), David Allan (first of what would become a regular column – still running, after a couple of breaks, in 2015) and no fewer than four by News Editor & Chief Feature Writer, Mr. Bob Powel:

Powel's Point of View (featured regularly throughout this first year and sporadically thereafter)

RCA Victor Country Show

British Scene

Bob Powel interviews Faron Young

The consensus, among staff and readers, was that this was a promising start – a good launch pad from which to build bigger and better things, but it wasn't long before problems arose, and the following summary of the next 11 issues, from March, 1970 to January, 1971, illustrates some of the tensions that existed during the magazine's first year:-

MARCH, 1970 – Judging by *Mailbag*, readers are impressed with both the layout and content of issue no.1. However, in a portent of things to come, the magazine appears 12 days late, albeit due to circumstances beyond anyone's control – a Trades Union dispute.

APRIL, 1970 – Larry, in his editorial, refers to a near-20,000 circulation, going on to thank his, "friend and colleague" Bob Powel, for "excellent biographies" on the Capitol/MCA artistes due to tour UK later that month. This issue also late (see JUNE for explanation).

MAY, 1970 – Larry expresses 'great personal satisfaction that the publication of a nationally distributed country magazine – his brainchild – has been one of the biggest factors in the growth of country music in the UK." It also contains a thoughtful reply by him to a crass anti-country piece by Peter Cole in the *Evening News*. (This issue also late). Additionally, page 33 features photo of Bob sporting a rather unflattering moustache, which, a year – and one runny nose – later, was gone.

JUNE, 1970 – Bob tackles Buck Owens over his failure to fulfil a touring obligation the previous November. Elsewhere, Larry apologises "to our readers, distributors, wholesalers, retailers and, not least, advertisers for late publication of April and May issues owing to a combination of circumstances, especially staff shortages owing to flu."

JULY, 1970 – Report on amalgamation of *CMP* with *Country Music* journal (run by Goff Greenwood and Alan Cackett).

AUGUST, 1970 – More favourable comments from readers in *Mailbag* – none, surprisingly, referring to publication delays.

SEPTEMBER, 1970 – Gordon Smith, in his *Out & About* column, has a none-too-subtle dig at Bob Powel for his connections with the *Ponderosa* – in particular its monopolising of top country acts in the area and publicising of the venue via his *CMP* column. Elsewhere, Bob reviews Jerry Reed's appearance at the *Nashville Room*.[56]

---

[56] Situated beside West Kensington Tube Station, West London, *The Nashville Room*, a converted pub, was opened on 5 March 1969 as a country music venue by no less a personage than Chet Atkins, who donated a guitar which hung on the wall until the club's closure. Calling itself 'The Mecca of Country Music', it hosted TV's *George The Fourth: A King in the Country* series featuring George Hamilton IV (11/70-1/71) and *Up Country* (1972-74). From 1975, it became a major pub-rock (evolving

OCTOBER, 1970 – Larry writes about the American *CMA (DJ) Convention* due to take place in Nashville this month.

NOVEMBER, 1970 – 'In-print' discord continues, Larry objecting to Bob's remarks (which he feels are aimed at him) made in this month's Tex Ritter interview concerning "other people on magazine who have ultra-modern tastes and don't like anything else." Meanwhile, Bob, in a full-page reply, defends his *Ponderosa* position.

DECEMBER, 1970 – Unsurprisingly, given last month's open disagreements, there is major 'blood-letting': Larry Adams, one half of *CMP's* founding team – and its main inspiration – is no longer involved in production. Now, just one name remains on page 3, as editor: Bob Powel.

JANUARY, 1971 – In this, his first 'proper' issue, the new editor expresses the desire for: a) greater coverage of British scene, and b) increased scope for non-recurring articles (i.e. fewer 'regular' contributors), even inviting submissions from readers. Plus, there are now 11 different names under 'Credits' on page 3, where all previous issues had just two, Larry Adams' and his own.

This, then, gives some idea of the turbulent undercurrents at work during the first momentous year in the history of *CMP*, which, miraculously, considering all this internal strife, is still functioning, 45 years later.

Bob stressed to me that his memories of this formative period may not necessarily concur with other people's, i.e. two people will often see the same incident differently –

---

into 'punk') venue, apart from a brief spell in between, 1974-75, when it featured cabaret. Closed 19 July 1980 when Fuller's decided to sell. Having reverted to its original name, *The Famous Three Kings*, it is now a 'sports' pub with multiple screens.

and, of course, our memories can play tricks on us. Nevertheless, as he recalled:-

"The late Reg Field, owner of Cray Press and now, owing to Larry's inability to meet the financial obligations incurred by *Opry*, also owner of *CMP*, was in poor health & struggling to cope with the extra responsibilities involved, chiefly:-

• trying to establish a good working relationship with Larry,

• achieving the target publication date (20th of previous month), consistently sabotaged both by an unnamed printing manager, who apparently 'had it in' for him and other factors outside his control,

• the Lucky Records venture. Having been persuaded by Gordon Smith to help finance this new label, launched (with noble intent) to promote the best in British country music, Reg had to sit by and watch as it struggled to make an impact (eventually folding).

"In fact, I had hardly any dealings with Reg, who, when not off sick, was based at the printers. However, as I remember, having presented an ultimatum that was refused, Larry resigned, leaving Gordon, unwilling to take on editorship, the task of finding a replacement. Alan Cackett, his first choice, declined, opting to remain in his full-time Night Manager's job at the *Kent Evening Post* newspaper, which left, presumably to Gordon's chagrin (bearing in mind his September *CMP* comments), me!"

Larry, in his '*CMP* Early Years' piece written for the 500th edition of the magazine (October 2011), states that part of the reason for his not getting on with Bob was the latter's objection to amendments of his copy, an accusation hotly denied by Bob in a letter printed the following month, and, being aware of his deficiencies in this regard (note teacher's comments on exam essay referred to in Chapter 2), it does seem more likely he would have been glad of such corrections. On the other hand, his 'Tex Ritter' comments in November's issue would surely have inflamed – and undermined – not just Larry, but any editor, causing something to give at that point. Whatever the truth of the matter, it's perfectly understandable Larry should feel somewhat aggrieved – bitter, even – at losing his 'baby' in this way, but such are the *Cold Hard Facts of Life.*[57]

With Larry gone, Gordon wasn't long in following. So, in precisely one year, the whole character of the magazine had altered, its co-founders departing in unhappy circumstances. Pressing on regardless, Bob and his team worked hard to overcome the losses. In *CMP*'s 100th edition (May, 1978), he outlines the problems faced:-

"When I took over…*CMP* was in a rather sorry state. We were thousands of pounds in debt and the future looked somewhat bleak. The main problem I had to tackle was that *CMP* never managed to come out on time, and it's amazing how much this affected the progress of the magazine. The readers would be unhappy, and many would blame their newsagents who in turn would get fed up with the hassle and often refuse to stock it. With a great deal of help from all at Cray Press, we put it right by March, 1971. For a long time it was a question of

---

[57] *Cold Hard Facts of Life* – Written by Bill Anderson, a No. 2 country hit for Porter Wagoner (12th August 1927-28th October 2007) in 1967 and reputedly among Bob Dylan's all-time favourite recordings.

producing the magazine for the least possible cost and I became quite adept at using old blocks and generally saving money. In my first year as editor, Wembley changed from a one day to a two day affair and slowly the music trade and media began to take us seriously."

He sheds further light on the situation in an interview with Don Ford for *Four-on-the-Floor* magazine (4 December 1976):-

"(*CMP*) was very much in debt and we had a very bad reputation with wholesalers and retailers with regard to delivery dates. One of the reasons for this, which people in the trade will understand, was that before I took over, the typesetters were about 5 miles away from the factory. This meant that if there was a line wrong, someone had to go back to the typesetters to get it corrected and bring it back, which meant a ten-mile round journey and the time involved. As a coincidence, the month I took over, the typesetters moved into our factory giving me a big advantage inasmuch as we were a self-contained unit and within two months the magazine was coming out more or less on time."

Upon taking over, one of his first moves was to draft in "two talented writers – Geoff Lane from Leicester and Tony Byworth" on a full-time basis. Tony, in particular, would become a close associate and, as future editor, a great asset to *CMP* in the years ahead. A Londoner by birth, he, like his new boss (and Larry Adams), had entered the music business following a spell of outside employment (import/export business). Joining the *BCMA* on its 1968 formation, he regularly undertook trips to Nashville's *DJ Convention*, including the very first one, in 1969. Summarising that experience for BBC Radio 2's

Country Meets Folk led to journalistic assignments – initially *Record Mirror* and then *Billboard* and *CMP*, enabling him to give up his day job and move into the music industry full-time. Several books followed, along with accolades, including *CMA*'s prestigious 'Wesley Rose (Foreign Media Achievement) Award' in 1993. After completing his spell as *CMP* editor in 1983, he formed the PR firm, Byworth-Wootton International (see Chapter 8). In 2012, in recognition of his services to the music, he was inducted into the British Country Music Hall of Fame.

The new editor had complete confidence in his two appointments, which proved well-founded, as the magazine soon began to function smoothly. Then, just as they thought they'd turned the corner, there came the postal strike to knock them for six. Lasting throughout February, it hit subscribers most of all and the problems it created through late publication were solved only by putting out two issues in one month. From then on, the magazine appeared on schedule, and kept appearing – surviving, as stated, to this day.

There now follows a record of some of the memorable items printed during Bob's first spell as editor – from January, 1971 to December, 1976:-

APRIL, 1971 – Enlarged 40-page issue with 15 pages devoted to 3rd *Wembley Festival*,[58] featuring Loretta Lynn, Hank Snow, Waylon Jennings and Bobby Bare. Mervyn Conn announces that a rodeo will be held at next year's event (an idea that, to the relief of many, failed to

---

[58] Brief details of each *Wembley Festival* from 1969-91 and 2012 can be found in the Appendix. A more comprehensive list (including names of performers) is available to view online at: www.stanlaundon.com/wembley.html.

materialise).

JUNE, 1971 – Tony Byworth resigns as staffer to pursue freelance activities (in his own words, "nearly starving," in the process), but continues to provide articles and sell advertising space.

JULY, 1971 – Special 'Jim Reeves' edition, issued to tie in with the 7th anniversary of his death.

SEPTEMBER, 1971 – Roy Acuff features on the cover of this issue, while there are no fewer than 30 different names listed among the credits on page 3. In his editorial, Bob recounts how, receiving details of Johnny Cash's upcoming tour late – so late that the magazine was already half-printed – he, by a stroke of luck (aided by an unexpected fault in production) managed to insert eight extra pages, including a hastily written article on Johnny Cash and supporting acts, plus, most importantly, the tour dates – and still the magazine appeared on time.

NOVEMBER, 1971 – Contains second part of interview with fiddler, Benny Martin, who, Bob claimed, dominated the conversation to such an extent he ended up titling the piece: 'BENNY MARTIN BY HIMSELF'.

DECEMBER, 1971 – Editorial reads: "This is an important issue for me. (It) brings to a close volume two of *CMP*. During the last year, I feel country music has achieved a great deal. I feel *CMP* has done the same. Our circulation has doubled. A great deal of the credit for this must go to the unsung heroes of *CMP*. The management and staff at Cray Press who have ensured that for almost a year now the magazine is completed by our target date, 20th of the preceding month."

Ever on the lookout for money-saving schemes, Bob, at this time, secured a special arrangement with *Harlequin Records* of New Bond St., London, W1 – "LONDON'S

LARGEST COUNTRY DEALER" as their ad boldly proclaimed. Being a keen – and impressed – customer of theirs and noticing that they already ran a regular ad in the magazine, he suggested a free half-page (sometimes a quarter, rarely a full page) in exchange for a selection of imported albums per month, an arrangement approved by owner, Reg Field, and one that continued to pay dividends for both parties up until the end of his first editorial spell.

MARCH, 1972 – Contains interesting article on origins and aims of *British Country Music Association*. Writer John Stafford also starts to make an impact.

On a sad note, this month brought news of Bob's father's death, the call from Marylee arriving while he worked at *CMP*'s Cray Press Office. Although not entirely unexpected (his father suffering from cancer), it still came as a shock and Bob's enduring memory was of sitting at his desk, "having a good grizzle," while co-workers gathered round to offer consolation and support. With Marylee at home to take care of funeral arrangements, his mother insisted that, instead of travelling over now, he visit later in the year, which is what he did, and each subsequent year until her own death.

Obviously, Mr. Powel had kept a keen eye on his son's activities over the years, and, although an opera fan at heart,[59] had at least made an effort to appreciate this vastly

---

[59] Mr. Powel's other great passion was golf. With more effort and commitment, Bob believed he might have attained professional standard. His sporting 'claim to fame' lies in achieving not one but two 'holes-in-one' in successive matches at Sidcup golf course, a feat that made the front page of the *Daily Telegraph* in 1937. (As with opera, the father's interest failed to transfer itself to son). By contrast, Mrs. Powel's return to the game she first played in her youth resulted in the club landing fifty feet away while the ball stayed firmly on the tee – ending

different genre, even attending a concert in London, where, for the only occasion in his life, he met a country performer – little-known British artiste, Billy Harris, who happened to be among the audience. Whatever the eminent gentleman might have thought of the entertainment on offer that night, it's certain he would have been too kind and tactful to express in negative terms. In fact, according to Bob, "I don't think he would remember it." Much more to his taste would have been the Elisabeth Schwarzkopf *Festival Hall* concert for which his son managed to obtain tickets. Reliving the experience the following day, Mr. P. revealed that some members of the audience had rushed the stage at the end, adding: "And I was one of them!" (So now we know the source of his son's enthusiasm). Bob could not recall the dates of these incidents but was certain they pre-dated his radio show "because otherwise I would definitely have taken him to that and I don't remember doing so."

Shortly after the funeral, Bob savoured a special moment. Receiving a letter postmarked a day prior to the death, he, upon opening it, was moved to read that this commanding, protective figure who he'd looked up to all his life, and who must have harboured reservations about his son's career choice, now felt "proud" of his achievements. Such affirmation helped considerably in the days ahead and in his efforts to move on – as he did shortly in more ways than one, for, within a year, having received a small inheritance, he was residing at No. 23 Broomwood Road, St. Pauls Cray, Orpington – next door to record filer, Dolly Waterton and three doors down from *CMP* owner, Reg Field.

The inheritance, as well as enabling the purchase of a

---

her comeback for good and ensuring she restricted her energies to other activities in future, notably knitting, at which she excelled.

new property, allowed Bob to come to the aid of friend, Doug McKenzie, whose Photographic Services business had expanded rapidly in a short space of time, leaving him in sudden need of funds. For Doug, official photographer for most major UK record labels and responsible for the bulk of *CMP*'s publicity shots, the interest-free loan ensured not only the fulfilment of this immediate commitment, but, effectively, his business's survival. Bob, in turn, continued to utilise his friend's services for future projects, including every subsequent *Wembley Festival.*

Back at Cray Press, the day-to-day running of *CMP* continued, the following being further significant items covering the remaining 4 and a half years of Bob's initial editorial spell:-

JUNE, 1972 – Includes useful summary of country music programmes provided by different local radio stations: Radio Bristol (Colin Mason), Radio Leeds (Goff Greenwood and Mike Storey), Radio Merseyside (Bill Holt and Don Allen), Radio Teesside (Stan Laundon), Radio Medway (Larry Adams, produced by Geoff Leonard), Radio Brighton (Neil Coppendale, produced by Jim Marshall) – and, of course, Radio London. Also, Paul Davis joins team of writers, specialising in gospel music, while the *David Allan Page* is conspicuous by its absence (reappearing in February 1974).

JULY, 1972 – Is Bob becoming cynical? He begins his Charlie Louvin interview: "Charlie Louvin, when are you going to come to England? I'll answer the question for you – when someone says the word and the word's money."

AUGUST, 1972 – Report on the decision to axe BBC Radio 2's *Country Meets Folk* (presented by Wally Whyton) after five years.

SEPTEMBER, 1972 – In his page 2 editorial, Bob expresses the opinion that new BBC Radio 2 programme,

Up Country, broadcast from *The Nashville Room* and featuring exclusively British artistes, is "a mistake (as) the majority of country listeners want American product." Issue also refers to formation of Saguenay Music,[60] under directorship of Craig Baguley and Bob, the first – and possibly only – songs published being *Tadoussac, You're Calling* and *Uncle Coosie* (see Chapter 1, footnote 14).

OCTOBER, 1972 – The special 'Canadian' issue featuring 'Bob-taken' cover photo of Tadoussac with an inset of Hank Snow was obviously a favourite, a framed copy of which hung proudly in his hall. In *CMP*'s 200th edition (September, 1986), he writes: "I won't say it was an unpopular issue but it is one of the few *CMP*'s from this era that we have still in stock." Also included is a letter from Bill Anderson, complaining about the omission of (his group) the Po' Boys' player, Sonny Garrish from May's 'Steel Guitar' issue – although the righteous indignation is blunted somewhat by a 'PS' advertising his new single.

JANUARY, 1973 – Approaching its third anniversary, *CMP* is far from sailing calm waters. In fact, money is so tight that, unable to pay the contributors, Bob ends up writing practically the whole magazine single-handed, even if some articles are credited to David Sharpe and William Harcourt (pseudonyms).[61] He also notes that P.M. Munsey

---

[60] Saguenay Music – A short-lived enterprise whose aim was to nurture and promote British country music talent (again). For the year of its existence (during which the only songs published were the Golbey-Powel composed *Tadoussac, You're Calling* and *Uncle Coosie*), Bob received regular royalty cheques from the *Performing Rights Society*, which, owing to pressures of work, he failed to cash, resulting in *PRS* cancelling his membership.

[61] Bob later confessed even he did not get paid this month (doing so, eventually). Within a few months, Cray Press went into liquidation, the liquidator, Granville White, buying up the company, employing Reg Field as managing director and

(who disliked 'Canadian' issue) has provided *CMP* with its "rudest-ever letter."

FEBRUARY, 1973 – Faron Young's[62] totally unprompted (tail-piece to his interview) comments re: *CMP* are worth reproducing. "I have a magazine, *Music City News*, and I know the work that goes into putting it together, travelling all over the world like you do for interviews, the money that's involved – the postage, printing, buying the paper, payment of staff, the telephones, and then you always have the people that won't pay you. You run ads and try to collect your money, try to break even; it's not an easy thing." With his photo on the front cover, a three-page interview inside, and *Four in the Morning* having recently made the UK Top Five, Faron was riding the crest of a wave at this time. Despite the fact he bore something of a hell-raising reputation, Bob always found him genuine and likeable.

JUNE, 1973 – Bob updates his *Up Country* assessment: "due to the many changes it has undergone, (it) now works and is doing much good for country music… producer Dennis O'Keefe has to be congratulated in trying new ideas and coming up with a winner." Elsewhere, he devotes a one-page article devoted to *Country Style*, about to finish its 5-year run on Radio 2 (replacement: *Country Club*, hosted by Wally Whyton). This issue also contains part one of an interesting article on the evolution of country-rock by Martin Hawkins.

---

allowing (for a price) *CMP* to continue using the printing works and to retain its office for "virtually no rent." (*CMP*'s 200th edition, September, 1986).

[62] Plenty has been written about the Louisiana-born singing star's less attractive traits (usually displayed when under the influence of alcohol). One little-known fact is that the cat owned by *Peanuts* cartoon character, Frieda, was named after Faron, whom Charles Schultz "admired very much."

JULY, 1973 – Features photo of Red Hayes[63] on front cover, plus short article by editor. *Tickertape* section begins – and continues under that heading for over four years.

AUGUST, 1973 – Price increase from 17½p to 22p, but, as Bob points out, "a 4½p price rise in three years is not, I'm sure you'll agree, excessive," especially when, as is the case, accompanied by a 4-page increase in size. First issue to feature a British country artiste on front cover – Tex Withers. Also includes a *Looking Back* feature, chronicling the first three years of his editorship, in which he notes:-

• Favourable comments from public outweigh unfavourable ones.

• Big rise in circulation.

• 'Album releases' feature removed, then restored, owing to public demand.

• Cutting of Irish & North Eastern items.

• Introduction of 'special' issues, including: 'Rockabilly' (Feb '72), 'Steel Guitarists' (May, '72) and 'Canadian Artistes' (Oct. '72).

---

[63] Joe 'Red' Hayes – Born 24 April 1926. Fiddle player, singer and songwriter, co-wrote *A Satisfied Mind* – a country hit for three different artistes in 1955: Porter Wagoner (No.1), Red Foley (No.3) and Jean Shepard (No.4). Later versions by Roy Drusky & Bob Luman (in the 70s) and Con Hunley (in the 80s) also made the country charts. Hayes died 2 March, 1973, after being taken ill on stage in Manchester, England, while touring with Faron Young and Vassar Clements. Just three days earlier, he had been interviewed for *London Country*, the show subsequently being broadcast, with his family's permission, on 6 July, and then, by public request – and for the only time in the show's history – repeated on 19 October, 1974.

• Removal of *British Scene*'s two-page spread, reasons for which clearly explained.

• Dropping of Jim Reeves' column (which did not result in expected sales dip).

• Old-time fans catered for by writings of Chris Comber who he describes as "surely one of the top writers in his field in the world."

• More record reviews, as requested.

One further change (not mentioned) is the introduction of 'news' pages in 1972, obligatory ever since. As for removal of the *British Scene* spread, it no doubt caused divided opinions. Some might have felt that an inordinate amount of space had been devoted to British country music in relation to its popularity (i.e. record sales), which, despite the efforts of so many, remains low to this day. Bob insisted the artistes did not want success badly enough, citing the "pathetic trickle" of information sent in response to his request for publicity material. This, and the fact that those who did respond were often sub-standard (reflecting poorly on *CMP*), led to his decision to remove the feature. However, one British country band member – John Martin of the Stetson Country Band – put the other side's case rather well via a letter to *CMP* in May, 1980: "There is no way we could promote our brand of country music without having to sell our souls (because) at least 75% of the record-buying public do not and will not buy country records, so just be glad you…can hear country music in some shape or form." Of course, it could be argued that British country music made a mark – of sorts – via the mild country-pop of Olivia Newton-John or the country-tinged sounds of Bonnie Tyler, Smokie and countless others, while some writers (Roger Cook, and, later, Paul Kennerley) based themselves in Nashville and took on, or, more accurately, worked in conjunction with, the Americans on their own turf – none of which would satisfy the purists. All in all, a highly emotive subject on which just about everyone has an opinion.

FEBRUARY, 1974 – David Allan (whose *Page* returns) reports on his visit to Anglia TV, where a new country series presented by Pete Sayers, *Country Hoedown*, is in production. Full of anticipation, he comes away "unimpressed and disenchanted," owing to "the whole thing being garnished with dancing ladies dressed as cowgirls doing lots of jolly little hoedowns with plenty of 'Yoo-Hoos' thrown in for good measure." He goes on to lament, "When will producers get the message that country music is a music for today, 1974, and not twenty years ago. Haystacks and log cabins went out with the 50s and it's high time we had a series on the box which reflects the scene as it is today."

MARCH, 1974 – Report on merging of Radio 2's *Up Country* with Wally Whyton's *Country Club* from April.

APRIL, 1974 – Biggest issue to date (44 pages) includes, for first time, back cover colour portrait – of Johnny Cash.

MAY, 1974 – In his editorial, Bob criticises *Melody Maker* for printing interview with long-time promoter and record label owner (Ember), Jeff Kruger in which he attacks *CMA (GB)*, Mervyn Conn, *Wembley Festival* and country scene in general.

JULY, 1974 – Jeff Kruger is granted full-page reply to Bob's criticism in May's *CMP*, his main point being that "20,000 fans packing Wembley proves nothing" when country giants are "playing to very poor houses on nationwide tours" and "country LP's are (nowhere) on our best-selling charts."

AUGUST, 1974 – Temporary (3 months) closure of

Nashville Room and axing of its all-country policy announced. Also, departure of staff member, Alfie Stillman, to concentrate on his country outfit, The Gentry. Elsewhere, Bob reviews – and approves – 'Opryland', new site for the *Grand Ole Opry*.

SEPTEMBER, 1974 – Special issue devoted to contemporary country, contributors including Brian Redworth,[64] Tony Byworth, Bob, John Stafford, Alan Cackett, and others.

OCTOBER, 1974 – First issue to feature colour photo on front and back covers (Slim Whitman and Larry Cunningham, respectively). Bob refers to October being "Country music month", owing to *Grand Ole Opry* holding its annual celebration in Nashville then. News of *Countrypolitan*'s (progressive country show hosted by Dave Cash) return to Capital Radio for one hour Sunday evenings.

NOVEMBER, 1974 – In his editorial, Bob comments on recent polls, lamenting the fact that the American *Country Music Association* axed the 'Comedian' category instead of the 'Instrumental', invariably won by Danny Davis & Nashville Brass (it was eventually axed in 1987). Meanwhile, the 'Letters' page returns after a short absence, and the following typical example must have brought a wry smile to the editor's face:-

"Dear sir, congratulations on the current (September) issue of *CMP*. For the first time since issue number one over five years ago, you have succeeded in publishing an entire issue that holds no interest for me whatsoever. Twenty two pence worth of waste paper! I like the idea of

---

[64] Brian Redworth – A pseudonym for David Redshaw, his real name was withheld because of obligations to rival mag, *Country Music Review*.

an occasional issue, such as the previous 'Canadian' and 'Steel guitar' ones, but at least these two held something of interest to all tastes in country music – the current 'progressive' *CMP* does not. I hope that you do an entire issue on the authentic side of country music in the future or even a 'bluegrass' special. I'm sorry that I have nothing good to say about it, Bob, but you did ask for readers' views on this. No doubt if you do follow my suggestions, then somebody else will complain about 22 pence worth of rubbish. It's a hard world." Clive Downes, Godalming, Surrey.

(According to Bob, generally, more readers were pro- than anti- the special issues).

DECEMBER, 1974 – A further price increase announced – from 22p to 25p, but pill is sweetened by news that, from following month, colour photos will be doubled to four. Elsewhere, Bob follows up last month's criticism of *CMA* Awards categories with full-page article on Danny Davis. Meanwhile, *CMA (GB)* Awards night is reviewed by him.

FEBRUARY, 1975 – Contains article recognising contribution to country music of producer Ian Grant, initiator of BBC Radio 1/2's *Country Meets Folk* (1967-72) and Radio 2's *Country Style* (1968-73), among many other varied, worthwhile activities within the genre. Issue also includes interesting John Stafford article on country comedy acts, e.g. Homer & Jethro,[65] Ben Colder, Don

---

[65] Homer & Jethro – Stage names of Henry D. Haynes (guitar) and Kenneth C. Burns (mandolin), a comedy duo much loved and admired by Bob. Formed in 1936, they separated owing to Army service in WWII but reunited in 1945. On signing to RCA in 1949, they switched from singing exaggerated versions of pop standards to parodies (penned mostly by Burns) of country and pop hits. Despite specialising in self-deprecation, both were accomplished jazz musicians (Django Reinhardt being a major influence). Haynes died from a heart attack in 1971, while Burns

Bowman, Simon Crum (aka Ferlin Husky), Jerry Clower, Archie Campbell, Roy Clark, Grandpa Jones, Stringbean, Shel Silverstein, Minnie Pearl and others.

MARCH, 1975 – Editorial states that "this month's issue is about *Wembley* and we will be taking an active part in the *Festival*, with a stand, where we can meet you, the readers." He goes on to praise both Mervyn Conn – for his achievement in securing George Jones, Dolly Parton and Marty Robbins (all making British debuts) for Wembley – and Jeff Kruger, for the Charley Pride package tour which sold out two houses at the *London Palladium*. Meanwhile, on page 5, two rare British triumphs are celebrated: Frank Jennings & the Syndicate on BBC's *Opportunity Knocks* (performing Tommy Overstreet's stateside hit, *Heaven is my Woman's Love*) and Haz Elliott with Feeling (singing original song) on ITV's equivalent, *New Faces*.

APRIL, 1975 – Bob gives *CMP*'s employees a "pat on the back," quoting three letters recently received from America:

• Jo Walker, head of *CMA* in Nashville, praising January's Tex Ritter article.

• Tex's widow, Dorothy, doing likewise.

• Bakersfield singer/songwriter, Red Simpson, who states bluntly, "I enjoy getting your magazine every month, it is one of the few GOOD country magazines being published."

Simpson's words were repeated often by performers, especially in relation to American magazines, letters to which were, apparently, "juvenile." Issue also includes a Bob-written one-page article devoted to Chris Forde's

---

briefly carried on with a new 'Homer' (Ken Eidson), before continuing as a solo act. He died in 1989 from prostate cancer.

Tennessee Club, Wimbledon, struggling to stay afloat just 15 months after opening.

MAY, 1975 – Editorial reports that this year's (7th) *Wembley Festival* is generally reckoned to be the best ever, "undoubted highlights" being George Jones and Marty Robbins. Additionally, there is a 3-page article on *London Country* – "Four years not out" (partially reproduced in Chapter 6).

JULY, 1975 – Bob, in his editorial, cites the "help from both our readers and advertisers" that has enabled *CMP* to "become Europe's largest-selling country music publication," adding that "this month we have been accepted into the Audit Bureau of Circulations with a proven sales figure of over 13,000 (equating to 40,000 readers)." He hopes this means that the days of struggle (see January, 1973 entry) are now over.

AUGUST, 1975 – First 'genuine' price rise announced – from 25p to 30p (previous increases were accompanied by extra pages and extended colour photos). This is the second special 'Steel Guitar' issue.

SEPTEMBER, 1975 – Contains news of *Country Club*'s change of producer – from Colin Chandler (position held since inception in July, 1973) to Bill Bebb, producer of *Country Style* for past three years. Meanwhile, Tony Byworth commences reviewing UK albums but finds level of product "not that inspiring."

OCTOBER, 1975 – Includes Bob-written reviews of two soon-to-be-released, country-based Hollywood movies: *W.W. & the Dixie Dancekings*, starring Burt Reynolds, which he describes as "enjoyable," and the more controversial, *Nashville*, his two-paragraph summary of which was partially reproduced 25 years later by Peter Doggett in his bulky history of country-rock, *Are You Ready for the Country?* (Penguin). Personifying *CMP*'s editor as a "country insider taken aback by [director] Altman's portrayal of the industry's greed and naivety," Doggett quotes him thus: "I would be a liar if I didn't admit to recognizing some of the bad things depicted, but it is certainly a gross and unfair exaggeration of the way Nashville is run." The review's concluding sentence (unquoted by Doggett) reads: "the music is quite terrible,[66] the singing worse and the whole thing is a bit sad." (David Allan, meanwhile, via his December *Page*, hails the film as "a glorious send-up" that he "thoroughly enjoyed").

NOVEMBER, 1975 – Bob, in his editorial, criticises Maurice Oberstein, managing director of CBS (UK), for failure to recognise the market for country music here, citing RCA's success with their mid-price range as an example of what can be achieved.

Around this time, Bob produced and edited a lavish 60-page souvenir booklet in tribute to the 'International Ambassador of Country Music', George Hamilton IV. With 12 full-colour pages (mainly courtesy of photographer, Doug McKenzie), articles by Alan Cackett, Tony Byworth, George and others, ample promotion via the pages of *CMP*, and an asking price of just £1.25 (including postage), it looked set to be a winner, but flopped badly. Fortunately, RCA A&R man, Shaun Greenfield, redeemed the situation by arranging for the booklet to be included in the double-album compilation, *The George Hamilton IV Story* (RCA, 1976).

DECEMBER, 1975 – Bob states that, halfway through the 70s, "country music has made tremendous strides…the great improvement being that its image has been totally reformed" and it has become "respectable." Continuing in upbeat vein, he applauds the "bumper year for tours, with

---

[66] *Nashville* actually won an Oscar (the only one gained by the film) for best song – *I'm Easy*, written and performed by Keith Carradine, son of actor, John – not that it's remembered much today.

Charley Pride, Ronnie Milsap, Glen Campbell, Johnny Cash, Charlie Rich, Hank Locklin, George Jones and George Hamilton IV, not to mention the highly successful *Wembley Festival* " in April. Only down side is Capitol Records' dropping of *Countrypolitan* so soon after its launch.

JANUARY, 1976 – Features Maurice Oberstein's reply to Bob's criticism of CBS's lacklustre promotion of country music (*CMP*, November, 1975), drawing particular attention to Wayne Nutt's forthcoming debut album on the label. *Tickertape* mentions Sonny James' refusal (via management) to grant *CMP* interview because "front cover could not be guaranteed," Bob adding (presumably tongue-in-cheek): "That's now happened twice, the first being another superstar, Jed Ford." David Allan, meanwhile, contends that "1975 was the year that more and more of the so-called 'general public' became aware that country music meant something other than Yoo Hoo's and six guns," adding perceptively, "perhaps the biggest factor in this conversion came in the form of the willowy lady who advised the populace to *Stand By Your Man*"[67] – the recording of which represents that rare occurrence, an authentic country song attaining No.1 position on the pop chart (by, of course, Tammy Wynette). Elsewhere, Bob (under pseudonym David Sharpe) reveals secrets of his record-filing system.

---

[67] *Stand By Your Man*. Billy Sherrill-Tammy Wynette composition – supposedly based on a Johann Strauss melody – first released in US in September, 1968, becoming a No.19 pop and No.1 country hit that year. It failed to break in the UK until 1975, when it went all the way to No.1. Song was selected by the Library of Congress as a 2010 addition to the National Recording Registry, which selects recordings annually that are "culturally, historically or aesthetically significant." Also rated No.1 of 100 greatest songs on Country Music Television. Covered by Patti Page (1968) and Candi Statton (1970).

FEBRUARY, 1976 – Announcement of Readers' Poll – co-sponsored by *CMA(GB)* Ltd., Mervyn Conn Organisation, *Country Music Review* and *CMP* – prizes to be presented at *Wembley Festival*. Other news: David Allan and Dennis O'Keefe set to replace Wally Whyton and Bill Bebb as respective presenter and producer of *Country Club*, Wally going on to present the more diverse *Both Sides Now*, also broadcast Thursday nights.

APRIL, 1976 – Editorial welcomes *NME* & *Music Week* writer, David Redshaw, to *CMP* staff. Specialising in progressive country, his first articles feature the Dillards, Country Gazette, Emmylou Harris (review of Hammersmith Odeon gig) and the Ozark Mountain Daredevils, whose 3rd album, *Car Over the Lake*, also happens to be reviewed by Tony Byworth (including the track, *Mr. Powell* – no relation!).

MAY, 1976 – Comprehensive report on *Wembley Festival*, Don Williams taking the major honours. Also features full-page photo-spread of George Hamilton IV's visit to Cray Press Ltd.'s factory and office.

JUNE, 1976 – Bob's editorial announces: "We can now make it official. Country music has arrived in Britain." The reason? *The Times*, no less (via Philip Norman's article), recently spent a whole page "having a hard-hitting and very amusing go at country music." As the cowboy gear seems to be the main focus of media attention, Bob feels it's a shame "the teenybopper writers" can't see that "for every hat, gun, sput and whatever, there are dozens, if not hundreds wearing John Colliers or C&A's best."

JULY, 1976 – The *David Allan Page* sees him praising totally diverse female country stars Dolly Parton and Olivia Newton-John, bemoaning country music's "minority taste" classification (quoting a 10,000-strong response to a recent *Country Club* competition), warning Merle Haggard/management against playing a waiting-game with his British fans (Merle never having visited UK up to this point) and criticising stars who spend a substantial amount of their performing time "sermonizing."

SEPTEMBER, 1976 – Having recently returned from a holiday in USA and Canada, Bob, in his editorial, suggests British country fans are not so badly off, radio-wise, at least. There, chances are, you can listen to country music 24 hours a day "but you will be lucky to hear 40 different tunes in one week," while in the UK, during the same period, "you can hear something in the region of 80 discs, with very few repeats." He continues, "TV, sadly, is another matter…"

OCTOBER, 1976 – On the same theme, Bob expresses "pleasant surprise" that 31 UK radio stations now broadcast at least one country music programme, compared to twenty years earlier, when Murray Kash considered himself lucky if his country show on the old Light programme was granted 7 hours a year! Betty Hofer, via a letter on behalf of her client, Canadian singer, Ray Griff, expresses "disappointment in the article you have printed on him in the August issue of *CMP* (because) you were to let him see copy prior to publication," Bob replying that he has "never promised any singer copy prior to publication as…it's a breach of journalistic freedom." (Mr. Griff, a virtual unknown in the UK, had been granted the equivalent of five full pages in the magazine). In contrast, this month's BP-interviewee, bassist, songwriter and manager, Tillman Franks, upon reading the finished article, expressed surprise and delight that his responses had been reproduced word-for-word.[68] Meanwhile, David Allan, in his column, refers to Ian Grant's series on *Country*

---

[68] According to Bob, only once did a guest insist on taping his interview: Oklahoma-born, cowboy singing star (and writer: *The Tex Ritter Story*), Johnny Bond, who featured in December, 1974's *CMP*. Bob, far from being offended, found him "a very charming man."

Club entitled, "The Rise & Fall of the British Country Scene."

NOVEMBER, 1976 – The merits – or otherwise – of British country music continue to stir controversy, both in Bob's editorial and 'Write-In' page.

DECEMBER, 1976 – Bob announces his departure from *CMP* editorship as follows: "The reason…is not a straightforward one. Certainly, there was a difference of policy with the publisher, Gordon Field, but more than that, I honestly believe that after 73 issues as editor, the time was ripe for a change. The move will, I believe, be right for both the magazine and myself…my ties with *CMP* will not be completely broken. I was asked by the publisher to remain a director and will continue to write for *CMP* as long as [successor] Tony Byworth so desires."

In his Don Ford interview for *Four-On-The-Floor* magazine (4 December, 1976), he elaborates further:-

"In the September issue (of *CMP*), Checkmate ran an advertisement on which there were references to some tape releases which were not correct.[69] I went into the office and…told them about the mistake…I thought it might be a breach of the Trades Description Act and that I thought it should not go through. Charles (Field) whose main interest is…to get the magazine out as quickly as possible…said, 'No, no…keep it as it is,' (to which) I replied, 'If we're going to keep it as it is, then I am not going to proof read any more.' Reg Field responded, 'Fine take three months' notice.' Instead of making up and being friends after cooling off, as we had done in the past, now I responded, 'Put it in writing,' effectively forcing the issue.

---

[69] These were eight cassette-only releases compiled by Bob, each containing 25 tracks. The 'Checkmate' ad listed them as containing 40 tracks.

Reg's first inclination was to close the magazine down, which I felt would have been a tragedy and I talked him out of that. In fact, a certain agreement that he has made with me [see Chapter 8, Footnote 100] made it impossible to close it down. I recommended, in fact, offered the job of editor to Tony Byworth…and I think he will prove to be a great success."

Ten years later, in *CMP*'s 200th edition (September, 1986), he states simply:-

"I was sacked. Six years is a very long time without a break and there's no doubt it was getting to me. The boss sacked me over an incident where I still believe I was right but it could easily have been the other way round. There are ways to treat the chief and keep your job, and there was my way. Reg Field could not have been fairer and we have remained friends all these years, which is just as well, as he and his wife, Margaret, live three doors away from me. The editorial control of course went into the hands of my successor and friend, Tony Byworth, as Reg never ever interfered with editorial policy, which is a rare thing, believe me. It was six exhausting but happy and eventful years."

He offers a similar (though less detailed) version in *CMP*'s 500th issue.

Tony Byworth, meanwhile, recalls that "Reg and Bob had one too many falling-outs, Bob resigned and Reg accepted it." His further assertion, following his appointment, Bob was on the phone, demanding, "How dare you be editor?" though denied by his predecessor, might suggest a case of overwork causing a heated, irrational reaction – quite understandable, given his many commitments at this time. By Tony's own admission, just editing a magazine alone is "a helluva job."

Whatever the truth of the matter, there is no doubting Bob's claim in (December issue) that "I leave the editorship of *CMP* with the magazine in a far healthier state than when I inherited it in 1970." Furthermore, Reg Field's comments in January's issue must have gladdened his heart: "My grateful thanks go at this stage to our ex-editor, Bob Powel. Bob has done a grand job over the past six years. In fact, but for Bob stepping into the breach six years ago and really putting his heart into the job, there would not have been a *CMP* today. I can honestly say that with all the discussions I've had with Bob, his first and final viewpoint was for the benefit of and image of the magazine, even doing extra work to find ways of increasing the revenue to keep *CMP* afloat. Perhaps his greatest spur was that the experts and critics only gave him three months." (The admiration was mutual, Bob appreciating his boss on many levels, not least that he paid for individual articles, something "not all owners would have done.")

Additionally, Tony Byworth, in his first Editorial (February, 1977 issue), states: "Under the dedicated editorship of its former editor, Bob Powel, [*CMP*] has established itself as a leader in its field...it's not my aim to detract from the preceding editor's work and the magazine's contents will remain basically the same, although the presentation will see changes."

Backing up his claim of leaving *CMP* in a "healthier state," Bob told Don Ford, "The print for the last issue I did was 18,000, an increase of over 2,000 from 1975, which I think is fantastic." Regarding overseas circulation, he confessed that *CMP* "has hardly any...but this will probably alter because, before I left Nashville in November, I negotiated with *Music City News* an exchange programme. The trouble is, going foreign is nice, but is no use to advertisers, who are your meat." Throughout his tenure, he ensured that all major US record companies were sent two copies of each month's edition of *CMP* – one for the office and one for reception – and, judging by the number of (invariably complimentary) letters received from industry people, especially stars, over the years, the magazine would appear to have been widely read Stateside (correspondents included Billy Deaton, Don Helms, Jerry Byrd, Bill Anderson, Red Simpson, Weldon Myrick, Johnny Gimble, Cliffie Stone, Lloyd Green, and Bob Everhart – the last two during Tony Byworth's editorship).

And so, the magazine continued without his authoritative presence – but he was not to be forgotten so easily, and, as we shall see, within seven years, was back in the hot seat.

Chapter 6

London Country: 1st Decade, 1970s

Gloryland March ("Glory Hallelujah, we are marching on...")[70]

The following are some of the responses – taken from a sample representing 7% of its 900-show output – by guests who appeared on London Country during its 17-year run:-

WARNER MACK: "I've had a great day, I really have!"

RONNIE PROPHET: "Listen, this is just a fantastic day, I mean it. Thank you so much!"

DUANE ALLEN (OAK RIDGE BOYS): "Any time you want an interview from me or any of the 'Oaks,' we'll always be here, because, even starting back in Philadelphia, I find that you are very interested in our business, enough to go back 14 years and find things I'd forgotten, and if you do things like that, I promise you, it's always exciting

---

[70] *Gloryland March.* Rousing country gospel chorus written by Johnnie Masters for his group, the Masters Family, Bob first heard the song performed by Hank Snow, and, according to *Powel's Page* (*CMP*, June, 1986), that rendition became the very first 78rpm single he bought.

to do an interview with you."

FELICE BRYANT: "You're surprising me with your history."

BOUDLEAUX BRYANT: "You're a better historian of country music than anybody I've seen in the past 25 years – or preceding that!"

PATSY MONTANA: "I've learned not to argue with Bob – he's always right."

ED BRUCE: "This is great! I'm getting re-educated here!"

BILLY WALKER: "Boy, you can pull some out of the hat, do you know that? Every time I come over here, you amaze me with what I've done!"

BILLY ARMSTRONG: "I learn a bit more about the business every time I'm around you."

If Robert Harcourt Powel had achieved nothing more in life than to present *London Country* on BBC Radio London (1458kHz/206 metres/94.9FM) between the years 1971 and 1988, that alone would serve as a fitting tribute to his abilities. It's said we're all called to some specific task, duty or work of art, and, if so, then this was his – except that to him it was always a pleasure, as Charlie Gillett discovered when, seeking support for strike action from his fellow DJ, he instead received the response, "Are you kidding – I'd do this job for nothing!"[71]

---

[71] Bob even funded some of the show's competitions out of his own pocket – as in the case of the Jimmie Rodgers' commemorative stamps. Issued on 24 May, 1978, these 13-cent stamps were designed by Jim Sharpe and depicted Jimmie wearing a brakeman's outfit and holding a guitar, while giving his 'two-thumbs up' sign, along with a silhouetted locomotive in the background. On a journey from Bangor, Maine, to visit his

Dutch performer Arie den Dulk speaks for many when he says, "His interviews were outstanding – the most informative and entertaining in the business. US presenters were a mile behind him – I'll cherish the memories of my appearances forever." The deep knowledge, the avuncular presence, the musical surprises sprung on unsuspecting guests, the authoritative yet mellifluous tone of his voice – all combined to make him, in Tony Byworth's words, "a unique presenter," albeit one who, conversely, could also stumble over words, play the wrong records, repeat certain phrases ("that's great", "well, that's really interesting", "oh yeh, nice one") and make almighty gaffes (examples of which are reproduced in the following chapter, with his full permission). Fellow BBC presenter David Allan recalls, "When it first began, you thought it couldn't possibly last because technically it was so awful, but it eventually achieved a cult following and we used to listen avidly every week."

Yes, he frequently 'boobed' and occasionally (though not often) got his facts wrong, but it didn't matter: Uncle Bob was where he belonged, where we all wanted to be – in the privileged position of being able to share hitherto unheard and unheralded country fare with hungry, deprived fans. Not only that, but above and beyond the formal duties, he appeared to be communicating on a deeper level, as if reaching out to the child still listening intently beneath the sheets in far-off Quebec or deepest Devon, entranced and enthralled as he had once been. The role seemed made for him, but just how had he got started in this competitive medium, one that is often looked down on by its more illustrious relative, TV, but which nevertheless has survived 60 years of competition from it – not to mention the more recent CD/video/DVD

mother, Bob stopped at every Post Office along the way to buy a 24-stamp sheet. Then, on his next show, he offered a stamp free to every listener who sent in for one.

onslaught – and thrives to this day?

It began early in 1970, when he and assorted *CMP* colleagues would join the studio audience for recordings of BBC Radio 2's *Country Meets Folk*, presented by Wally Whyton from the *Players Theatre*,[72] tucked away in Hungerford Arches, beside London's Charing Cross station. After transmission, cast and privileged members of the audience retired to a nearby pub, and it was here that producer, Bill Bebb, remarking on the quality of Bob's speaking voice, offered him a featured spot on another Radio 2 show he was producing at the time, *Country Style*, presented by Pat Campbell.[73] Bob always wondered what

---

[72] *Players Theatre.* Founded in 1936 as a Club by Leonard Sachs (of *Good Old Days* fame) and Peter Ridgeway. Original site was Covent Garden. Soon became established as a 'little theatre', attracting leading actors to perform and leading members of London society as patrons. After World War II, moved to Hungerford Arches, going from strength to strength and leading to *The Good Old Days*, which ran on BBC for 32 years, and *The Boyfriend* stage musical written by Sandy Wilson. Moved from Hungerford Arches to Duchess Theatre, near Aldwych, 1987. Later, moved again to Villiers Street (arches). Spawned Craven Players c. 2010.

[73] Pat Campbell. Genial Irish host, record executive, singer. With Val Doonican in folk group, Four Ramblers early 50s. Replaced David Allan as presenter of *Country Style* in 1969 until its demise in 1973. Compered *Wembley Festival.* While working for RCA label, arranged single release of album track, *I Love You Because* by Jim Reeves, which became huge hit, also pushed for UK release of *Four In The Morning* by Faron Young. Later director of Major Minor label. Although generally not hitting it off with Campbell, whose concept of country music differed from his own, Bob was nevertheless impressed with one of his on-air ad libs. This followed an item read by *Ponderosa* owner, Tom Butler, who, being unused to radio announcing, was affected by nerves to the extent he had difficulty holding the sheet steady, creating a clearly audible rustling sound. Afterwards, Campbell quipped, "That was Tom Butler, the rustler from the *Ponderosa*."

prompted Bebb to offer him the post. Undoubtedly, he had a fine speaking voice, but, just as the novelty of his 'Englishness' helped gain him admission to the *Grand Ole Opry* in Nashville, so now, perhaps his Canadian 'twang' aided his entry into the (then) somewhat privileged world of the BBC. This, in turn, poses the intriguing question: had he spent his entire life in Canada, would he have enjoyed the same degree of success?

For now, his chance came because *Country Style* was about to be moved from its 9.15pm slot to a more favourable 7pm, accompanied by a 15 minute extension, 10 minutes of which would be allocated to guest record reviewers, the first – for a four-week stint – being himself, with more to follow. Thus, in April, 1970, Bob, punctual as ever, arrived two hours before transmission at BBC's studios in Portland Place, London, to run through his (fully scripted) sequence. Although nervous, with a little rehearsal, he performed his first 'on-air' performance without hitch, thereafter growing in self-assurance, until, noticing he was becoming over-confident, Mr. Bebb, at the next run-through, laid into the newcomer with critical comments – "too rushed", "too relaxed", "not relaxed enough." Somewhat taken aback, Bob momentarily lost his composure, before realising the reprimand had a purpose, from which point he recovered and never looked back.[74] In later years, he described this episode as "good experience." In fact, it might have proved a wasted experience, but for his next career development: a simple case of mistaken identity that was to prove most fortuitous for him. Enter Duncan Johnson.

Born Gerald Clement in Toronto, Johnson had done

---

[74] Bob related an occasion during this period when, on air, and with the script directly in front of him, he seized up completely – a frightening experience and one that he believes never recurred because he went on to the unscripted and less regimented atmosphere of local radio.

radio work in Saskatchewan before moving to the UK where he became a DJ for off-shore pirate station, Radio London (no connection to BBC Radio London), which operated from 1964 until silenced by the launch of BBC Radio 1 in 1967. The idea for *London Country* supposedly originated in a pub conversation between himself and BBC head of music, David Carter. Having decided on the format, Johnson, seeking a bright, personable assistant, recalled conversations he'd had at Wembley's 1971 Festival with just such a person – a knowledgeable country enthusiast whose name escaped him, their never having been properly introduced. However, he remembered that the young man worked for *Country Music People* magazine...

Placing a call to the *CMP* office, he got through to the editor, with whom, coincidentally, he had also conversed at Wembley. Result: confusion, leading to Johnson unwittingly hiring the wrong man. One can only imagine his shock when this large, vaguely familiar figure presented himself at the studio on day one. However, amazing though it seems, everyone, out of embarrassment or whatever, apparently carried on regardless. By such twists of fate are careers won or lost. Naturally, the victor felt rather guilty of this incident thereafter, especially since the legitimate 'heir' was none other than good friend, Tony Byworth, whom he always believed to be unaware of the subterfuge.[75] In fact, Tony knew from early on, yet remained on good terms with both colleagues for life. He says of the incident today, "To be fair, Bob was probably more suited to the role than me – and he certainly took his chance well!"

So, what of this new station? With a catchment area

---

[75] This incident has echoes of Genesis, chapter 27, where Jacob (through his mother's conniving) receives his father Isaac's blessing instead of Esau, thus cheating his brother out of his rightful inheritance.

encompassing all of Greater London and beyond, and a potential 10 million listeners, Radio London had been launched on 6 October, 1970 (3 years ahead of commercial rival, LBC), following a successful pilot project headed by Frank Gilliard, who based the format on those observed in the United States. The original broadcasting studio was located at *Harewood House*, Hanover Square, near Oxford Circus in London's West End, subsequently (1980s) moving to Marylebone High St., about ½ mi/¾km away, at a building formerly occupied by the *Radio Times*, without windows but boasting an enormous sub-basement studio and here it remains to this day.

The new station immediately targeted a broad, mainstream audience, offering a lively sound and featuring (as it still does) extensive traffic reports, phone-in programmes (it pioneered the daily phone-in in the UK) and much contemporary and middle-of-the-road music. The musical diversity is, in fact, what distinguishes it from LBC.[76] FM stereo began in 1981, leading to improved audience figures (averaging half a million listeners) and a string of awards and accolades. Re-launched in 1988 as GLR (Greater London Radio) and again in 2000 (BBC London Live) and 2001 (BBC London 94.9), the current presenters include phone-in show hostess, Vanessa Feltz, ex-*Big Breakfast* presenter, Gaby Roslin and veteran *Top of the Pops*/Capital Gold Radio DJ, Tony Blackburn (who ran a show in the 1980s, subsequently leaving, then returning).

Bob's role in this new show – launched on 21 May and called *London Country* from the very start – was to present a short news feature, with his more experienced colleague hosting. Although an accomplished performer, the deep-voiced Johnson was no country music specialist, and,

---

[76] In fact, in its early, Gough Square days, LBC featured some genre music programmes, including a country show presented by American Jim Keltz, on which Tony Byworth guested regularly.

when, just three weeks into the programme, his source of material – basically, the station's slim library plus his own limited stock – began running low, he turned to his better-equipped colleague, who also provided and interviewed guests (including Roy Acuff). After two months of this imbalanced arrangement, Johnson, sensing the way the wind was blowing, resigned (later appearing on Radio 2), leaving producer Irvine Brookes and head of music David Carter with just one realistic choice to replace him: the ubiquitous Mr. P.

However, this presented an immediate and major problem: obviously unaware of how things would develop, the new presenter had booked a month's holiday in advance, set to commence, coincidentally or not, on the first transmission date – furthermore, it was too late to cancel. Again seeking advice from a higher authority – Mr. Brookes – it was decided they had no alternative but to pre-record the first four programmes, something that occurred only rarely during the show's run. And so, as *London Country* aired on 27 August, 1971, the host with the transatlantic tones, although seemingly at the helm, was literally trans-Atlantic – halfway to Canada!

Having solved this early hitch, Bob, on returning to England, quickly settled into his new role, the relaxed atmosphere of local radio suiting him down-to-the-ground: no script, no run-throughs and no one telling him what to say – or play. He alone decided every note of every record, drawn exclusively from his vast musical reservoir. Now he could introduce to the British public those obscure artistes whose output he had accumulated over two decades of dedicated listening – acts such as bluegrass duo Moore and Napier, smooth baritone George Morgan, pint-sized Jimmy Dickens, and hundreds more.

Bob: "Apart from the 'Requests' shows, I simply played what *I* liked."

Aided by producer Brookes – shortly to be replaced by

Margaret 'Maggie' Tschirren – and programme secretary[77] 'Amazing' Grace Talbot (later Valerie Clayton, then Chrissie Davy, then Grace again), what could go wrong? Quite a lot, actually, but that only added to the fun. It was a show where anything might happen, and where anything country-flavoured might be – and generally was – played.

Operating on an informal, 'live' basis, the programme ranged in length from 1 hour 20 minutes to well over 2 hours, as did the time – and day – of transmission: from Friday evenings to Saturday mornings or afternoons, and even Sundays. Such decisions were out of the presenter's control, though at least one change came about as a direct result of his influence: feeling it would be more logical for Robbie Vincent's 'Soul' show to follow his own, he requested that it be swapped with a Marjorie Bilbow film presentation, which currently filled the spot, and this is what happened (at least, until his show was switched to a completely different day).

At this early stage, no one was thinking long-term, just glad of the present air-time – although the host would have liked more. Producer Irvine Brookes recalls, "He had so many contacts and so much enthusiasm (but) he was very frustrated by the limitations on the programme imposed by budget facilities, production staff (i.e. ME!) and the time available." In fact, its host never had a contract, the team merely told that, after six weeks, "We'll see what happens." Nothing further was heard, so technically, he remained freelance. While seemingly no more than a follow-on from previous BBC radio shows,

---

[77] Irvine Brookes and Maggie Tschirren were official BBC producers – or, to give them their proper title, 'station assistants' – while the programme directors (Grace, Valerie, etc.) were recruited by Bob himself at around £5 per show. Names of other helpers (phone-answering, etc.) mentioned at the end of the programme include: Don Glace, Jill Burrows, Dee, Jude Taylor, Lin, Phil Hughes, Steve Iles, Stephanie Gresswell.

Country Meets Folk and *Country Style*, in retrospect, there were differences – and a number of factors in its favour from the start:-

• The first *Wembley International Festival of Country Music* (organised by Mervyn Conn) had taken place just two years previously, providing a shot in the arm to the industry and helping the careers of many country artistes.

• *Country Music People* magazine, in its second year, was regularly out there on news-stands, maintaining the high profile, fuelling enthusiasm and keeping fans informed of events and happenings.

• All country artistes were benefiting from the huge, extraordinary wave of enthusiasm for the 'twin icons' of country music, Jim Reeves and Johnny Cash.

• The 'outlaw' movement of the late 60s/70s/80s, spearheaded by Willie Nelson, Waylon Jennings and Cash himself, brought to the genre a completely different type of fan, who subsequently discovered that traditional acts such as George Jones and even Hank Williams and Lefty Frizzell were not so far removed from this 'new' music.

• Hugely talented, diverse acts like Tammy Wynette, Dolly Parton, Kenny Rogers, Don Williams, John Denver and Crystal Gayle emerged, each with great individual commercial appeal.

• Last, and not least, teenage record buyers of the 50s and 60s were simply growing up and looking back fondly rather than derisively at music of the past – country music has always had a strong 'nostalgia' pull – aided by newcomers like Emmylou Harris, who, as well as providing a trendier, more glamorous image, were respectful, reverential, even, towards the music's roots.

So, the *LC* team had quite a lot going for them – as their leader later admitted: "I was lucky to be in the right place at the right time." However, they still needed to produce the goods – so how exactly did he go about planning each show? Answer: with simple logic. Thus, the appearance of Dennis Weaver, Hollywood actor and part-time country singer, was supplemented by music from comparable artistes, e.g. Walter Brennan and Robert Mitchum, the acquisition of relevant material presenting little problem, given Bob's outsized collection. The format may have been decided in advance, but there needed to be plenty of scope for spontaneity, one of the show's great attributes being that it had an instinctive, 'live' feel, without ever resorting to gimmicks or glib 'DJ-speak' to remind listeners of the fact. Around one in three of the shows featured guests and as many as it has been possible to trace are listed, with year of appearance, at the back of this book. Obviously, the studio's location in central London helped attract people, as did the fact that Bob was known amongst stars, having interviewed them in Nashville and elsewhere for *CMP*.

Whenever possible, the show featured an outside broadcast and the annual *Wembley Festival* provided a perfect opportunity – as on the evening of Friday, 31 March, 1972, when, with the pre-Festival *Grosvenor House* party in full swing, five of its most renowned participants – Loretta Lynn, Conway Twitty, George Hamilton IV, Bill Anderson and Tom T. Hall – dropped in to say hello to the *LC* team broadcasting 'live' from the famous venue. The same show saw its host put out an appeal on behalf of another *Wembley* act, the Stoneman Family – in particular, mandolin player, Donna, whose baggage had not arrived at the airport that day. No sooner had the request for a replacement instrument been made than one was provided by listener and professional musician, John Cowling.[78] Just

---

[78] Fiddle player, steel-guitarist and mandolin player John

to round off the fairy tale, the Stonemans were the hit of the *Festival* that year.

London Country also broadcast, on a couple of occasions, from *The Ideal Home Exhibition*[79] and – once – from *The Motor Show*,[80] which tested Bob's abilities as a performer among the public, instead of within the close confines of a studio. A recording from the latter of these two events (featuring Chet Atkins and dating from October, 1983) indicates that, while still competent, he does not seem quite so comfortable in the outdoor setting. On other occasions, the entire programme was recorded in America, as happened on three successive weeks in 1974, the first,

---

Cowling is typical of many British folk/country/bluegrass musicians and occasional writers/DJs – Wally Whyton, Bryan Chalker and Stan Laundon among them – who started out in the skiffle era and whose love for the music survived the fluctuating trends of successive decades. John has worked with just about anyone who is anyone on the British country scene, as well as several visiting American musicians, including Mac Wiseman, Connie Smith and the legendary Guy Mitchell. Other activities include hosting off-shore radio shows, compiling boxed-set compilations for companies such as Jasmine and Bear Family and writing a limited edition book, *British Skiffle*, published in 1989. He remains active to this day. (John also provided this writer with recordings of several *London Country* shows, including that featuring Lester 'Roadhog' Moran and the very last one).

[79] *Ideal Home Exhibition* (now called *Ideal Home Show*). Annual event in London held at Olympia, 1908-78, and Earls Court, 1979-present. Devised by the *Daily Mail* newspaper and run by them until 2009, when sold to events and publishing company, *Media 10*. Radio London would hire a stand at the event, usually for one complete day, its presenters taking it in turns to host individual segments.

[80] *Motor Show*. Event held regularly between years 1903 and 2008, initially in London – at Crystal Palace, Olympia and then Earls Court, before moving to the National Exhibition Centre in Birmingham in 1976.

on June 2nd, coming from Bakersfield and featuring Buck Owens, Susan Raye, Buddy Allan and David Frizzell, the second, from Nashville: Johnny Rodriguez and Narvel Felts, the third, also from Nashville: singer-songwriter Jimmy Payne. Many more were to follow in subsequent years.

Occasionally, guests would appear fortuitously, as in the case of Emmylou Harris. Aware the highly acclaimed singer was in London to perform a concert, Bob had attempted to arrange an interview through her promotions team – without success. Carrying on regardless, and playing and discussing tracks from her current album with another guest, fellow Alabaman, Jo Ann Steele, who should telephone halfway through but the lady herself, having stumbled across the show by chance while twiddling with the dial. Only too willing to grant an interview ("no one asked before"), all ended happily, in this instance.

Of course, when a highly rated performer was booked, the result could be disappointing – either for the host, listener or both. One that fits this category might be California-born, ex-Kingston Trio member John Stewart, most famous for penning the Monkees' 10 million-seller, *Daydream Believer*, and certainly no country purist – decidedly an acquired taste, in fact. His 1974 appearance was fraught with difficulties and distractions within the studio, which possibly affected their rapport – whatever the reasons, it's a show Bob preferred to forget, calling the end result "a terrible embarrassment." (As a matter of interest, Tony Byworth endured a similar experience with Stewart, describing his *Record Mirror* interview as "the worst I did for the magazine.")

For non-guest shows, the approach was simpler: decide on a theme (listeners often being consulted for ideas), identify appropriate tracks and place them in some sort of logical order, the tricky part being those occasions when it was decided to link up different versions of the same song. Then, Bob enlisted the services of friends Alfie Stillman and the late Eddie Pearson, who sorted out key/tempo variations to ensure a seamless flow. Themes featured include: Irish artistes, 1950s recordings, mono recordings, Hawaiian music, 78s, Western ('cowboy') music, Australian country, listeners' requests, No. 1 hits of the year, bluegrass, yodelling, 'old' songs, new releases, Christmas songs, music of deceased legends such as Hank Williams, Bob Wills and Jimmie Rodgers, etc., etc.

The formula worked well, and, in the following extract from an interview given to David Redshaw of *New Musical Express* pop magazine, printed in *CMP*'s May, 1975 edition, entitled 'Four Years Not Out', Bob elucidates on the show's appeal:-

DR: What kind of budget do you have to spend?

BP: Our budget is a clean piece of paper. It's literally nil. The salary we all get, as freelancers, is not what it should be, of course. One of these days, hopefully, the BBC will be able to allocate – and what it knows it should allocate. The way we work with British artistes singing – we haven't got a budget, so we pay basically expenses. We'll book them up maybe two weeks in advance. I'll say to Brian Golbey or someone, "You working in a fortnight?" Well, if they're not booked up by then, they're not going to work on that day, unless it's a local gig, so they'll just come in and do two sets of three numbers, usually with just a guitar. Suzanne Harris brought in a guitarist and so did Jon Derek, who brought in Graham Walker.

DR: What are the balance problems of having people perform on this informal basis?

BP: It's only when you start using electrical instruments. The most surprising one that succeeded very well – that I was quite pleased with... we had a group we called the London Country Quartet, consisting of Chas Hodges on fiddle, Dave Peacock on bass, Keith Nelson on banjo and Albert Lee, no less, on lead guitar – all acoustic. We thought we had swing arm mikes, but we found out that they were assigned somewhere else that day so we only had one mike. So we stuck them all around the one fixed mike and said, "Anyone who does a solo, lean in." And the sound balance was fantastic. We've had the Southern Ramblers on two mikes. We were a bit worried about it, so we got people like Tony Byworth and Roger Camden, lead guitarist of *The Gentry*, to ring in if they thought there was anything that could be improved, because you can hear it better in your own home on the radio than you can in the control room, and Tony rang up and said, "The bass player's a bit loud," so we told him to stand away a bit.

DR: You retain a strong affection for fifties country music – something of a golden era for country – but how wide is your musical taste?

BP: Oh, I like them right up to date. More than the fifties nowadays. I started as a diehard country fan, mainly because when I started in the business, the music was the stringy, Eddy Arnold type, which I still don't like. The music of today is, I think, the best country music ever. As regards choice of material, I try to make it as liberal as possible. See, the programme is based on what went before. Last week, we had one hour of pure bluegrass, with Mac Wiseman and Country Gazette, followed by Mary Lou Turner and Jimmy Gateley. So, this week the idea was to play pretty straight country records. Next week, it's Gary Stewart, who's modern country, and then probably the week after that it'll be bluegrass and some contemporary – although contemporary is one side of it that I'm not as well informed on as I'd like to be. Tony Byworth was going to make me a list of contemporary records which I was going to play, but he hasn't got round to doing it.

DR: How about Tom T. Hall and the 'Outlaw' movement?

BP: What upsets me… these fellas came into Nashville three or four years ago, and they were rebels – they were different. But now you look at the street corners around Tompall Glaser's studio and Waylon Jennings' office – they're wearing a uniform, a denim outfit with a cowboy hat… and they all look the same and sound the same – I'm not talking about the really successful ones… it all seems so phoney to me.

DR: Some very big names have featured on London Country. Which interview sticks out most in your mind?

BP: I would say Red Hayes. I've never actually told anyone this. The way we work… Faron Young was coming in, so we were going to record a programme with Faron and Connie Smith on the Thursday and put it out Friday night (this was before the change to Sundays). It was all arranged, but Faron was very tired, so was Connie. Jeff Kruger and Phonogram had a reception and they were coming up to me literally every ten minutes and changing their minds – "Faron was going to be on the programme the whole two hours, Faron was not going to be on for two hours, he was going to be on twenty minutes, he was going to be on half an hour…" I was at the point where I was about to tell Faron to get stuffed. So we got back to the office and finally it was agreed that he was going to do an hour and Connie was going to come in and do some, and that left us with half an hour to kill, so we asked Red Hayes if he'd come along to fill in. (Half of the programme was being broadcast on Radio Merseyside, by the way, the first time that ever happened). Well, the reaction to Faron, who was at his sarcastic best, and to Connie, was very little, but the reaction to the little bit that Red Hayes did was fantastic, and I was completely enthused with it. It had the makings of a good programme. He was such a likeable guy, a sort of gentle giant, and it came over how pleasant he was. He portrayed this to the listeners and I had a lot of phone calls. I still think I've had more reaction to that particular programme. There have been other programmes I've enjoyed a great deal, such as Tex Ritter live on the programme, Tompall Glaser singing old-time songs live…

DR: *You had Roy Acuff on, too.*

BP: Yeah, that was the second or third week of our existence, in Duncan Johnson's days. We had him in for about a twenty minute interview and we also had all his band in. The Bill Anderson programmes were particularly good because he's so good to work with. We've done two complete Bill Anderson shows, now.

DR: *How about your scheduling slot?*

BP: I was much happier going against BBC Radio's *Country Style*, which was slickness, one type of country music only, and I was so against that programme – I didn't like it at all towards the end. The presenter of that programme [Pat Campbell] was always telling me that the programme was not for the country fan but for the people who were getting into country music; and I thought, 'Well, let's do a programme for the country fan,' and that's exactly what we did.

DR: *In this game, you must always keep an eye on audience figures. Do you have any idea at all how many people are listening each week?*

BP: Bill Anderson's manager tells us that in the States if they have a phone-in competition they multiply the response by three thousand for each call. Now, on our Bill Anderson programme, we got five hundred and forty six replies, which is over a million listeners. Now I don't believe for one moment that we get a million listeners; but I do believe that we get one hell of a lot.

DR: *What sort of people listen at that time of day? Sunday weekend motorists?*

BP: I would say that in the south of England, if there was a most popular programme for men doing the washing-up, it would be *London Country*. All these middle-aged guys come up to me and say, "It's my day to do the washing-up and I always listen to your programme while I do it." I think it's that time of day. Basically, from our phone-calls, in respect of nationalities, I would say probably besides English people, Irish people listen a great deal, and the amazing and pleasant thing is the amount of black people and Indians that are now ringing in. At least they sound like Indians and West Indians. They seem to be interested and it's very pleasing to me because I don't really believe it's a specialist music.

The Bill Anderson comment – "he's so good to work with" – is particularly interesting, as he and Bob were to experience a see-saw relationship through the years, typified by a barbed response from the polished writer/performer to an emailed communication: "Bob Powel? Oh yes, I remember you – you're the guy who suggested I cut out the narrations, which have proved to be the biggest money-spinners of my career." Leaving the host unsure whether to be offended – or impressed at his long memory! At least one person – a representative from Anderson's UK fan club – believed Bob *was* offended, even suggesting to the singer that his music was being boycotted on *London Country*, an accusation met by the host's simple retort: "Hardly – I wasn't playing any Bill Anderson beforehand!" (Which probably did little to thaw out relations).

By the mid-70s, *London Country* was beginning to earn something of a reputation. Firstly, it was learned that, in the sincerest form of tribute, many listeners were taping the show[81] to send to fans living outside the catchment

---

[81] Fans would occasionally ask the host why he insisted on

area. Then, TV started to take an interest…

The well-spoken young executive sounded keen over the phone and a visit to *London Country*'s studios was soon arranged. On arrival, however, the gentleman – accompanied by a colleague – immediately seemed rather ill-at-ease. Bob, sensing this and knowing the importance of physical appearance in the world of television, enquired tentatively, "Would I need to be in full vision?"

"Yes," came the joint reply.

"Oh…" Embarrassed silence, until the situation – and their anxiety – was rescued with the pre-emptive: "You don't really want me, do you?" The short, one-word answer was delivered cruelly and with barely disguised relief. Unbothered, the presenter returned to his patch, comforted in the knowledge that "I have the perfect figure for radio." Mind you, it seems more than a little unfair that the – at least – equally rotund Johnny Russell's shape didn't hold him back – and he had a beard, and was no prettier – though I suppose it helps if one of your compositions happens to have been recorded by the Beatles. (Russell's stock response to digs about his weight: "I'm not really fat – just short. I used to be seven foot eight, but someone dropped a piano on me and spread me out a little!")

Despite this rebuff, the (generally) unseen radio presenter enjoyed a couple of minor TV appearances, the first while visiting his sister, who was studying midwifery in Scotland: on a day trip to the small coastal town of Inveraray, he somehow managed to get caught up in a TV recording of the *White Heather Club*, sandwiched between hosts Robin Hall and Jimmie MacGregor, for a two and a

---

talking over the intro of records. Bob had a stock response to this question: "Be honest with me – is that because you're taping the show?" The answer would always be 'yes', so, taping being illegal, "I felt justified in ignoring their requests to refrain."

half minute 'knees-up' appearance. "I didn't do it on purpose," he claimed, none too convincingly. The second occurred during a Speedway Final at Wembley Stadium, where cameras recorded him carrying one end of injured rider Barry Briggs' bike. There may also be odd clips floating around America, as he participated in several US networked items relating to the UK country scene, notably a Walter Cronkite CBS news programme (reported in *CMP*, April, 1978) and an NBC feature (*CMP*, May, 1987).

One incident that gave rise to notions of genuine stardom came via the spate of fan-messages that appeared on *London Country*'s answerphone around this time – all singing his praises as a wonderful DJ, adorable human being – sexy, even. The presenter couldn't help feeling that perhaps here at last was recognition of his finer qualities. His head was halfway in the clouds, until, finally managing to speak to the person (there was just one), he discovered her to be an overly hysterical teenager besotted with Radio 1 DJ, *Peter* Powell – a sickening eight years younger and six stones lighter, into the bargain! Upon explaining exactly who he was, the line went suddenly dead (he got over it, eventually).

Bob never met the aforementioned Mr. Powell, but occasionally encountered other DJs, one of whom was fellow Radio London presenter, Tony Blackburn. An abiding memory was the sight of this eternal optimist leafing through a bundle of carefully compiled joke books, recounting selected examples to his somewhat bemused colleague (not unknown to deliver a corny gag or two himself), in the process, supplying enough jokes – and laughs – for both of them.

Back in the world of serious broadcasting, Bob, via *Powel's Point Of View* in *CMP*'s August, 1977 edition (commemorating the show's sixth anniversary), explains the differences between *London Country* and networked shows – in particular, Radio 2's *Country Club*:-

"A team of three is involved in (our) show. I have had a producer ever since I have been on the air, but the role of the producer is a little different from that of Colin Chandler on *Country Club*. Colin's main job is *Country Club* and he and his secretary devote most of their working day to the programme. It, as befits a network show, takes a week to plan – not so on a local show. My producer, Maggie Tschirren works two days a week on *London Country*. Unlike *Country Club*, the show is not scripted, so the timing is only informed guesswork, and on the show, it is the rule rather than the exception that records have to be cut or added to the running order. Like most of the other local DJ's, I 'self-op,' which means I play in my own records and mikes, compared to *Country Club*, where the producer oversees one engineer who operates the board and another who plays the discs and tapes. So, the operation is totally different and so is the result. You can get away with more mistakes on a local station and things have been known to go wrong but it all adds to the atmosphere."

Irvine Brookes concurs: "Our programme was, I think, rather unfairly compared to the network BBC country programme. The concept of a BBC local radio station (and all that meant in terms of staffing, facilities and funding) in the capital city was hard – if not impossible – for some to grasp."

He proceeds to shed light on the amount of work involved behind-the-scenes to produce the show:-

"There were just two of us involved – myself and (news department) secretary, Helen Ronald. All the logging of timings had to be done in our own time, when other broadcast shifts permitted, so we played back a recording of the programme and 'logged' the relevant details, record number, label, duration, writer and publisher of every piece of music broadcast. It was very time-consuming but had to be done – by law. We Radio London station assistants also had to make and operate other programmes on shift from the early morning rush-hour (starting around 4am) to the late evening special strands for other producers. This involved weekends on sport and religion."

Brookes (a non-Southerner) returned North in 1972, finally quitting the BBC in 1992.

As for actual content, thanks mainly to keen listeners, there are, of around 900 made, some 66 recordings of entire or partial programmes known to exist (see *Appendix*), the earliest of which dates from 27 February, 1973 and features singer/songwriter/musician, Red Hayes. This show, a recording of which is lodged with the *Country Music Foundation*[82] in Nashville, was not broadcast until 6 July, owing to its subject's sudden death 3 days later, and it contains some poignant exchanges, including the following:-

RH: "I want to say something about this song (*Sunset Years of Life*), if I may."

BP: "Please do."

RH: "I wrote this song from a letter that I got from my mother just a few months before my mum and dad's 50th anniversary and it was such a beautiful letter – almost

---

[82] *Country Music Foundation.* Chartered by the state of Tennessee in 1964, this is a non-profit organisation based in Nashville dedicated to the preservation and education surrounding country music.

everything in the song is something she said in the letter. I've still got the letter – written on the outside of it (is) 'KEEP' in big letters... I think the song is really my favourite of everything that I've ever written."

Later, on the subject of Red's best-known composition, *A Satisfied Mind*:-

BP: "Have you ever worked out how many copies (it) has sold?"

RH: "Oh no, I don't have the slightest idea..."

BP: "It would be well in the millions, wouldn't it?"

RH: "Oh yes... thank goodness! Close to 200 have recorded it. I wish I had a copy of each one for my collection, but I don't have – I think maybe I have 4 or 5 copies, one (of which) is my own..."

BP: "Has anyone in the pop field recorded it?"

RH: "Oh goodness, yes. At the time it was big in the country field, Mahalia Jackson had a spiritual record on it, which was wonderful, Ella Fitzgerald had a jazz record on it, which was real fine, a group from Chicago by the name of Betty & Jack – The Keens, I believe – they had a good record on it, Hugo & Luigi... Joan Baez recently in the last two or three years. The Byrds had a fabulous record on it, Bobby Helms in the pop field had a great record on it... I could go on, but I won't..."

BP: "But the best version was Red Hayes, right?"

RH: (After consideration) "My mother liked that one best..."

The disappointing aspect of this particular show was that regular producer, Maggie Tschirren, owing to another commitment, missed out on the recording, her place being taken by Tony Fish. So, as Bob lamented, "Tony did one programme and got in the *Country Music Foundation*, and Maggie isn't!"

In a totally different vein, the show recorded 16 March 1973 features the Statler Brothers, plus special 'shock' guest, Lester 'Roadhog' Moran (actually the group's bass singer, Harold Reid), whose gimmick involved speaking in an ultra-deep, exaggerated Southern growl.[83] With uncommunicative, guitar-playing sidekick, Wichita, dire backing group, the Cadillac Cowboys, sponsor, Burford's Barber Shop (sideline: illicit whisky) and a limitless supply of homespun philosophy – *Be good to your neighbour, Keep smiling, May the good Lord take a liking to you*, etc. – Moran's presence promised something out of the ordinary, and so it proves, from the moment he is introduced by (actual) brother, Don, as "a gentleman we met back in Virginia and invited to join us on our latest album."

LM: "Thank you very much, glad to be here with you, Tom."

Rest of group: "Bob!"

LM: "Bob, yeh – it don't matter…"

Later:-

BP: "I believe you were in the Navy with Johnny Cash…"

LM: "I was in the Navy with Johnny for two years – he got out early on a dishonourable discharge. We were

---

[83] Reid eventually quit playing this role, as the effort of making the deep, guttural sounds adversely affected his singing voice.

stationed in Norfolk, Virginia – do you know where that is?"

BP: "It's in Virginia, isn't it?"

LM: "That's right, Bill."

Rest of group: "Bob!"

Further on:-

BP: "Do you write any songs yourself?"

LM: "I wrote a few."

BP: "Do you know any titles of them?"

LM: "Er, one title was, 'I Love You Darling' – have you ever heard it?"

BP: "I've heard the words before – in just about every song that was ever written, actually."

LM: "Well, Tom…"

Rest of group: "Bob!"

LM: "Bob, that's right. Well, this here's a love song – I said it with a lot of heart and soul."

BP: "Now, do you ever go out of tune – or do you ever get *in* tune?"

LM: "Far as I know, the Cadillac Cowboys always finished up together."

Don: "Didn't you write a Christmas song once?"

LM: "Well, Gene Autry wrote *Rudolph the Red-nosed Reindeer*, while I wrote *Do You Think It's Gonna Rain, Dear?* but it didn't take off – unlike the reindeer…"

And finally:-

BP: "I'd like to thank you – I think – very much indeed for coming on the programme because I can honestly say if you hadn't come on, *London Country* listeners would not have... had a show like this."

Harold Reid (as himself): "Will it be played?"

BP: "Once Margaret gets through with a little red pencil – YES."

HR: "Think you'll get 20 useful minutes out of it?"

BP: "I doubt it."

Lecturer and film critic (specialising in science fiction) Philip Strick presents no such worries when guesting in 1976. At the time, Strick was running country music courses in South East London, and the host, having established that the two-hour sessions often stretched to three, probes further:-

BP: "You've got very definite opinions on country music...When you lecture, do you make sure people know this or do you keep your opinions to yourself?"

PS: "I think there's nothing worse than telling people what their opinions should be and no lecturer should ever come out with ideas which are so strong that his students get all cowed and say, 'Oh my God, that's what I should be thinking,' and they don't do any thinking for themselves. Obviously, it's important for me to have very firm ideas of my own and to be able to back those up. But chiefly, what I hope I can get the people who come to these sessions to do is talk for themselves about how they feel about country music and that's far more important than them hearing me waffle about it."

Strick (who passed away in 2013) conducted courses from 1975 to 1978 before switching attention to his many other activities. Someone much more firmly rooted in country music was Faron Young. Making his second appearance, on 7 February 1977, he immediately reveals himself as someone with whom the host is able to engage in easy banter. Opening with a recording of his greatest American pop and country success, *Hello, Walls*, the conversation proceeds:-

BP: "Good afternoon! Today on *London Country*, we have a special 'live' guest – one of the great stars of country music-"

FY: (Interrupting) "Are you sure I'm 'live'?"

BP: (Thrown) "Erm…"

FY: "I feel dead today…"

BP: "Do you?"

FY: "After my appearance, I'm tired."

BP: (Regaining composure) "I haven't read out what I'm going to say about you yet – hard-working, never swears, sober… (laughter from Faron) of course, who can it be – anyone *but* Faron Young!"

FY: "Thank you, Bob. Don't ruin my reputation – I've spent all these years cursing and drinking to build up my reputation and you're going to ruin it!"

BP: "I will never be able to ruin the reputation you've got!"

In fact, Young's other reputation – as an exceptional 'live' performer – prompts the host's next suggestion:-

BP: "I've said for years – and you've ignored me, like

everyone else does – that you should do a 'live' album, because you're one man that does entertain on stage."

FY: "Well, I was the first guy, I think, to have this idea, and I went to Capitol years ago. I said, 'Let's go to some good place and do a 'live' album.' 'Oh, that's not a good idea, nobody's gonna buy that.' And by the time we got around to thinking of doing it again, 150 people had done it, and they said, 'Hey, I got an idea, let's do a 'live' album!' I said, 'That's nothing new.' So, I won't do it now."

BP: "Well, you should-"

FY: (Interrupting) "Bill Anderson did a 'live' album, but he recorded it at the studio and put applause in, so he could go over as big as he wanted to." (Laughter)

BP: (Laughing) "You say lovely things about your friends, don't you?"

FY: "Well, when Buck Owens was here recording 'Buck Owens Live at the London Palladium', he didn't have about 300 people-"

BP: "He had a darn sight more than 300 people!"

FY: "–and then he had to add the applause!" (Laughing)

BP: "That's not true at all! The place was as good as packed – I was there, actually…"

FY: "I'm only kidding with you."

Later, in a scenario that would be repeated regularly, Faron disputes the line-up of his backing group, the Country Deputies, on a disc Bob is about to play. Finally, conceding that Bob is right, he exclaims: "I'm gonna have to check with you to see exactly what I'm up to!"

The same show features a good example of Bob's eclecticism within the country genre: a four-minute plus, jazzed-up, 3/4 alternating with 4/4 version of Roger

Miller's *King of the Road* by fiddler Vassar Clements that, aided by some inspired sax and fuzz guitar playing, really swings! Another Powel 'special item', American Forces Recruitment Shows[84] – 'live' recordings never officially released yet somehow acquired by him – regularly 'throws' guests, who, more often than not, are unaware of their existence and only vaguely recall their participation. Faron Young, after he'd got over the shock – "How d'ya get your hands a-hold of *that*?" – proves no exception, managing to date it only through the inclusion of a record on release at the time. As well as providing a novel diversion from the programme's standard fare and – at an average 12 minutes duration – an opportunity for Bob to relax and take a break, these shows, which he described as "a godsend," enabled him to keep within the bounds of 'needle-time'

---

[84] American Forces (Army, Navy & Air Force) Recruitment Shows. Special recordings made by famous – and not-so-famous – country performers, these were broadcast by American radio stations with the aim of encouraging enlistment. Featuring accompaniment from top Nashville session-men, they were (some – certainly Bob – would say, mercifully) free of the heavy orchestrations, including obligatory Anita Kerr Singers, that featured on many recordings of the day. (The musicians were also called upon to supply the applause, which involved clapping in double-quick time – and volume!) Upon obtaining these – 400, in total, and all free – in two separate batches: the first from Tom Perryman, long-time Jim Reeves associate and General Manager of WMTS Station, Tennessee, the second from Bill Ormes, of WAGG, Franklin, Bob was amazed but delighted to discover both dated from the 1970s, the latter commencing at the exact point the former terminated. Earlier batches – dating from the 1950s and obtained from Ray Avery's Rare Records, Hollywood, California – were 16-inch transcription pressings designed to be played from the *inside* of the disc out, allowing Bob to have great fun with Radio London technicians unused to the format. (His laughter soon turned to tears of frustration upon attempting to transfer the discs to tape – a problem eventually solved with the aid of a giant gramophone machine).

(set by the musicians union at 20 minutes per two-hour show), which, being non-commercial recordings, they did not count towards. When a guest appeared, the problem did not arise, as you were "illustrating his or her career with music" – likewise, record reviews were exempt. In such subtle ways was the restriction worked around.

Another noteworthy show, of which a recording exists, dates from 23 March, 1978, and features American country DJ, Ralph Emery, virtually unknown in the UK but considered the best among his peers. Bob's opening remark betrays his feelings: "I have never been more nervous as a country music disc-jockey." He needn't have been, as he acquits himself well in Mr. Emery's company and they enjoy a good rapport from the start:-

Ralph: "I was looking at the music sheet – I'm amazed at some of the things you've planned."

Bob: "Well, it gives me great pleasure to do things like that because you pull dirty tricks like this on artistes all the time in the States."

Ralph: (Feigned innocence) "I don't know why I have such a bad reputation because I'm really a nice guy…"

Bob: "Really? Oh, I'm not."

Ralph: "I need to get on a few people to relieve my boredom…"

Bob: "Exactly – that's why I do it. If you just play the latest records, it gets dull, doesn't it?"

Later, as Bob is about to play *Rainbow Road*, an early Emery attempt at vocalising:-

Ralph: "I don't know why you want to do this to me because… I have never, never told anyone I can sing."

Bob: "Do you want me to explain, because, you won't remember it, but I've been on your programme once, and the door was open while I was talking to you and I couldn't see who it was, and you said, 'What do you think of Marty Robbins – he's not very good, is he?' And this sort of thing, and I said, 'Yeh, I think he's good.' And you said, 'You've said to me off-mic…' (To which I replied) 'I never said to you off-mic.' And it turned out Marty Robbins was behind us and you were trying to get me going, you know."

Ralph: (Nervous laugh).

Bob: "So, you deserve everything you get, really."

Ralph: "Oh, did I do that to you, Bob?"

Bob: "Yup."

Then, after playing record:-

Bob: "Different."

Ralph: "You didn't say 'good', I notice, just 'different.'"

Bob: "Yes, well, one has to keep one's reputation – I wondered why you stayed at being the No.1 *disc-jockey* in the world… No, I think it's not bad, really – I wouldn't say it's good…"

Ralph: "Bob, I'm not trying to beg for a compliment – I know what it sounds like…"

Bob did not often play – or comment on – his performances, but roared with laughter when listening back to this exchange (as he also did with Faron Young's 1977 ones).

One guest whose talent is unquestionable (if – beyond country music circles – virtually unrecognised) is fellow Canadian, Ronnie Prophet – singer, musician, impressionist, mimic, and occasional *Wembley Festival* compere. On his 30 December, 1978 appearance, the host, after playing Ronnie's 'Donald Duck' version of *Help Me Make It Through the Night*, asks when he first realised that, in the music business, a performer has to really entertain:-

RP: "Well, I've always been involved in country music, and I saw so many artistes come out and do what I call 'jukebox': 'Here's a song that I cut last year and it goes something like this' – it doesn't even go like 'this', and the next tune is: 'Here's one that I've just cut and you'll hear it on your radio station…' Well, who gives a damn, you know – come out and do something that's different, perform, give the public their money's worth."

BP: "But then again, it's a two-edged sword, in that, I believe you haven't really achieved the record success you should and I think the same goes for Roy Clark, who's another great entertainer. Is it that you can get such a reputation as an entertainer that the producer says, 'Well, I don't really know what to do with him?'"

RP: "Oh yes, I've sat down and talked with Chet (Atkins) and said, 'Why don't we go into the studio and you produce me?' And he's said, 'I don't know what to produce you on.'"

Later…

BP: "Who would *you* go to see to be entertained?"

RP: "Barbara Mandrell is a great artiste… I understand that, musically, Donna Fargo has a great show…"

BP: "It's interesting you mention those two because… neither of those went particularly well at *Wembley* because they were too 'Las Vegas-y' for the *Wembley* audiences, yet you went down a storm."

RP: "I think because my type of act is 'off-the-cuff'… I play to the audience itself… you couldn't say to (Barbara) 'do this' in the middle of her show because there's just no way, (while) Roy Clark is flexible like myself."

BP: "It's funny, because when Roy was on, I played a 'live' recording he made in 1959 and he said he's got to change some of his jokes – he didn't realise he'd been doing them all those years!"

RP: "But there's something about our business… if you've got a piece of material that works… never drop it. You'll have people who'll say, 'I heard him say that before,' but you'll still get a laugh out of it. I will not drop it, it's there for keeps and it's a part of me."

In the face of so much American talent, British country artistes had a hard time establishing themselves and a *London Country* show dated September 1979, illustrates the difficulties on both sides (performer and presenter). Rusty Douch, a British singer/songwriter/musician, is touring at the time with Patsy Montana, and Bob invites him onto the show, along with Patsy, to perform a few songs, introducing him as "a young man who I've known for many years, and I'm looking forward to this spot because I know he's a great singer and guitarist." Then, "Rusty, my boy,[85] what are you going to start off with?" There follows a lengthy pause before the hopeful, young troubadour

---

[85] Although he would have denied it, the evidence suggests Bob displayed a different attitude towards British country artistes – it's somehow hard to imagine him introducing Merle Haggard or Tom T. Hall this way.

opens his 4-song (12-minute) set with an obscure Mickey Newbury number entitled, *Frisco Depot*, delivered in obligatory American drawl, followed by another obscure, though marginally better, piece (from a Tompall Glaser album), *A Phoney World*. Third up comes a tune in honour of his daughter, *Tara*, which, while original, is heavily American-influenced. His closing – and best – performance, *Steel Guitar Man*, contains some neat references to American country stars, Merle Haggard, Slim Whitman and Don Williams. Although Bob commends the singer for a "superb job," perhaps a more telling comment follows Patsy's observation that "you've got a lot of good talent here in England."

"We've got even better talent when you come over."

Bob, in many of his shows, reveals an interest in song-writing, using every opportunity to elicit secrets of the art from guests, as with Red Hayes, in 1973:-

BP: "You've written a lot of unusual songs – do you get ideas early in the morning or do they just come to you, or what?"

RH: "Now, that's a hard question…"

BP: "Do you have a tape recorder by the bed, that sort of thing?"

RH: (Laughing) "No… I don't use a tape machine until the song's finished in my mind. I don't even write it down until it's finished."

And Jim Glaser (24 March, 1979):-

BP: "Do you write with people in mind?"

JG: "I may have once or twice...there was one time someone was looking for a soundtrack for a movie and Jimmy Payne and I wrote a song for it and another of our writers, Hoover, wrote one (but) neither one of us got the song in the movie, but each of us got the song cut by someone else..."

BP: "When you write, do you go to each other's house and sit down, or how does it happen?"

JG: "We do it all different ways, sometimes we go to one another's house, many times we've gotten in the car and rented a cabin in some obscure place...one time, we went to St. Louis, more recently, we went up to one of the lakes 60 miles outside Nashville, spent a day or two...whatever it takes, you know."

Glaser then relates the story of his (minor) contribution to brother Tompall's composition, *Stand Beside Me*,[86] recorded by Perry Como, and later successfully revived (in a more up-tempo version) by Daniel O'Donnell:-

JG: "Chet Atkins picked the song (for) Perry Como (who) didn't get involved in picking material at all...but (he) can sight-read music, so the arrangements were written and he would walk into the studio, pick up the music and sight-read the song for the first time he was recording it. So, when he got to the second verse of the song where it made a reference to...'growing old is fun when your heart is true to one,' he threw down the piece of paper with the lyrics on it and walked out of the studio,

---

[86] *Stand Beside Me* provided Jimmy Dean with a No.10 country hit in 1966. Other artistes to have recorded the song (apart from Perry Como and Daniel O'Donnell) include Connie Smith and Nat Stukey. (Not to be confused with a similarly titled song by Jo Dee Messina).

saying he refused to record a song that says, 'growing old is fun!' So, Tompall called me at home about four in the morning, saying if we wanted to get a Perry Como cut on this song, we'd have to write a different second verse – he couldn't do it…so I roused brother Chuck out of bed…and we wrote a new second verse, which Perry then did find satisfactory and recorded."

Occasionally, guests would comment on other writers, as when Hank Locklin, appearing 24 June, 1978, acknowledges the contribution made by Fred Rose to Hank Williams' music. *May You Never Be Alone*[87] has just been played:-

BP: "Beautiful song, Hank, isn't it?"

HL: "Oh yeh, Williams just had the right songs, every time. Fred Rose worked very closely with him…Hank would write a song and Fred would take it and look at it – and he was near-sighted, he had to look real close at it. He was a genius, he'd take lines out and put the right ones in it for him."

Felice and Boudleaux Bryant, in their 1981 appearance, go further in their assessment of Rose's contribution:-

Felice: "People will not own up to it, but it's a fact…" (i.e. that Fred Rose virtually wrote Hank's hits)

Boudleaux: "He (Rose) was the greatest song doctor in

---

[87] *May You Never Be Alone* – Self-composition recorded by Hank Williams on 1 March, 1949 and issued as the 'B' side to *I Just Don't Like This Kind Of Livin'* which reached No.5 on the country chart the following year.

the world."

BP: "Do you think Hank would have been a great writer without Fred Rose?"

Felice: "No."

BP: "You don't?"

Boudleaux: "I don't know…"

Felice: "He (Williams) was charismatic, he was a great singer, he had tremendous presence on record, I mean he came through like Presley on record – and on stage – but without Fred Rose – no…"

Boudleaux: "Fred Rose was a genius, he was a song-writing genius, really…"

Felice: "The first song that Hank Williams ever brought into Acuff-Rose was *Lovesick Blues-*"

BP: (Interrupting) "Oh no, he didn't write that…"

Felice: "No, that's right, but he told Acuff-Rose he wrote it!"

BP: (Laughing) "Oh, did he?"

Boudleaux: "His name was on the first record. Hank was an extremely talented singer and a great 'idea' man…"

Felice: "And *he* was a title man, Hank was…"

Boudleaux: "Yes."

What sort of person made up *London Country*'s audience? An item in January 1979's *CMP* provided an indication, albeit obliquely:-

(Heading) "CONTEMPORARY LONDON GETS THUMBS UP

"In a swing away from the normal, Radio London's Bob Powel presented a wholly (contemporary)-orientated U.S. Country Chart Show on his *London Country* programme, Saturday, November 25th. Usually, Powel presents what he considers 'a more balanced programme of old and new records rather than a continuous stream of chart recordings which make overtures to both pop and rock markets.' At the same time he asked for listeners' response and admits that he was surprised to find a slighter percentage of phone-calls received during a 30-minute period were in favour of the contemporary recordings. 'I think it's worth noting, though, that at the time the show goes out (Saturday 2-4.30pm), we have more than a *country* listenership and I think the phone response proved it,' says Powel. He later added that letters received following the show's transmission provided an opposite viewpoint; a greater preference to more recognisable country recordings."

Which proves nothing, really, other than that, like the music itself, *London Country*'s audience probably comprised a varied mixture. An earlier telephone survey, in February, 1978, revealed that 77.7% of listeners favoured contemporary sounds (*CMP*, March, 1978). And Bob himself confessed to me, "If there's one gap in my knowledge, it's the contemporary West Coast scene."

No analysis of the show would be complete without mention of Dolly – not the famous Parton, but Bob's lesser-known though more important (to him, at least) next-door neighbour, Dolly Waterton. Identifying individual titles among 10,000 records was obviously a mammoth task, especially when, as often the case, a songwriter featured on the show. Enter our unsung hero, or heroine (albeit a paid one). This diligent lady's task was to examine records individually, copying details of each featured songwriter onto index cards, which then cross-referenced with the appropriate album/EP/45. The records themselves were filed via the first letter + one vowel, e.g. under *S*, there would be *Sa, Se, Si, So, Su,* for which Hank Snow, say, would be filed under *Si,* different records being numbered accordingly, *Si1, Si2,* etc. These five segments were marked with five different coloured stickers. It all seems rather archaic – and arduous – compared with modern-day computerised methods, but, in fact, it worked most effectively, ensuring each and every obscure title by any composer was 'captured.' This, in turn, helped make those moments of surprise, as the writer is confronted by some long-forgotten gem, all the more magical.

Bob's favourite Dolly story concerns the occasion he mistakenly referred to a payment she was receiving as a pension. "I'm not a pensioner!" came the indignant response. She was, in fact, 59, and, six months later on his show, knowing the milestone had now been reached, the mischievous DJ couldn't resist playing a song "dedicated especially to my next-door neighbour, Dolly: Roy Acuff's *When the old-age pension cheque comes through the door.*"

Calling round to her that evening, he was greeted with, "I hate you!" followed by a door slammed firmly in his face! (Though they later shared a cup of tea). Dolly passed on shortly after the turn of the millennium, but her place is forever assured in *London Country's* history.

Chapter 7

London Country: 2nd Decade, 1980s

Everything's OK ("We're still a-livin'…")[88]

Bob's second decade at *London Country* continued in much the same vein as the first, one notable difference being that country music now had a far higher profile, thanks in no small part to him, and to reasons mentioned previously. By this stage, without *CMP* editorship, he had more time to indulge his hobbies, which, while numerous, tended to revolve around familiar themes such as music, film and sport. Friends recall seeing the evidence of such activities…

Bryan Chalker "envied the *Wurlitzer* jukebox he had sitting in his lounge" (according to its owner, this was actually a *Seeburg*), while Marie O'Connell was astonished at the amount of space taken up with archived music: [the room] "was filled from floor to ceiling with shelving containing some of the rarest original country recordings in existence. On his lawn, meanwhile, stood the biggest

---

[88] *Everything's OK.* Droll, Hank Williams-composed novelty number, recorded by him in 'Luke the Drifter' guise. According to *Powel's Page* (*CMP*, June, 1986), this was the second 78rpm single Bob bought, after *Gloryland March*.

satellite dish I had ever seen – outside of an international space station. Bob could operate it from inside the house, enabling it to turn (making quite a loud buzzing noise), I'm sure much to the annoyance of his neighbours, as he would do it in the middle of the night whilst watching North American sport and music."

Never having married nor learned to curb his less moderate inclinations, the independent-minded DJ believed firmly in 'doing his own thing' about the house, consequently leaving himself open to the charge of being 'eccentric.' Add in an – otherwise delightful – cleaning lady with a loose tongue and tendency to exaggerate, and you have a recipe for, at best, misunderstanding, at worst, scandal…

In fact, the said lady, Mary (now deceased), by virtue of unswerving loyalty and dedication, became very dear and important to the not-so-tidy bachelor, which is why he generally ignored her gossip. Until, that is, she began telling neighbours she had to empty and clean out his bath "every day of the week," at which point he felt compelled to act, since it was an outright lie, though, as is often the case, it contained an element of truth: occasionally, if the phone rang while he was so indisposed, he may have neglected to do the necessary, especially if the call required an urgent departure. There were probably other stories that never made their way back to him – and perhaps just as well.

Nevertheless, the relationship survived and, on the whole, seems to have been happy – and certainly jocular. As on the occasion Bob, repeatedly discovering cigarette ash on his pillow, asked the good lady to "please go into the kitchen to smoke, and, when you've finished, carry on with the housework." Taking his request a stage further (or perhaps to heart), she decided to kick the habit completely – whereupon her cheeky employer promptly deducted the amount she would have spent on cigarettes from her next wage packet (but only in jest!). Mary eventually retired, aged 86.

Back at *London Country*, Felice and Boudleaux Bryant, prolific husband and wife song-writing team who were as comfortable operating in the pop as the country field, reveal, on 27 June 1981, how they pitch their material:-

BP: "Do you sing your own demos?"

Boudleaux: "We don't make many demos, actually, because we've never had any success that way."

BP: "That's unusual."

Felice: "You should have heard the demos!"

Boudleaux: "Yeh, right. Our demos must have been the most terrible in the world – even some people around Nashville used to collect them simply because they were so bad. Most of the songs that we've ever gotten on record were shown in person to the artiste."

BP: "What, you sing them…?"

Boudleaux: "Right. For some reason, people, when you sit down and sing a song, they don't expect too much. If you push a button or turn on a switch, they say, 'Ah, this is gonna be good.' And when you push a button with *my* demos on it (laughs), it ain't gonna be good!"

Later, the host reads out a list of the many versions of Felice and Boudleaux's *Rocky Top* that he has in his own private collection:-

BP: "Paul Franklin (did an instrumental version of it), Diane Sherrill, Flying Burrito Bros., Concrete Cowboys, Dottie West, Otis Williams, Jimmy Crawford & Russ Hicks together, Dillard & Clark, Jimmy Dean, Everly

Bros., Danny Davis, Buck Owens, UK group The Maverick, McPeake Bros., Rose Maddox, Charlie McCoy, Lynn Anderson, Bill Anderson, Barbi Benton, Porter Wagoner, Buddy Spicher, Carl Smith, Nitty Gritty Dirt Band, Tokyo Matsu, Dave Dudley, Dick Curless, Randy Corner, Vassar Clements and Maybelle Carter."

The Bryants, like many songwriters before and since, are both amazed and impressed at the number of hitherto unknown recordings of their songs unearthed by the host. However, on this occasion, their response is rather different – and amusing:-

Felice: "Don't you have the Czechoslovakian record?"

BP: (Unfazed) "No, I missed that one."

Boudleaux: "It's one of the best records of all and I will make sure that you get a copy just for your own collection."

BP: "Right, well, until then, I'll have to make do with the Nitty Gritty Dirt Band version!"

Towards the end of (the first part of) this interview, Bob asks "the question everybody asks you – how did you get your name, Boudleaux?"

Boudleaux: "I was named after a French soldier by my father. This soldier happened to save my Dad's life during the First World War and he thought that it would be a tribute, some sort of recognition to name his first-born after him and that's what he did."

BP: "Did he stay in touch with him?"

Boudleaux: "I don't believe so. As far as I know, he

didn't.''

BP: "Was it his surname, or his first name?"

Boudleaux: "I think it was his surname…"

BP: "Oh, interesting. And this is a question you won't answer – what's your real first name, Felice? I heard you on the radio saying you won't tell anyone…"

Felice: "Oh, my gosh…my given name?"

BP: "U-huh…"

Felice: "No…"

BP: "'*No* Bryant' – I can see why you didn't want to tell us…"

Felice: (Laughing) "That's right, yes." [It's actually Matilda].

Aiming for as much diversity as possible, the show could not ignore country music's all-acoustic relative, bluegrass – thus, on 1 November, 1981, little-known contemporary practitioners the McPeake Bros. are featured. After establishing that only one of the original three brothers, Larry, remains, and that guitarist/banjoist Richard Skaggs is unrelated to his more famous namesake, Ricky, the host enquires if there is a market for their brand of 'progressive' country:-

Larry McPeake: "It seems to be, especially in the states of Florida, New York or somewhere like that, they still lean towards the Stanley Bros. style or the old Flatt & Scruggs style , for some reason. You can get away with playing the progressive stuff if you can balance it out with the old-time music."

BP: "Can you make a living playing bluegrass?"

LM: "Not much, but it's a heck of a lot of fun!"

BP: "Do you have a job in the winter, to help?"

LM: "No. Right now, we're solely supporting ourselves on bluegrass and it's working out right well. The more you play, the more albums you get out, and, of course, the more money you can make. You can't make as much as the country people do – you can make it, but you won't live as the king does, or whatever."

While he may not claim to be 'king' of the genre, one bluegrass performer who manages to live very well is the aforementioned Ricky Skaggs. During his 19 May 1985 appearance, he explains how he sustains success without compromising his style:-

RS: "Well, I felt like there was a hunger out there and we were supplying the food for the hunger. 'Crossover' country music had kinda swept the country and it replaced so much of the tradition and so much of the roots and so much of what country music is all about. Sorry to say, but it really did happen. And we came along four years ago and started doing something that all the people started really liking."

BP: "When you first started, did the WHNs (New York radio station) of this world hold back from playing your stuff?"

RS: "I'm not really sure, I was in contact with quite a few of the radio stations in the early days, and still am in contact with many of them. I think WHN has been a supporter of Ricky Skaggs, even though there were a couple of times they were afraid to play *Uncle Pen* and some of the stuff (but) once they realised there was a big New York market out there for Ricky Skaggs, they knew when the other stations were taking it to No.1 and it was going No.1 nationally and they weren't playing it how foolish they looked, standing there with egg on their faces, so they've been a supporter of mine for quite a while."

One thing for sure is that *Uncle Pen* would have been played on *London Country* regardless of performer or whether or not that particular style was fashionable at the time. However, the policy of featuring anything and everything country-flavoured – the further back and more obscure the better – occasionally rebounded on its host, as the Boxcar Willie episode demonstrates. The Texan-born singer, christened Lecil Travis Martin, achieved UK prominence through his *Wembley Festival* appearances, commencing in 1979, but 20 years earlier, he had recorded an album under the name Marty Martin. Managing, as only he could, to obtain a copy from Boxcar himself, Bob wasted no time in playing some tracks on his show, with the star's permission. As if in confirmation of *London Country*'s attraction to all sorts of listeners, these happened to be heard by a quick-thinking Swedish entrepreneur, who promptly tracked down the label owners, obtained rights to the material and re-issued the entire package in updated format, which included listing the artiste as 'Boxcar Willie' (his 'justification' being that this also happened to be the title of one of the tracks). Needless to say, Lecil was not pleased – and to compound his annoyance, the album was advertised in *Country Music People*, available by mail order at £5 a time! (Though, to be fair, not during Bob's tenure). As with 99% of such fall-outs in the world of country music, all was eventually forgiven.

Country stars, unlike their pop counterparts, are, in fact, renowned for exuding warmth and good humour, not just to each other but to fans and media alike, and Bob generally found this to be the case, experiencing very few examples of tantrums or ego-tripping throughout his career. One exception was Dave Rowland of Dave & Sugar ('Sugar' being his two attractive female co-

performers), who arrived at the *London Country* studio in
full tennis gear ready for a 10-minute spot – and not of
tennis – despite having previously consented to a full one
and a half hour appearance. A heated discussion ensued,
resulting in Bob's obtaining the majority of his interview,
but resolving to avoid this individual in future, if at all
possible. Another who failed to comply with the scheduled
terms was, surprisingly, Charley Pride, who showed up an
hour late for each of two appearances, disrupting the
programme's flow and ensuring he was not invited back a
third time.

Visitors to the show also experienced the hospitality –
or otherwise – of their heroes. British country artiste Dave
Travis recalls attending the studio at Bob's invitation, and
as rep for Southern Music, who at the time controlled the
European publishing for Merle Haggard, that week's guest.
It was in the star's interest to show courtesy, but, for
whatever reason, the only response Dave could muster
from either Merle or any of his band members was stares
at the floor. Thankfully, the singer's then-wife, Leona
Williams (a fine performer, in her own right) compensated,
with her winning charm. Additionally, she forever earned a
place in Dave's affections by remembering the encounter
the next time they bumped into each other – 20 years later,
in Green Bay, Wisconsin! (Perhaps lady country singers
have a soft spot for their British male counterparts, Patsy
Montana – an unqualified *London Country* success – inviting
UK tour support act, Rusty Douch, to stay with her in
California for 16 days, an experience that inspired his
album, *California Bound*).

Bob could recall only one artiste who declined to
appear on the show, although it was more a case of
indecision on the part of the star, Britain's 'king of skiffle',
Lonnie Donegan, who changed his mind so often, the host
felt he had no option but to drop him. However, there
were several names Bob later wished he had approached,

notably the heroes of his 1950s youth: Hylo Brown, Lefty Frizzell and Lee Moore. Also, songwriter Don Robertson, who, as well as composing some of Elvis Presley's most poignant country ballads – *I'm Counting On You, There's Always Me, Starting Today* and *Anything That's Part of You*, among them – initiated the 'slipped-note' piano technique later developed by Floyd Cramer to become a standard ingredient of the Nashville sound.

While some guest appearances, such as John Stewart's, proved disastrous, others were merely disappointing: Don Williams' renowned laid-back style and minimal responses ensured the host needed to work doubly hard during his 1983 appearance – and still the show finished early that week, evidenced by the extra-long closing music. At least he managed to make his laconic guest laugh heartily at one stage, when, referring to his decision to retire from the *Grand Ole Opry*, it was suggested he might miss the $60 appearance fee! Daniel O'Donnell (1986), meanwhile, just sounded shattered, prompting the sympathetic observation, "I think they're making you work – you look tired."

Daniel responded wearily, "A wee bit, it's like the middle of the night, now, I should be still in bed, but never mind." (One guest actually did nod off mid-interview, though ace steel guitarist Buddy Emmons insists he was just fooling around!)

Asked to identify the guest who caused him most anxiety, Bob had no hesitation in nominating cult singer-songwriter, Townes Van Zandt, whose reputation for drinking, drug-taking, bad language and general unpredictability preceded him, ensuring the presenter could not relax throughout his 1987 appearance – especially since the station, unlike some, did not have an eight-second delay. In fact, the most tense moment occurs early on, when Van Zandt, fixing his interviewer with a stare, declares, "You're nervous, aren't you?"

"You're damned right I'm nervous!" came the short, sharp reply. Things settled down after this, and the show is noteworthy only because a film crew shot some footage, subsequently used in a documentary on the artiste, entitled, *Be Here to Love Me*, issued by Rake Films in 2004. The two-minute segment featuring a couple of exchanges between host and guest hardly stands out, but at least provides some sort of (the only, in fact) video evidence of the show.

One astonishing fact revealed by Bob to Don Ford is that "I have never looked up any details or written any questions down before an interview. It's a little difficult to explain but it means that, although I don't prepare myself physically, I am prepared mentally." He also claims not to listen to certain tracks – and this applies particularly to contemporary country – before playing them on his show: "This is not laziness, but if I don't play a track because I don't like it, it means that everything I play, I like!" Trying to pin down his tastes, Mr. Ford ventures:-

"Would you care to put yourself in a category, then?"

BP: "No, it depends on what mood I'm in. I could go home and play the Skillet Lickers, Bob Wills, Red Foley, Hank Williams, Webb Pierce, Hank Snow – the only period I didn't like was the 'stringy' era: Eddy Arnold, Jim Reeves – full of strings – and when the Anita Kerr Singers were not background but foreground."

Away from the studio, Bob, without the responsibility of *CMP* editorship, found his thoughts returning to the days of his youth. The family had previously owned a dog, and now, as 1982 dawned, he felt the need of canine company once again. So it was that a furry bundle of fun called Casey joined the Powel household, courtesy of Foal

Farm, in Downe,[89] Kent. Being a second-hand dog, it was not quite love at first sight – however, within a month of meeting, they had become firm friends ("Both very intelligent and a bit crazy at the same time." – Marie O'Connell) to the extent that he occasionally attended *London Country* broadcasts, where his on-air growling – or more commonly yawning – drew from his master the firm reprimand, "Quiet, hound!" Officially a chow mix, Bob maintained he was more collie, a view supported by the photographic evidence (he appears in October 1983's *CMP*, seated beside "Britain's first lady of country music," Tammy Cline).

Although small, Casey had a big personality, illustrated by two particular episodes, both of which occurred at 1986's 'alternative' *Peterborough Festival* (Bob having departed the main affair to assist his friend, Goff Greenwood). The first involved a conversation between Bob, Goff and fellow *CMP* contributor, the late Al Moir, during which Moir exclaimed loudly, "There's only one thing wrong with this Festival – there's no bloody food available!" Bang on cue, who should emerge from nowhere with an enormous hamburger wedged between his jaws but the star himself! The second occurred when the faithful pet, sniffing around to pick up its master's scent (in the process, rather amusingly following his exact route), alerted a spectator, who, assuming it to be stray, secured a collar around its neck. Meanwhile, Bob, ready to depart, began whistling, the loyal pooch's signal to head home – fast. So fast, in fact, that before our helpful friend realised it, his captive had slipped the lead, leaving him holding thin air! (He seemed to like Peterborough – a titbit from October 1984's *CMP* refers to his chasing rabbits around the *Moat House Hotel* grounds in the early hours of the

---

[89] The home of English Naturalist, Charles Darwin (1809-1882). Down (spelt without the 'e') House is situated immediately adjacent to Foal Farm.

morning, aided by some unnamed "clowns.")

Photographer Marie O'Connell recalls Bob's unconventional method of dog-walking at this time. Accompanying master and pet in the car one evening, she was amazed to see the animal dropped off at the roadside while owner and car accelerated away. Then, looking behind, she could barely believe the sight of this wonder-dog whizzing along on the grass verge, managing not only to keep up, but (she swears) "grinning from ear to ear!" (Bob confirmed this story, adding that he had a top speed of 32 mph!). Marie puts down such boundless energy to the raw eggs Bob occasionally fed him.

Was he a good guard dog? Possibly not, but reliable and honest: at the first sight of an intruder, his tail would unfailingly form a question mark (unless the offenders happened to be gipsies, in which case he would probably go for them – quite why, it was never discovered). His bid for glory via Hewitt Farm's mongrel equivalent of *Crufts* – 'Scruffs' – was abruptly curtailed by Bob's holiday to Thailand, a trip that was to tragically, if indirectly, end his life, when, with his owner 6,000 miles away, he perished in a house fire. Although neighbours had charge of him at the time, Bob apportioned no blame, regarding it as an unfortunate accident.

Meanwhile, back on *London Country*, Roy Drusky's 7 February, 1982 appearance is progressing smoothly enough (rather like the guest's singing), until some typical Bob 'business' shakes things up. Having already played one incorrect record, another is about to follow…

BP: "Well, here's one you both (Roy and Vic McAlpine) were involved in – I think there's a third name here as well: a George Hamilton IV version of *Before The Day Ends*."

RD: "Yes…Marie Wilson, is her name on there?"

BP: "Quite likely, but I can't look now – keep talking for ten seconds and I will."

RD: "OK, I think it's Marie Wilson and Vic McAlpine and myself that were on the song..."

BP: "You're absolutely right. Those were my keys jingling, by the way, while I was doing that…"

RD: "And I remember this song, too."

BP: "You do? What's the first line?"

RD: *"They say that my kind of love is blind…"*

BP: (Over song's introduction) "We'll soon see…"

George Hamilton IV: (Singing) *"Take my hand for a while, explain it to me once again…"*

BP: (Fading out record, annoyed) "I don't *believe* this! (Sound of Roy laughing in background). Not *two* in twenty three minutes! (Regaining professional calm) But I'm always prepared for emergencies – and we're not going to have George Hamilton's version of it, now, we're going to have Eddy Arnold's."

RD: "You just wanted me to have the wrong first line, didn't you?"

BP: "Exactly!"

(As an anecdote to his bloopers, Bob related the story of fellow host, Pat Campbell, who claimed that, because the public enjoys these disasters so much, he occasionally threw one in. Bob's response: "Oh, I don't need to do that – they just happen!")

Among the mild mishaps were scattered absolute clangers that, for sheer originality, take some beating. Now, with his kind permission, just a few of these are revealed, perhaps for the first time:-

• Bjoro Haland, a Norwegian singer (born, coincidentally, the same year as Bob, 1943), emigrated to America in 1960, working as a builder and singing in bars and clubs, before returning to Norway six years later. In the course of his career, he made 22 albums garnering sales of 4 million, but his main claim to fame, as far as British country fans are concerned, is that his voice bears an uncanny resemblance to Jim Reeves. Whether this is the reason he was invited to appear at the *Wembley Festival* is not known, but he certainly went down well, prompting Bob to play a track from his 1980 album, *To My Friends*. Reading from the sleeve, the host proceeded to announce the singer as "Tomy (pronounced 'Tommy') Friends," even spelling it out, and failing to notice the error until a listener phoned in. (He wasn't quick – or duplicitous – enough to pretend it was a 'spot the deliberate error' competition!).

• At least Bjoro wasn't physically present to witness his embarrassment. When Irish country singer, Philomena Begley, guested and was introduced: "Good afternoon, Philomena, and welcome for the very first time to *London Country*," instead of the expected response, "Thank you, Bob, it's nice to be here," he was met with the devastating: "I was on two years ago!" (And, unfortunately, his witty riposte, "Oh, was that *you*?" took 30 years to dream up!)

• Relying solely on his record collection for the show's content ensured a disaster-in-waiting. Perhaps, therefore, it's fortunate he forgot to bring in the week's 'supply' only twice. The first time, making the mistake of confessing his 'sin' on air, he received a deluge of complaints. Learning his lesson, on the second occasion, he kept his mouth shut – no one was any the wiser and no criticism ensued. In both instances, the station's meagre library supply sufficed.[90]

---

[90] At the other extreme, Bob, uniquely among his DJ colleagues, kept a complete programme "in reserve" for emergencies. This

• Although DJs may appear to have all the time in the world, there can be moments of panic. One such incident occurred when a record finished playing, and, with nothing ready, Bob hastily flipped the disc, discovering, to his horror, it was a double 'A' side (mono/stereo versions of the same song). Trying to remain calm, he turned to the only other sound source available – an 8-track cartridge machine, and, pressing the play button 'blind', was hugely relieved to hear the silence broken by a jingle from TV soap, *East Enders* – not quite what he had in mind, but it could have been much worse!

• One blooper even made it to the illustrious 'Colemanballs' column of satirical magazine, *Private Eye*. Named after the late BBC sports presenter, David Coleman, this feature exposes wonderful gaffes made by unwitting radio presenters, Bob's entry being: "Let's stay with the colour green, because the next track is called, *New Shade of Blue*." (Bob claimed this was an intentional joke, all part of his whimsical sense of humour!).

When called upon to recount odd or memorable *London Country* incidents, Bob, as well as celebrated bloopers, tended to recall dramatic news items of the day – like the occasion he was caught off-guard – and on-air – listening to the 1978 university boat race in which the Cambridge boat sank. On a more tragic note, the Tupolev Tu-144 ('Concordski') plane crash in which 14 people lost their lives, brought back sad memories, the incident being reported during the 3 June 1973 show. And he could never

---

was dedicated exclusively to deceased performers, ensuring that, whenever broadcast, it would remain valid. Additionally, if for any reason, this became unviable, there was a cabinet stocked with assorted 45s – usually minor label issues – which arrived at the station periodically. Not that Bob worried unduly about such things, but his show being 'live', nothing could be left to chance.

forget the 9 April 1988 broadcast, which coincided with Rhyme 'n' Reason's Aintree *Grand National* victory. Not that he backed the winner – just that, apart from the musical coincidence of 'rhyme', the horse was ridden by namesake, B(rendan) Powell.

Through the technical chaos and general confusion, the host's basic knowledge of the genre shone like a beacon. Fans Alan and Jean Earle, who attended *London Country*'s studios at his invitation several times and who are on friendly terms with many country music stars, quote what has been repeated to them often: "Bob Powel knows what he is talking about, does not ask a load of silly questions and consequently gets the best out of us." The secret to his interviewing technique? A simple six-letter word, delivered at a critical moment with just the right degree of curiosity. The word: "Really…?" Seldom used in common parlance, but one that ought to be top of the list of required vocabulary for all dedicated listeners. Of course, having a genuine love of and interest in all things – and people – country helps. While on the subject of Alan and Jean, as well as being huge Faron Young devotees (they ran his fan club at one stage), Jean is a talented artiste, having, over the years, sketched many country stars (see illustrations). *London Country*'s host occasionally obtained autographed copies of her sketches from the show's guests before returning them to her.

Presenters – of radio or TV – need to negotiate a skilful path through difficult terrain: technical challenges of every kind, stars with wildly varying temperaments – and egos – and the ever-present demands, rules and regulations inherent in the medium. Although Bob was not blessed with great technical ability, he managed to get by, while country music has traditionally been less prone to the 'diva-type' behaviour associated with other musical genres (a trend that has possibly changed[91]). As for operating within the broadcasting medium as a whole, he was fortunate to enjoy an excellent working relationship with producer Maggie Tschirren (later Gamwell).

A BBC staff producer of the first order, Maggie, of Swiss descent, and her less-experienced front man bonded instantly, part of their rapport involving a gentle running gag, which consisted of a double catchphrase: one observing, "It does happen," the other responding, "You do get this."

Another ongoing joke originated in a remark Bob overheard a performer make to his boss[92] at a different studio, following some disagreement: "You're only the producer, I can get rid of you just like that!" This lodged itself in his brain, subsequently becoming a stock warning, delivered at opportune moments. Unfortunately for him,

---

[91] An example might be Lucille Starr. Born Lucille Savoie, this Franco-Manitoban-British Columbian singer, songwriter and yodeller is best known for her 1964 hit single, *Quand le Soleil Dit Bonjour aux Montagnes*, a.k.a *The French Song*. Working out of Nashville from 1967, she enjoyed a long and prosperous career, while never matching the success of her initial hit, which sold over a million copies, making her the first Canadian artiste to achieve this. Always – and still – a big fan of her music, Bob, upon finally interviewing her (not for *London Country*), was somewhat disappointed by her 'starry' pretensions (a case of name reflecting nature, perhaps). According to him, "it was a bit of a shock, because we didn't have divas in my day!"

[92] This particular producer, like many at the BBC, was known to be gay. Bob, secure in his own inclinations in this regard, remained non-judgmental. Nevertheless, he enjoyed tremendously the sign another producer had attached to his office door which read: "WE'RE NOT ALL LIKE THAT, YOU KNOW!" (It was also once – jokingly – pointed out to him that if all the 'gays' and Jews were barred from holding positions of responsibility within the Corporation, he would be Director General!)

the person who made the original remark was shortly thereafter sacked, meaning the boot was now on the other foot – and his producer was not slow to remind him, "Hey, you're only the *presenter*, I can get rid of you just like that!" After Maggie transferred to another show in the mid-1980s, Bob found the (several) replacements wholly inadequate, persuading him to carry on without anyone at the helm for the remainder of the show's term. As for his "ideal" producer, she died tragically at a premature age.

Throughout the show's existence, Bob remained wary of certain dangers. There was the occasion, during his second spell as editor of *CMP* that he agreed to publicise a certain event on *London Country* and the recipient promised to take out an ad in the magazine, implying that it was a return gesture. Bob responded, in no uncertain terms: "Let's make it clear: I've decided to proceed with your feature on *London Country*, but whether you take out an ad or not has nothing to do with it." (He may have been thinking of Pat Campbell, who had earlier been dismissed by the BBC owing to publishing connections with the song, *It's Not the Miles You Travelled*, 'B' side of Faron Young's *Four In The Morning*, which he had promoted heavily on his show, *Country Style*). Likewise, Bob refuted Tony Byworth's claim that he (Tony), during a period when *London Country* was followed by an Indian language programme, announced on-air: "Well, you've heard the cowboys, now the Indians are coming."

"A remark like that is unprofessional and could put me off the air," he said, "so I think I would remember it."

Tony responds: "Remember, this was around 35 years ago – in the age of Alf Garnett, 'curry & chips' and *Love Thy Neighbour* – when political correctness didn't rule our lives. It was meant as a humorous remark by a guest on the show – and hardly reflected Bob's professionalism, especially as he didn't know the remark was coming up."

While naturally anxious to keep his employer happy,

the vigilant host remained equally keen not to upset the sensibilities of his audience by playing – or saying – anything inappropriate or which contained bad language. Consequently, criticism of this nature was rare, the only example recalled being a complaint following his mention of the movie, *The Best Little Whorehouse in Texas*, starring Burt Reynolds and Dolly Parton. The listener in question claimed to be offended not so much for himself as for his children, who happened to be beside him.

Such concerns were unnecessary on 28 March, 1982, when Billy Armstrong guested. The award-winning fiddler proves refreshingly open and willing to laugh at himself, but also makes some astute observations regarding the American country club scene. Bob has just devoted a full six minutes to the 'What's On' feature, in the process naming an impressive fourteen local clubs:-

BA: "Sounds like there's a lot of country music around the London area…"

BP: "It's amazing how many clubs there are…this is just in the south. Although a couple have closed with the recession, I'm happy to say that the majority seem to be hanging on, and let's pay credit to the club organisers because they do it for love…"

BA: "That's right, there's not that much profit in it at all…but we have had the same problem in the States recently with our recession…some of our clubs have folded and I think, in a way, it's beneficial because, with the *Urban Cowboy* (movie) and everything, clubs sprouted up all over and consequently, you got a poorer grade of country music – there were a lot of out-of-work rock musicians trying to play country music and I don't believe you can play country music unless you understand the music and I think we had a lot of bad country music for a while…"

Very few country records make it to the top of the UK pop charts, especially ones featuring a narration. However, J. J. Barrie managed to achieve the feat in 1976, courtesy of Harlan Howard's *No Charge*. Appearing on *London Country* eight years later, on 29 April, 1984, the Canadian-born singer reveals how he came to record the song and his subsequent rewards – or lack of:-

BP: "How many copies did it sell?"

JJ: "In the UK, almost half a million – and worldwide, several hundred thousand more."

BP: "Right."

JJ: "Never did get a penny for it, by the way…"

BP: "You're kidding!"

JJ: "'Not Quite No Charge' is the title it should have been…the company folded and all the receipts got tied up in litigation."

BP: "Oh, no..."

JJ: "Great title for it, wasn't it?"

BP: "How did you hear of it, because it was a hit for Melba Montgomery…?"

JJ: "Well, to be really truthful, I heard someone singing it over here in £-s-d and I wrote it down fast because (although) it sounded a little bit gimmicky, I liked the idea. And we were travelling to Toronto at that time to record the album, and we were in the studio Christmas Eve, putting some tracks down…I had the idea of actually talking the song and having girls sing behind me – we had Madeleine Bell, Kay Garner and Joe Brown's wife, Vicki. And Vicki was so sensational with that soul-country sound that we just pulled her voice out, and I think that was a strong reason why it was such a success – because it reached every mother in the world."

After playing record:-

BP: "A song like that is almost impossible to follow up with another hit, isn't it? Because you can't do a similar one."

JJ: "That's right. You know, I was offered *Teddy Bear*! Red Sovine's demo of *Teddy Bear* was offered to me to follow up *No Charge* and I said, 'No way, I couldn't do that,' because I daren't get into a bag. I mean, that was accidental, and it's wonderful that it happened, but it's been hard enough to get out of the bag, even up to now. If I'd done two like that – wow…"

BP: "What was the follow-up, actually?"

JJ: "It was a song called *Boys Will Be Boys* – a nice, sentimental song, but a bit too slow…"

London Country guests were not confined to musicians, singers, songwriters – or even lecturers! On 16 November, 1986, Chris Martin of 'Martin Guitars', in England to promote the famous brand, appeared on the show, at one point explaining Willie Nelson's attitude to his much-cherished Martin model:-

CM: "He (Nelson) plays a nylon-string Martin guitar, which doesn't have a scratch-plate. He plays it with a pick and he's scratched right through the top."

BP: "Hasn't he asked you to repair it?"

CM: "He has had the internal struts re-done to make sure that structurally it's sound, but he's so in love with his guitar (that he calls 'Trigger') that he wouldn't have it changed for love nor money."

BP: "He's got autographs of everybody on it and all sorts of things, hasn't he?"

CM: "Right. To him, it's a part of his life."

BP: "And you've actually had it back at the factory, then, have you?"

CM: "It's been rebuilt to the point where it won't collapse."

BP: "Yet."

CM: "Yet."

BP: "It used to belong to Roger Miller, I believe – my joke was, he kept half of it…"

CM: (Laughing) "He's seen other Martin guitars and he just said, 'The one I have is the one I like.' And Bob, that's true of so many customers – they all swear that the Martin guitar they own is the best one ever made!"

Pursuing his interest in song-writing, Bob enquires of Felice and Boudleaux Bryant, during their 1981 appearance:-

BP: "Do you sometimes add a couple of things on Boudleaux's name, for tax reasons, or whatever?"

Felice & Boudleaux (in unison): "Oh, no, no!"

Felice: "We're too vain."

BB: "We never do that. If you see Felice's name on it, you know that she contributed a lot to it, maybe wrote most of it. If my name's on it, I wrote some of it, or maybe most of it, or certainly contributed. No, we write separately and together, and if Felice writes a song by herself, such as *We Could* and various others, her name is the only one on."

Later, after playing that very song:-

BP: "That's the only song I've got that you've written by yourself. Have you written many more?"

Felice: "I have a thing about…I don't like to finish material without Boudleaux, I feel he has a lucky touch and I don't like to send a song out without it, but a couple did escape – one is *We Could* and the other one is *I'm Not Afraid* by Ricky Nelson."

BP: "Oh yes, right. Well, I'm surprised you say that – *We Could* is one of the most beautiful of all songs, in my opinion…"

Felice: "It was an act of love."

BP: "The one question that I ask every song-writer…talking to many, I find that some are 'title-writers', some aren't. In other words, do you think of the title first, then write the song around it?"

Boudleaux: "We seem to write all kinds of ways. Maybe some little snatch of melody will activate some process in the mind, maybe a title, or maybe just a line that you build to, you know…"

BP: "Harlan Howard told me that he always wrote six songs or so at one time – do you do that? He always has them in an unfinished state and will go back to them…"

Felice: "We have unfinished songs that we go back to, but we don't have a formula."

Boudleaux: "We write in large ledgers. A long time ago we used to lose a lot of songs because we wrote on napkins, anything that was handy. One evening, we went out to Fred Rose's house, I had on a raincoat with nine new songs in it. I forgot the raincoat. Eventually, Fred began to wonder whose coat it was and his wife said, 'I don't know whose it is.' Finally, they gave it to the gardener, didn't check the pockets, and so I don't know what those nine songs were, but I hope they were hits for somebody."

BP: "There might be a rich gardener around somewhere!"

Having surprised the duo with several recordings of their compositions they are unaware of, the host gets around to asking "the impossible question":-

BP: "How many songs have you actually had recorded?"

Felice: "Well, it's harder now than it was before because you've come up with some we didn't even know about!"

Boudleaux: "I think we've had, all in all, a thousand…we've written probably around five or six thousand, but a lot of them we don't show because, well-"

Felice: (Interrupting) "They're not any good."

Boudleaux: "Cos' we don't like them…"

BP: "Well, now be fair – name one of those songs that you didn't particularly like – I bet you, you won't!"

Felice: "I can't think of one, because after it hit, we loved it!"

Boudleaux: (Laughing) "Yeh, after somebody said, 'I like it and I'll do it,' we loved it!"

Later, the host observes:-

BP: "I notice now you write more together than you

used to – you used to write a lot by yourself in the old days, didn't you, Boudleaux?"

Boudleaux: "I used to get up earlier than she did!"

BP: (Laughing) "Really?"

Felice: "The orders came too fast and Boudleaux had to sit down and deliberately go at it and he'd write on the way home and on the way to the studio…"

BP: "While you were doing the housework and things…"

Felice: "While I was taking care of babies and doing housework and so on and so forth…"

Bobby Bare, during his 12 September 1981 appearance, explains the reason for his lack of recent compositions:-

Bobby: "I was writing a lot during that period (early 60s), but then, when I started having a lot of hit records, I didn't have the time to write, and I had a lot of excuses not to write – and I'm basically lazy, so I didn't write nearly as much as I should have, from that point on."

BP: "Are you back into it again – you're not, really, are you…?"

Bobby: "When you have friends like Tom T. Hall, Bob McDill, Shel Silverstein, Kris Kristofferson, Willie…actually, it humiliates me. Seriously, I used to come to Nashville loaded with songs and we'd all sit around at the hotel – the Andrew Jackson Hotel before they tore it down – me, Willie, Roger Miller…a bunch of us. And we'd sit around, and I'd listen to all of their songs – Willie singing *Funny How Time Slips Away, Hello, Walls*, and then Roger Miller singing *Dang Me*, and all those Roger Miller-type songs, I'd come down with 25 songs and I might wind up singing one or two!"

Roy Drusky (7 February, 1982) confesses to being a 'title'-writer:-

BP: "You were really a commercial songwriter for a while, weren't you?"

RD: "Well, that's what moved me to Nashville, and yes, I was. I think we had over one hundred songs recorded."

BP: "Were you a 'title' man – did you take a title and expand upon it?"

RD: "Yeh, that's the way I did it – melody and words at the same time, they just kinda come together, you know."

BP: "When you worked, say, with Vic (McAlpine) and with other people, did you contribute ideas together or did you start a song and Vic end it, or vice-versa?"

RD: "One of us would have the idea and then…"

BP: "You didn't sit in a room together…?"

RD: "Yes, we did – one of us would come in and say, 'I heard a line' or 'I heard something that I really like – let's see if we can write this.' And we'd just sit down with the guitar and start writing it, you know."

Hoyt Axton, on 14 November, 1982, reveals his simple, straightforward song-writing technique:-

HA: "I just write little folk songs…I write when the muse comes down out of Heaven and hits me upside the tempo with a little tuning-fork and says, 'Write a song, Hoyt…'"

Don Williams, appearing on 8 May, 1983, discusses the

origins of his biggest selling UK hit, *You're My Best Friend*:-

DW: "Wayland (Holyfield) and I worked a lot together on that song…Wayland brought the original idea to me and we talked about it and he went off and worked on it and came back and we did that back and forth for about a year until the last time he brought it, I said, 'You nailed it, that's it.'"

Although uncredited on that particular song, Williams is less sure with another of his recordings:-

BP: "Let's go…to your compositions again…one of your numbers, *Too Late to Turn Back Now*, that you did write, didn't you?"

DW: "Er…no…no, that's Allen Reynolds."

BP: "It's got your name on it."

DW: "On *where?*"

BP: "On the record, I've got it right here…"

DW: "Let me see it."

BP: "All right."

DW: (Muttering) "Some of these co-written songs, I can't remember…"

BP: "You remember the song, though, don't you?"

DW: "Oh yeh, I remember the song very well…(after reading credits)…you may be right… (sound of Bob's laughter). One of the problems that I do have, really, is, er…there's very few songs that I don't do work on before I record it and I don't…you know, it's strictly to make it fit the way I feel and exactly what I want to say, and when it goes back to (Bob) McDill and (Allen) Reynolds, especially those two, and Wayland Holyfield, there are songs that I worked on with them that I just can't remember for sure, you know. It's not that I don't remember the song, it's just I don't remember what my involvement was."

BP: "As a matter of fact, many songwriters forget they've written songs that I've had on this show, so it's no problem."

The host's forthright attitude ensured he did not hold back when questioning the originality – or otherwise – of guests' material. He has just played *The Man Who Turned My Mama On*, sung by Tanya Tucker and written by guest Ed Bruce (13 November, 1983):-

BP: "I could feel traces of *Delta Dawn* in that…do you accept it?"

EB: "I was trying to capture that gospel feel that was on *Delta Dawn*…"

On this occasion, he does not follow up his observation, but on a later show (4 April, 1984), after playing *Buford Pusser's Walking Tall* by guest Eddie Bond, he notes melodic similarities to the Tom T. Hall-composed *Harper Valley PTA*:-

BP: "Thank you, Tom T. Hall, for the tune! A little similar to *Harper Valley PTA*, but that's called, *Buford Pusser's Walking Tall*…"

EB: "Well, I wrote the words to the song and had it out, and I'm going to blame Jerry Chestnut for putting the Tom T. Hall thing in! When I got to Nashville to record it, he'd already cut the tracks for me, and there it was!"

When challenged by David Redshaw (*CMP*, May, 1975) to name "the interview that sticks out most in your mind," Bob makes a popular choice: Red Hayes' 1973 appearance, for obvious, if possibly tragic, reasons. He also mentions Tex Ritter, Tompall Glaser and old sparring partner Bill Anderson. Asked more recently to recall his most enjoyable show, the answer is different:-

BP: "Well, I'd need to listen back to the show, if I could get hold of it [it is not among those available], but Boxcar Willie and Johnny Russell were on tour here in Britain [1987] and I was on the bus for a couple of gigs. Now, the following day, both were due to appear on *London Country*, having been guests several times previously. While on the bus, we were just talking about country music and things like that. So, when it came to the next day, I said 'on-air' (without advance warning), 'I spent a really enjoyable two or three hours yesterday just talking about country music with Boxcar Willie and Johnny Russell and because they've been on the show a lot...that's exactly what we're going to do, now – but with music. So, that's what we did. It had the same atmosphere, too, and was really nice. Of course, I haven't heard it back for many, many years – if I ever did – but, to me, it seemed like a good idea."

London Country's host is renowned for his formidable knowledge of country music, rarely getting his facts wrong. Occasionally, however, he is caught out, as the following exchange with Ed Bruce, dating from 13 November 1983, illustrates. They are discussing Ed's daughter, Ginny:-

BP: "How old is Ginny?"
EB: "Almost 18, now."

BP: "Because I know you had her while you were on RCA."

EB: "Right. (Reconsidering) No, it was on Monument. I gotcha, Bob!"

BP: "Oh yes, Monument."

EB: "At the time, she was about two years old…"

BP: (Laughing) "I'll edit that bit out, by the way."

EB: "Oh no, you won't!" (He – obviously – didn't).

London Country had been airing happily with BP at the helm for over seventeen years when the sad news arrived that, in a decision taken by the 'powers-that-be', Radio London would disappear from the airwaves to be replaced with, or – in broadcasting speak – 're-launched as' the 'radically different', 'irreverent' GLR (Greater London Radio), the final broadcast being scheduled for 7 October, 1988 (GLR commencing 18 days later on 25 October). Saddest of all, although some of the presenters were being kept on, 'Uncle' Bob, as a freelancer, was not among them, nor his comrade-in-arms, Stuart Colman, whose show, *Echoes*, preceded his, covering similar ground, though focussing more on the rockabilly side of things. Why the axe? As ratings were stable, one can only conclude that neither presenter was 'irreverent' enough. *CMP* editor-at-the-time Craig Baguley summed up the feelings of many with a paragraph in November's issue of the magazine:-

"Radio London has been taken off the air to be replaced by the new look GLR (Greater London Radio). Fair enough. Change the name and reorganise things a bit. But what is hatchet man Trevor Dann doing taking two well-established and successful programmes off the air completely? I refer to Bob Powel's *London Country* and Stuart Coleman's *Echoes*, programmes which have given enormous pleasure to Londoners for years. *London Country* has been essential listening for both traditional and modern country music fans inasmuch as Bob's vast personal collection meant that we got to hear many rare as well as well-known records, and he was a popular figure with visiting US stars, major and minor, who were only too willing to appear on his show." He concludes, "Bob's loss is our loss."

The final *London Country* show, which also happened to be the station's last 'live' programme, broadcast on Saturday, 1 October, 1988, and is, fortunately, among those that survive on tape. This is how it is introduced:-

"My name's Bob Powel and I'd like to welcome you to – sob, sob – the very, very last *London Country* and we're going to take the opportunity to look back over the years…"

He then proceeds to choose a track by one artiste who appeared on the show for each year of its existence, working through from Tex Ritter (1971) to Randy Travis (1988), on the way, choosing titles, some of which perhaps betray his feelings:-

Guess Things Happen That Way – Charley Pride (1972)

Whatever Happened to Randolph Scott (Has Happened to the Industry) – Statler Bros. (1973)

Take Me Home – Boxcar Willie (1985)

Making Plans – Johnny Russell (1986)

It's Out of My Hands – Randy Travis (1988)

With his radio career stuttering and the CMP Shop in financial difficulty, Bob appeared to be drifting. So, how about his third 'baby' – *Country Music People* magazine?

Chapter 8

Country Music People, 2nd Term: 1983-1988

Under Your Spell Again ("I've gotta take you back just one more time...")[93]

Since taking over editorship of *Country Music People* in January, 1977, Tony Byworth had seen the magazine's fortunes, along with those of country music generally, soar. In an article for the 200th edition (September 1986), he outlines his editorial approach:-

"(My basic objectives are) backed up by my wholehearted conviction of the commerciality of country music – a conviction that still remains the prime motivation in my activities within the music industry today."

Later, in the 500th issue (October, 2011), he

---

[93] *Under Your Spell Again*. Co-written and originally recorded by Buck Owens, for whom it provided his first major country hit (No.4 in 1959), this proved almost equally successful for Ray Price, whose version reached No.5 the same year. The song subsequently charted for Waylon Jennings and Jessi Colter (No.39, 1971) and Barbara Fairchild (No.65, 1976).

acknowledges the factors in his favour: "These were boom years for *CMP*. The industry looked on country music with interest…and most record labels had someone taking responsibility for this music. It was also the period that saw magazine sales expanding and *CMP* was no exception, with its sales reaching new heights around the turn of the decade."

The following is a brief summary of Tony's tenure:-

APRIL, 1977 – Biggest ever issue, running to 76 pages (many March and April editions of this era were extra-large, owing to *Wembley Festival* write-ups). Also contains feature on the Cotton Mill Boys, *Opportunity Knocks* winners last November.

AUGUST, 1977 – "All-Time Favourite Country Record" readers' poll launched in conjunction with BBC Radio 2's *Country Club* (Don Williams' *You're My Best Friend* triumphing). Meanwhile, an article by Gerry Wood reprinted from *Billboard* reveals that 12% of titles appearing in the magazine's Top 100 Pop Singles chart classify as country, compared with 2% the previous year.

JANUARY, 1978 – Launch of *Critics' Choice* column, whereby *CMP* writers list various likes and dislikes of previous 12 months.

MAY, 1978 – 100th edition. Front cover features conceptual design: a stack of past editions of *CMP* laid out amidst a selection of musical instruments. To coincide with the centenary, Tony, via Sonet Records, markets an album entitled *Country Music People*, comprising tracks by artistes from the Rounder and Flying Fish labels, which proves so popular a second volume emerges 18 months later.

SEPTEMBER, 1979 – Includes (generally favourable)

report by editor on "the first concentrated attempt to package contemporary country music" before European audiences, Roy Clark, Barbara Mandrell and the Oak Ridge Boys being the featured artistes.

OCTOBER, 1979 – Editorial points to the increasing role of cinema in the promotion of country music, citing *Every Which Way But Loose, Coal Miner's Daughter* and *Urban Cowboy* as three prime examples of the trend.

JANUARY, 1980 – Editorial's reflection on 1979: "The record industry has been beset by one pitfall after another. Record sales are down; record companies and retail outlets are folding; promotional budgets are being cut; redundancies occur weekly; and major companies appear the objective of continual takeover bids. Simply...the music industry is in a state of recession." (Country music obviously bucking the general trend).

FEBRUARY, 1980 – 10th anniversary edition. Second readers' poll, for "Artiste of the Decade," sees Don Williams again taking the honours. Issue includes centre-page spread featuring specially commissioned painting, *Country Landscape*, by renowned artist, David Oxtoby (available on poster), comprising "most important artistes of 1970's in the opinion of this editor based upon significant career and popularity strides in either British or US markets." Tony's choices in alphabetical order:-

1. Boxcar Willie
2. Johnny Cash
3. Crystal Gayle
4. Merle Haggard
5. George Hamilton IV
6. Emmylou Harris
7. Waylon Jennings
8. Loretta Lynn
9. Willie Nelson

10. Olivia Newton-John
11. Dolly Parton
12. Charley Pride
13. Kenny Rogers
14. Billie Jo Spears
15. Slim Whitman
16. Don Williams
17. Tammy Wynette

Issue also includes an assessment of "the music's most significant developments...over the past decade...together with significant artistes" by Tony and six other regular *CMP* writers, details of which are briefly summarised below:-

▪ TONY BYWORTH: "Emmylou Harris, I'd rate, as the real saviour of the 70's, while Don Williams proved...it was still possible to sell records in spectacular quantities."

▪ DAVID ALLAN: "My greatest impression is of the way country music has gradually become 'respectable.'"

▪ JOHN ATKINS: "The Gram Parsons, Emmylou Harris wave of country music...has added a dimension...that has been missing for many years."

▪ ALAN CACKETT: "I guess it was Waylon, Willie and the rest of the so-called 'Outlaw Movement' that made the biggest impression."

▪ MARTIN HAWKINS: "My overwhelming impression...is one of expansion – in specialist shops...and in country music's increasing share of the market."

▪ JOHN STAFFORD: "The ten year period in question...has been the most impressionable in history (particularly in terms of 'image')."

▪ RICHARD WOOTTON: "(The decade) , via artistes such as Rodney Crowell, Waylon Jennings and Joe Ely –

inspired by Kris Kristofferson – provided an alternative to the increasingly bland, heavily orchestrated 'Nashville Sound.'"

APRIL, 1980 – Mervyn Conn article commends *Wembley Festival* off-shoots in European countries Germany, Switzerland, Sweden, Holland and France, estimating that the ten-day round of activities will attract between 120,000 and 140,000 customers and a TV audience of up to 90 million.

JULY, 1980 – Editorial focusses on "the most predictable activity on the local scene – Festivals," concluding, "wouldn't it be better if some of the energies and monies backing the festival operations be re-routed in other directions and help create something fresh on the British scene."

AUGUST, 1980 – Report on *CMA*'s annual 'Country Radio' survey, revealing an 8% rise in full-time country stations.

MAY, 1981 – *CMA*'s 1981 'Country Radio' survey shows another big swing to country music, with 21% more stations now broadcasting country than in 1980. The report follows hot on the heels of country music's increase in record sales – up to $438 million from $427 million at a time when total industry sales suffered a fall to $3.7 billion from $4.2 billion in 1978.

OCTOBER, 1981 – Editorial reports on yet another survey by the 'National Association of Recording Merchandisers' (NARM) showing that country music in the USA represents "14.3% of all records sold – up from 11.9% in 1979 and second only to rock music."

JUNE, 1982 – *Faces 'n' Places* reports that Bob Powel "is now a lawman, having been appointed a Chief Inspector with the Police Dept. of Finger, Tennessee – the appointment being made by the Chief of Police, McNairy County, Tennessee. The Chief there is no one less than Eddie Bond. 'Now,' says Powel, 'I can point the finger of suspicion.' (That's one of his awful Radio London funnies!)" Issue also reports that North London's *Grosvenor Rooms* is "packin' 'em in constantly on Friday nights…compered by Radio London's Bob Powel."

JULY, 1982 – *CMA* survey reveals that 44.5% of US/Canadian radio stations currently programme country music – nearly double the number of three years previously.

Tony, whose last issue as editor was August, 1983, concludes his *CMP* 200th (September, 1986) article:-

"The face of country music…was changing during my years as this magazine's editor, the decade of the controversial 'crossover' movement led into the short-lived but highly successful *Urban Cowboy* trend of the early 80's highlighted by movie box office smashes such as the aforementioned Travolta vehicle and the Loretta Lynn biopic, *Coal Miner's Daughter* and today Nashville mourns falling record sales with the music slipping away from the glorious mass attention that it enjoyed just a few short years ago."

As for the 'BP Interview', a mainstay during his predecessor's six-year term (featuring on 76 occasions in 83 issues), this did not appear once during Tony's near seven-year reign, though the occasional *Powel's Page* compensated. However, Bob had other journalistic assignments to keep him busy: apart from album compilations, there was a 'Country Music Extra' supplement for *Weekend* magazine, part of the *Daily Mail* group of newspapers, an opportunity that came about through his friendship with the *Weekend* editor. He said of this venture: "Sales were healthy, but, owing to poor advertising revenue, the supplement lasted just two issues."

So, how did Bob come to regain editorship of *CMP*? The following is Tony Byworth's account – in his own words – of events leading up to the September, 1983 'coup' as he describes his departure in that 500th issue:-

"By this time (1983), I was developing a PR business with Richard Wootton because, basically, I'd been going to the States a lot, covering events for magazines and I'd got to know a lot of management and artistes (who) would say to me, 'How do you get something going in Britain?' And it crossed my mind to set up a publicity company representing artistes in Britain, rather than dealing with record companies here who didn't really want to know half the time about country music. If I was working directly with the artistes in Nashville then the record companies would have to listen to me a bit because I was representing the artistes' interests. So, anyway, I was planning to quit the magazine. Also, part of my personality means I get bored doing the same thing after a period of time – my music business has covered different areas: I've music-published, worked in a record company, I've done all sorts of things – so, I was getting tired of editing the magazine.

"Well, I was away in Florida and I had a call from Wally Whyton, who said, 'Do you know Bob Powel's editing the magazine?' I said, 'What!' Apparently, he'd done a deal with Reg to buy the magazine, so obviously, I got the shove. If you ask Bob, he'll say, 'We were thinking you'd start selling the front cover to your artiste friends,' (an idea) never in my mind. As I said, I was about to quit anyway, as I intended building a national operation. I was actually out of work for a few months and I wrote a book, *Giants of Country Music* (Littlehampton Book Services Ltd.,

1984), during that period to get some funds together, then moved on to set up the PR business, which became very successful, I hasten to add – obviously, as other people then set up their own operations in competition with us."

Unsurprisingly, his replacement offered an alternative view. Firstly, in *CMP*'s 200th edition (September 1986), he writes:-

"By 1983...sales...had dipped alarmingly...so that *CMP* was facing a loss again.[94] Tony by this time had formed the PR firm 'Byworth-Wootton International' and in the summer of 1983, he left *CMP* to concentrate on 'B-WI' which had gone from strength to strength."

To me, he elaborated further:-

"By mid-1983, Reg Field, in poor health throughout his time at *CMP*, was contemplating retirement. Aware of Tony's business plans – which I believe were already operational at this stage – and anxious there should be stability following his own departure, he (Reg) contacted me with a view to sharing ownership until such time as he made the final break, which happened to be exactly a year later. Regarding the 'Byworth-Wootton International'

---

[94] This seems odd, given that as recently as September 1980, Tony Byworth, in his editorial, was claiming an increased circulation figure of 20,000 (equating to 80,000 readership). However, in an earlier quotation of this chapter, taken from *CMP*'s 200th issue of September, 1986, the same writer laments "falling record sales with the music slipping away from the glorious mass attention that it enjoyed just a few short years ago," indicating that, while the 80s may have started impressively, there was a fairly rapid decline.

enterprise, although not doubting for one minute Tony's integrity, I honestly felt (as Reg did) that such dual interest would inevitably lead to suggestions of preferential treatment to 'B-WI' acts (regardless of whether or not true) and thus compromise his – and *CMP*'s – position."

In response to which, Tony immediately points out the new editor's own "vested interests – *London Country* and the CMP Shop!!" Whatever the rights and wrongs of the matter, from September, with Bob once more in charge, it was business as usual at Cray Press, although there were some differences, one of which involved the editorial comment itself, referred to in his first issue:-

SEPTEMBER, 1983 – "(The editorial) will be printed when I believe a point should be made. Otherwise, the space will be available for other *CMP* and even guest writers." He goes on to lament that the country music "boom period has long since passed." However, the magazine is as good as ever, with a feature on Merle Haggard, a Q & A page from Spencer Leigh, a father-son and mother-daughter singing connections article (John Stafford) and part one of a three part feature on country fiddlers by the editor.

OCTOBER, 1983 – Contains four-page country radio supplement, detailing stations/wavebands/d-js for 56 different cities/areas of UK and Eire, plus, a four-page review of 4th *Peterborough Festival of Country Music*.

NOVEMBER, 1983 – Bob's interview reappears, with Boxcar Willie featured.

JANUARY, 1984 – After an unbroken ten-year run in the magazine, the *David Allan Page* is set to be dropped for the second time (the first being early in Bob's initial editorial term, though he did also reinstate him). Here, in his last entry for a long while (over ten years, in fact), he looks back fondly to his two-year spell aboard pirate Radio 390 in the mid-sixties. Plus, Bob-written four-page country comedy feature.

MARCH, 1984 – Editorial refers to *CMA*-commissioned survey into British attitudes towards country music, results to be presented to April board meeting in Houston, Texas, and then made available to record companies worldwide. Also contained is an eight-page *Directory of Fan Clubs & Mailing Addresses*.

APRIL, 1984 – Strongly worded letter from Mr. Tommy Sexton of Clwyd sums up feelings of many re. *Wembley* (now *Silk Cut*, sponsors since 1981) *Festival*, suggesting that, by inclusion of acts such as the Osmonds and Ray Stevens and exclusion of Ricky Skaggs, Whites and Hank Williams, Jr., country influence is diminishing – he goes on to predict ticket sales will slump by 50%. (In total contrast, Mick Green of Bexleyheath, in an earlier letter to *CMP* – September, 1979 – maintained it was "absolutely vital that country goes pop," pop being definitive for popular, and, in hindsight, this is what happened, to a large degree).

JUNE, 1984 – Review of *Silk Cut Festival* is shared among four different writers and spread over eight pages, with plenty of photos. Despite concerns expressed in above letter, event appears to have been as successful as ever, Ray Stevens and headliner Glen Campbell being among the most popular (though no mention is made of attendance figures).

JULY, 1984 – Don Ford article (referring to *CMA*-commissioned survey – see MARCH entry) reads: "Those in the UK country music industry who have long held the view that a vast untapped market for the music exists here in Britain were thoroughly vindicated by the findings of the recently completed extensive three-part survey conducted for *CMA* by MORI, (which) revealed that 49%

of the British public enjoy country music compared to 51% who listen to pop music, country music being more widely enjoyed than classical, light orchestral, disco, soul, jazz or reggae. (Additionally), a number of country artistes, notably Johnny Cash, Dolly Parton, Crystal Gayle and Kenny Rogers are as well-known in Britain as many established British pop and rock acts, including David Bowie, Culture Club and the Eurythmics." Article concludes, "Increased radio airplay and television exposure are seen as critical to the development and promotion of country music in Britain. Increased marketing co-ordination and financial backing by the record companies, along with more co-operation between dealers and record companies also appeared as essential elements." Elsewhere, advertisements for August's *Peterborough Festival* (the 5th) reveal it is starting to attract top names – Porter Wagoner, Hank Locklin, Barbara Fairchild, Tommy Cash, Ronnie Prophet and Hank Williams' Drifting Cowboys Band among them.

SEPTEMBER, 1984 – Retirement of Reg Field announced in editorial, Bob, "new publisher of *CMP*," adding that this will be the last issue printed by Cray Press and the new headquarters will double as a shop, the grand opening of which (on 15 September) is announced in a full-page advertisement.

NOVEMBER, 1984 – Two-page article on 'Grand Opening' commences, "At time of writing, the *CMP* shop has been open three weeks, and they said it would never last!" In fact, the day was a great success, 200 fans turning out "to welcome *CMP*'s latest venture into the world." Celebrities lending support included George Hamilton IV and surprise last-minute guest, Patsy Montana, as well as Cynthia Leu (*CMA*'s European representative) and *CMP* stalwarts, Tony Byworth and the late Paul Davis.

MAY, 1985 – Under heading, "COUNTRY SALES PLUNGE", news item refers to declining sales of country records in America, as highlighted by *Billboard* magazine's *Nashville Bureau*, citing a 50% drop in sales figures for some leading artistes and quoting 1979-83 as the industry's boom years.

JUNE, 1985 – First of a new item, *Powel's Page*, sees the editor reflecting on *London Country*'s 14th anniversary, listing some of the artistes that have appeared during that time and gone on to greater success (or anonymity), relating the true story behind *Ruby, Don't Take Your Love to Town*, as explained by its writer, Mel Tillis, in his autobiography, *Stuttering Mel*, plus, a blunt assessment of Jed Ford's forthcoming *Peterborough Festival*: "Every single act...appeared first at that other festival in West London...the show will be good but we know what to expect." (This criticism was nullified in next month's issue, following Slim Whitman's withdrawal and the addition of four new acts).

JULY, 1985 – Report on decision to print UK album charts in *Billboard* and *Music Week*, which, according to *CMA* Manager of European Operations, Cynthia Leu, "should augur well for the future development of country music in the UK."

AUGUST, 1985 – Continuing on from May's "sales plunge" item, this issue quotes US nightclub operator, Jerry Garrens, who blames over-exposure of country acts, the fact that "you can't tell most of the new performers one from another," stars with an excessive number of hangers-on ("some of them even have bodyguards") and record label bosses who are 'computer buffs' and know as much about country music as James Brown. Nashville DJ, Charlie Douglas, takes a different slant, singling out the movie, *Urban Cowboy*. "Radio had all these stations which were unsuccessful. Then *Urban Cowboy* came along and these stations grabbed a sackful of country records and went country. The new-born country stations didn't know country music and played what they felt comfortable with, and when that happened, the record companies had to supply the stations with what they wanted. That's the type of music coming out of transmitters of country stations today – and that music has hurt the industry." Meanwhile, *Powel's Page* previews the forthcoming all-British *Worthing Festival.*

SEPTEMBER, 1985 – *Powel's Page* refers to the completion of Bob's first year as publisher *and* editor: "I never really knew what my friend and ex-partner Reg Field did – now I know and it is a great deal." He proceeds to list recent changes implemented in *CMP* production: new printers, Development Workshop, replacing Cray Press; new distributors, Seymour Press (replacing Surridge Dawson); new computerised addressing machine, courtesy of Target Addressing. Most importantly, the shop-cum-office, opened 12 months ago, following Reg Field's retirement, has "worked out very well." He concludes, "Every issue in the last year left our premises days before the end of the month – before that it appeared some two to three weeks late. I hope also you have enjoyed the magazine the last couple of years. Either way, we would like you to tell us…who and what you would like to see featured."

OCTOBER, 1985 – *Peterborough Festival* review (by John Stafford) spread over eight pages, Al Moir continues his reviews of videos with a country connection, while *Powel's Page* enthuses about forthcoming TV documentary, *Route 66*, tracing the history (and course) of the famous highway.

DECEMBER, 1985 – Price rise – from 80p to 90p – announced, commencing next month.

JANUARY, 1986 – Report on "United Front" marketing campaign co-ordinated by *CMA* and endorsed by Byworth-Wootton International Ltd., entitled *Discover New Country*, to be launched by 5 major UK record labels in March, with special promotion granted to ten chosen acts[95] – a direct result of MORI survey (see MARCH & JULY '84 entries).

FEBRUARY, 1986 – Includes three-page tribute to Rick Nelson who died in a plane crash on New Year's Eve. Also, Bob's interview returns after a five-month absence, Merle Haggard featured.

MARCH, 1986 – *Powel's Page*, referring to the *Discover New Country* initiative, commends "a brave campaign…that deserves to succeed," but doubts that it will "get the very young audience, as they have a habit of following acts who, if not in their teens, are not that far removed from it." Of the ten acts chosen for the campaign, he concludes, "Let's face it, there is a lot of grey hair in that lot, and even a grey beard or two."

MAY, 1986 – Contains four-page *BP* interview (plus back cover photo) with 1950s star, Tommy Collins,[96]

---

[95] The 10 acts were:-

1. Alabama (RCA)
2. Rosanne Cash (CBS/Epic)
3. Exile (CBS/Epic)
4. The Judds (RCA)
5. Gary Morris (WEA)
6. Oak Ridge Boys (MCA)
7. Sawyer Brown (EMI)
8. George Strait (MCA)
9. Don Williams (EMI)
10. Hank Williams, Jr. (WEA)

[96] Born Leonard Sipes 28 September 1930, the much-loved Tommy Collins, along with Buck Owens, Wynn Stewart and Merle Haggard, helped create the 'Bakersfield (West Coast's equivalent to Nashville) Sound', enjoying a string of hits in the 1950s. By the time Bob got to meet him (mid-70s), the star had fallen on hard times and was living out of his car, which so moved his fervent fan that he ended up paying for his stay at a hotel. Managing to get back on track, Collins eventually (early

bidding for a comeback with his first major album for 17 years, *New Patches*, issued on future editor Craig Baguley's Password label. Also, 12-page review of *Silk Cut Festival*, shared among three writers, Johnny Cash and Nitty Gritty Dirt Band proving to be the highlights.

JULY, 1986 – *Write to Reply* includes a long letter from Cynthia Leu, *CMA*'s European Director of Operations, in response to a previous communication (from Alan Sands) deriding the *Discover New Country* campaign, her letter closing: "*DNC* can be judged a resounding success by anyone's standards." Although records indicate that none of the ten specially promoted acts achieved any sort of UK pop chart success, a 1988 *Gallup* poll revealed that country music record sales in the UK doubled between 1985 and 1988 (*CMP*, January, 1989). Meanwhile, *Powel's Page* reprints Bob's first ever article for *Country & Western Roundabout* – published 20 years earlier – detailing his 1965 trip to America.

AUGUST, 1986 – Under heading, "*FAN FAIR RECORD*", a report that registration for the 15th Annual *Fan Fair* in Nashville set new attendance records for the event with registration closing prior to the opening ceremony – a total of 21,500 fans paid $60 each for the five-day tickets. Elsewhere, in *Write to Reply*, the *DNC* controversy continues to rage, as Alan Sands is granted over a page to respond to Ms. Leu's July letter, his final words being: "I believe your campaign to be unnecessary,

---

80s) began writing and performing again, leading to his Password series of albums. The pair last met on 17 October, 1989, when Bob accepted an invitation to join the singer at his small, neat home in Franklin. Settling down to watch a World Series baseball match between Oakland Athletics and San Francisco Giants, they instead witnessed the Loma Prieta earthquake, ABC's Al Michaels' skilled commentary ensuring they stayed tuned throughout. Collins passed away on 14 March, 2000.

poorly conceived and, ultimately, a waste of money."

SEPTEMBER, 1986 – 200th issue contains stories (plus back cover picture) of "only three editors *CMP* ever had." (Essentials of these stories are reproduced in both Chapter 5 and this Chapter).

OCTOBER, 1986 After *Write to Reply*'s war of words over *DNC* campaign, Cynthia Leu resigns (to join RCA), her replacement being named as Martin Satterthwaite, former General Marketing Manager with MCA Records (later Island Records). *Powel's Page* focusses on the increasing number of country music festivals (he mentions five) being held at the same time of the year and the adverse effect they have on each other. He also condemns the poor security arrangements at festivals generally, *Wembley* included.

Throughout his work commitments, Bob always found time to return home,[97] planning his visits to coincide with local baseball matches. Following her husband's death, Mrs. Powel had moved to a flat not far from where she was living in Quebec City. Later still, she moved into a home, Bob, when visiting, staying at a nearby motel. Sadly, his mother's mental health deteriorated to such an extent that, on his final visit, she failed to recognise him, launching an attack with her cane – no doubt, a distressing incident for the son who described the healthy Mrs. Powel as "a lovely lady." She passed away within a year.[98] Again, Bob did not attend the funeral (he claimed never to have

---

[97] The parental home was 1170 Bougainville St., Quebec, close to the Plains of Abraham, scene of the decisive 1759 *Battle of Quebec*, where Wolfe defeated the French forces under Montcalm, thus adding Canada to the British Empire.

[98] Just as Mr. Powel met only one country performer, so did Mrs. Powel – in this case, French-Canadian singer, Willie Lamothe (and son), who Bob invited round to his mother's flat for a cup of coffee one day.

attended one in his life), and it was on with work.

FEBRUARY, 1987 – *CMA*'s newly appointed Director of European Operations, Martin Satterthwaite, announces that, commencing this year, the UK country chart will be revamped, meaning, essentially, that artistes regarded as more rock or pop (e.g. Eagles, Lone Justice) will be omitted, paving the way (theoretically, at least) for newer country acts such as Ricky Skaggs, Randy Travis, Reba McEntire and the Judds. Tony Byworth comments: "This decision caused Satterthwaite a considerable problem, as several Daniel O'Donnell albums were removed from the chart (all there, obviously, because he was selling more records than the other artistes). The news hit the Irish national press, creating such reaction that the decision was reversed. The incident hardly did Satterthwaite or the *CMA* any favours." Issue also features centre-page photo spread of Boxcar Willie and Johnny Russell during visit to *CMP* Shop.

MARCH, 1987 – Contains details of forthcoming five-part (one hour each) Channel 4 TV documentary, *A-Z of C&W*, presented by Hank Wangford. Meanwhile, Martin Satterthwaite insists 1986's *Discover New Country* campaign was successful, pointing to: a) rise in country album sales generally, and b) *New Country* category becoming established in minds of media. Therefore, new campaign – *New Country 87* – planned, featuring seven fresh acts,[99] plus the Judds, who were among original ten. Also contains interesting reply from Spencer Leigh to a question regarding country stars' nicknames. He lists fourteen of the most famous, namely:-

---

[99] Of these seven acts, just Steve Earle, with nine chart albums (highest position 22) and two minor hit singles (45,75), and Randy Travis (No.55 with the radio-friendly *Forever & Ever Amen* and 64 with accompanying album in 1987) achieved success. (Reba McEntire's lone chart single – No.62 – came in 1999, well after campaign ended).

Bill Anderson –*Whispering Bill*

Johnny Cash – *Man In Black*

David Allan Coe – *Mysterious Rhinestone Cowboy* (now dropped by Coe)

Tom T. Hall – *The Storyteller*

Johnny Horton – *Singing Fisherman*

Jerry Lee Lewis – *The Killer*

Jim Reeves – *Gentleman Jim*

Charlie Rich – *Silver Fox*

Jimmie Rodgers – *Singing Brakeman*

Hank Snow – *Singing Ranger*

Ernest Tubb – *Singing Troubadour*

Hank Williams – *Drifting Cowboy*

Conway Twitty – *High Priest of Country Music* (described by Leigh as "a bizarre choice")

George Hamilton IV – *Ambassador of Country Music*

Missing are:

Eddy Arnold – *Tennessee Plowboy* (because he was born and raised on a farm)

Jack Clement – *Cowboy*

Tennessee Ernie Ford – *The Ol' Peapicker* (from his catchphrase, "Bless your peapickin' heart")

Red Sovine – *The Old Syrup Sopper* (earned through selling *Johnny Fair* syrup via his KWKH radio show)

Tammy Wynette – *First Lady of Country Music*

Faron Young – *Singing Sheriff* (originally *The Young Sheriff*, the winning entry in a name-finding competition)

Elsewhere, John Stafford devotes a six-page article to country artistes who have yet to tour UK – and there are many of them.

MAY, 1987 – Report on visiting NBC film crew whose feature on country music in Britain is set to be screened on US prime time TV Easter Monday. Plus, announcement of 'live' country music from *The Tramshed*, Woolwich, S.E. London, commencing 3 May, with resident compere, Bob Powel. Elsewhere, Al Moir analyses airtime granted to country music on TV (2%), concluding, in light of MORI poll, it is "given a raw deal." *Write to Reply* includes three letters referring – all unfavourably – to Hank Wangford's *A-Z of C&W* documentary, comments ranging from "what an awful series" to "the repulsive and boring Hank Wangford" and "leave it to the experts…the programmes could be put into the hands of Bob Powel and the staff of *CMP* (where) everybody who is or was anybody gets a fair crack of the whip."

JUNE, 1987 – *Round The Country* reveals promoter Harvey Goldsmith is organising a country tour of China for later in year, headed by…Jerry Hall (Mick Jagger's then-wife – Dolly and Willie also being mentioned). Balancing things up a little, *Write to Reply* features two letters praising Hank Wangford series. (There are also two from disappointed Wembley fans).

JULY, 1987 – Announcement of *CMP* magazine sale to Craig Baguley and Jon Philbert (effective from August issue), owing to "other commitments."[100] Bob's statement

---

[100] Bob held the rights to all *Country Music People* magazines from the first issue in February, 1970 to July, 1987 inclusive, as he owned the publishing company, *Country Music Press Ltd*. (From August, 1987, the magazine was published by *Music Farm Ltd*.)

continues:-

"...I have known Craig Baguley and Jon Philibert for over fifteen years and I think that they will do a first rate job with the magazine. I am happy to say I have been asked to remain as editor...As both Craig and Jon have been involved in country music for many years, I am looking forward to their input...Craig Baguley is a well-known music publisher and producer who has been involved with *CMP* for the last two years behind the scenes as proof reader. Jon Philibert is a noted writer both as journalist and songwriter...Craig and Jon also own Password Records which to date has issued LP's by Tommy Collins and Jimmy Payne...the magazine will undoubtedly go through changes...Basically though Craig and Jon's opinion of country music and the magazine is similar to mine so there will be no drastic change..."

His faith in the new owners was not misplaced, the background of both being firmly rooted in music of just about every kind. Baguley (whose parents were in show business) was general manager of Robert Mellin Music (*Stupid Cupid, Only You*, etc.) in the 60s and 70s, before he moved into the country field, via the Jonny Young Four's Philips' releases (including 1972's *Country Pride* album) and, later (80s) the Password series of albums mentioned above. He went on to edit *CMP* for a record-breaking 22 years.

Equally, Jon Philibert's musical credentials can be traced back to the 60s, when, as a flatmate of Pye A & R man, Dave McAleer, he began embracing country music, in preference to the previously favoured soul/R&B sounds. Forming a publishing company (I Love Music)

He had hoped to put all 210 of these issues 'online'.

with Craig and writing reviews and articles for *CMP* helped establish his reputation, boosted further by the success of his composition, *I've Been Rained On, Too*, a No.13 US country hit for Tom Jones in 1983.

Elsewhere in this issue, an item from Nashville reveals that it is among America's top ten metropolitan destinations, being visited by some seven million tourists annually, bringing in $776 million. Plus, news of forthcoming "Country Music Chart Countdown" show to be produced in London, presented by Doc Cox and syndicated to various local stations around the UK. *Write to Reply* now contains no fewer than 4 letters in support of Hank Wangford series and none against.

AUGUST, 1987 – Page 3 lists Craig Baguley as *CMP* 'Managing Editor' and Bob Powel as 'Editor'. Impressive line-up for August's (8th) *Peterborough Festival*, including Johnny Cash, Billie Jo Spears, Nitty Gritty Dirt Band, Kris Kristofferson, Hoyt Axton and Ed Bruce. 50 radio stations will attend the event, which (for the second year) is presented by Jeffrey and Howard Kruger. *Write to Reply* prints one final (anti-) Hank Wangford letter, making 6-4 printed replies spread over three issues in favour of the series, though Craig Baguley, in a comment, states that "from the correspondence received, the majority are of the view that the series left a lot to be desired," which coincides with his own opinion that it was "a missed opportunity."

SEPTEMBER, 1987 – Magazine has a new look – larger size, name in bigger, bolder print on cover and improved quality of paper. Unsurprisingly, this is accompanied by price increase – from 90p to £1.10. Letter from Managing Editor, Baguley, stresses that "I personally enjoy the whole range of country music…and shall ensure the continuation of all the regular and popular features while…introducing new ones." Included this month are, "a *New Faces* section and a look at the historical roots of country music."

OCTOBER, 1987 – Includes 12-page review (by four different writers) of four-day *Peterborough Festival.*

DECEMBER, 1987 – *Round The Country* reports that Nashville's *Country Music Hall Of Fame & Museum*, celebrating its 20th anniversary, has attracted 6.5 million visitors in that time.

JUNE, 1988 – *Round The Country* reveals the mildly surprising fact that Anne Robinson, acid-tongued host of TV's *The Weakest Link*, loves country music. Meanwhile, among *Write to Reply*'s letters are several defending *New Country* acts Randy Travis and Dwight Yoakam, plus one heavily criticising Bob Powel's review of Dolly Parton's recent 'pop' album release, *Rainbow*. (Issue also happens to include an appraisal of Dolly's career by Steve Derby).

JULY, 1988 – Previous eleven issues – from August, 1987 – listed Craig Baguley as *CMP* 'Managing Editor' and Bob as 'Editor'. This month sees a change with the former becoming Editor, the latter Editorial Consultant, and this is how the position remains up to and including December, 1988, Bob's last month of direct involvement with the magazine in an official capacity. Issue also contains Bob's detailed reply to pro-Dolly/*Rainbow* letter, closing, "Dolly is still a great star and I'm sure will be so for many years, but I think she will be even more popular when she realises that record buyers, both young and old, will accept the real star, and the real her is country," the last point made in response to the letter-writer's assertion that Dolly "knows what her fans want."

AUGUST, 1988 – Following on from the popularity – or otherwise – of Dolly Parton, *Round The Country* reports on dropping of US ABC Television's "costly and much-vaunted extravaganza," *Dolly*, which critics slammed and which "achieved such poor ratings." Very next *RTC* item reveals that Emmylou Harris' 14-year association with

Warner Bros. yielded equivalent record sales, i.e. 14 million.

SEPTEMBER, 1988 – Craig Baguley, via *Soapbox* ("an occasional column for him to get things off his chest"), slams the BBC for the appalling sound quality of *Wembley Festival* transmission, contrasting it with the "professionalism that went into recording the recently televised Alexander O'Neal concert." Meanwhile, *Write to Reply* prints a long, articulate letter from Michael Malone of Leicester, condemning "record companies' hyping of *New Country* acts who are no more country than David Bowie." Despite granting it 'WINNING LETTER' status (possibly because of its eloquence), editor Baguley disagrees: "There are some fine 'New Country' artistes out there…time was when both drums and the steel guitar were frowned upon in country music circles…the promotion of *New Country* acts can only serve to heighten the public awareness of the older, established artistes as witness the re-emergence of Buck Owens."

NOVEMBER, 1988 – *Soapbox* returns, editor Baguley criticising the BBC once more, this time for axing *London Country* (see Chapter 7).

"DOLLY TO SPLIT FROM HUBBIE CARL?" poses the dramatic headline. In what would become an obsession (in the tabloids, at least), the stability of Dolly Parton's 23-year marriage is questioned, following reports that reclusive husband Carl Dean "has not seen his wife since last November and is so fed up with her prolonged absences from home he is ready to file for divorce." Despite being linked with, among others, Burt Reynolds and Sylvester Stallone, the superstar is adamant: "He is the only man in my life…he loves me to death…and we're really happy." 27 years further on, the couple are still together, so one can only conclude that she knew better than outsiders all along.

Meanwhile, a lively *Write to Reply* features three letters

disagreeing with Mr. Malone's anti-*New Country* stance, comments ranging from, "Please Mr. Malone, wheel your wheelbarrow through streets broad and narrow…to a Daniel O'Donnell concert," to "If Mr. Malone took off his rose-coloured glasses and really looked (and listened) to today's country music, he might actually realise how good so much of it is." Page also prints a letter from Nick Barraclough of BBC Radio 2's Music Dept. defending his "light-hearted" decision to appoint *The Archers'* Eddie Grundy (alias actor Trevor Harrison) as Wally Whyton's (one-week only) deputy on *WW Show*, his letter concluding: "Go on, Craig, it was funny." Craig's response: "No, it wasn't."

DECEMBER, 1988 – Includes coverage of the *BCMA* 1988 Awards, featuring photo of Bob holding trophy for "Outstanding Services To Country Music In Britain," accompanied by Craig Baguley's words of approval, "the most deserved award of the night…I doubt if there's anyone in Britain who knows more about country music," adding, "let's hope he acquires a new radio vehicle ASAP"

As a matter of interest, in the near-18 year period between issue No.1 in February, 1970 and No. 227 in December, 1988, there were eleven price rises – taking the cost of the magazine from 17½p to £1.10. Obviously, there are many factors that affect this figure – from the general economic situation to production costs, from the size, quality and quantity of the pages to advertising revenue. Nevertheless, for what it's worth, here is a breakdown of each price rise, the amount and frequency of which would always be determined by the owner:-

1. *August, 1973* - 17½p to 22p (26%) Bob's editorship)
2. *January, 1975* - 22p to 25p (14%) " ") 6 years
3. *August, 1975* - 25p to 30p (20%) " ")
4. *January, 1977* - 30p to 35p (17%) Tony's editorship)
5. *January, 1978* - 35p to 45p (29%) " ")
6. *February, 1980* - 45p to 50p (11%) " ") 6½ years
7. *January, 1981* - 50p to 60p (20%) " ")
8. *January, 1982* - 60p to 70p (17%) " ")
9. *January, 1983* - 70p to 80p (14%) " ")
10. *January, 1986* - 80p to 90p (12½%) Bob's editorship)
11. *September, 1987* - 90p to £1.10 (22%) " ") 5 years

Despite, from January, 1989, severing his editorial links with *CMP*, Bob continued to provide the occasional article, as in February, 1991, when, at the request of current editor, Craig Baguley, he, in a two-page item, "looked back at the changes in the country music scene since Issue No.1, twenty one years ago."

Then, 20 years later, for the 500th issue (October 2011), he, along with Larry Adams and Tony Byworth, "traced the history of *CMP* and reflected on their time in charge," extracts of which are quoted extensively in this chapter and Chapter 5.

For a near three-year period between September 1984 and July 1987, Bob had simultaneously held down three highly responsible positions within the UK country music industry – *London Country* radio show presenter, editor of *Country Music People* magazine, and owner of the CMP Shop. Now, with his radio show and involvement in *CMP* at an end, he was left with just the shop. So, how had this enterprise come about?

Chapter 9

CMP Shop: 1984-89

Window Shopping *("Just trying to find the best deal in town...")[101]*

As with his journalistic career, which happened almost as a by-product of his love for country music, so, according to Bob, the CMP Shop came about because of a need for office space – a need hastened by the retirement of *CMP* editor, Reg Field, in September, 1983:-

BP: "Reg, after a year, as agreed, said he was going to quit, and Cray Press said they didn't want to print the magazine anymore, so it was the perfect time, as Reg didn't want to have to find new printers. And I don't think he charged me for his share, I think he just gave it to me. So, we were using a spare room in his house. I jokingly complained to Reg that he didn't give me travel money to go into this new office – which was three doors away from where I lived! But, basically, I needed a place."

---

[101] *Window Shopping.* Marcel Joseph composition recorded by Hank Williams on 13 June 1952 and issued as 'B' side to *Jambalaya*. Although having a different rhythm, the melody of Elvis' *You're a Heartbreaker*, recorded 2 years later, is very similar.

How did you decide on the location?

BP: "I tried where *Abba Dart* mini-cab firm are now [at the top of Sidcup Hill]. They wanted something like £120 a week – really high rates…and then I had the bright idea…we used to do a lot of mail-order stuff and I stopped going to the Post Office in Cotmandene Crescent, which was always very busy and went to Grovelands Road, which is about two streets over and then up a little street, where there was a sub-Post Office, and I noticed there was a grocery store there, which, through time, would open, last about six weeks, stop, the guy would go broke, then it closed and opened again. Well, at the moment, it was closed. So, when I went up to send the magazines off, I said to the guy running the Post Office: 'That grocery store up the road – what would the rent be?' He said straight away: 'You can't sell food!' Because he was selling food then, since the grocery store last closed. So, I said, 'I don't want to sell food – basically, I want it as the headquarters for my magazine.' 'Oh,' he said. So, he had the key, and I had a look around, got in my handyman, Rob Waterton (Dolly's son), also. I said, 'That would be perfect, plenty of room for the magazine.' More than we needed, really – best of all, the rent was only £30 per week!"

So, how did you get started?

BP: "I contacted the man at the Council and the first thing he said was, 'You have to sell something.'

I said, 'Oh, that's all right – bung a few records in the front, you know. You don't actually have to sell them, do you?'

He said, 'No, no, just as long as they're there.' And it

just so happened that the bloke with a shop in
Cotmandene Crescent, Peter, was giving up his records, so
he sold me about seven or eight racks for a fiver [per rack]
– no records – and then I wrote to the seven dealers or so
that took adverts from us and said to each of them, 'Can
you send me 100 different albums at £1 each, postage
paid?'

They all said, 'Yes,' so we got 700 records and we put
them in alphabetical order and then we got from the Post
Office a phone number because when it was actually
opened, I had no phone – it hadn't been connected – and I
got friendly with the butcher, I gave him my card and said
if anyone needed me and told him where I was, etc."

And so, Saturday, 15 September, 1984, the day of the
Grand Opening of the CMP Shop at 78 Grovelands Road,
St. Pauls Cray – an off-the-beaten-track location, albeit one
just 10 minutes' walk from his home – became another
milestone in Bob Powel's life. With a guest list that
included George Hamilton IV, Patsy Montana (an
unscheduled, late appearance), David Moody of the
Moody Brothers, *CMA* head of European Operations
Cynthia Leu, past *CMP* editor, Tony Byworth, Christian
music disc jockey/writer Paul Davis, the Waterton clan,
Chrissie Davy, manager Eddie Pearson in the back room
selling items, various *CMP* scribes and photographers and
200 country music fans, the event proved a resounding
success, even if, as Tony Byworth recalls, "a number of
LP's were hanging up on butcher's hooks in the window!"
But would interest and enthusiasm continue?

BP: "About three days after the opening, the butcher
rang and said, 'Where are you?'

I said, 'I'm at home, working.'

And he said, 'Well, there's people here, waiting to get in.'

I said, 'What for?'

He said, 'To buy records!'

I said, '*Really*?' So, I rushed over and sold them records – and soon the phone got put in and we had no problem. During the week, quite often, you didn't get any customers, maybe three or four, but on a Saturday, it was really busy. So, I don't think we sent off one packet or did one wrapping-up on Saturday, because we were busy serving or taking telephone orders. At other times, we were spending our time wrapping up magazines – we'd deal with mail order items as they came in."

The success really took you by surprise?

BP: "Absolutely. When I read stories from famous shop owners saying, 'I opened this or that shop by accident,' I think, 'Yeh, I'm sure you did,' but mine really *was* an accident, I had no idea it would go, but it went bloody well and I was making far more from the shop than I was from the magazine. That's why I sold the magazine to Craig."

Having a stall at the *Wembley Festival* helped, presumably?

BP: "Yes. Since the early 70s, we had had a deal with Mervyn Conn to operate a *CMP* stall at the *Wembley Festival* in exchange for advertising space. This worked OK and we made a small profit, though I needed to renegotiate terms each year and ask for the details in writing, since Mervyn had a tendency to forget key points. Then, when we were able to sell records as well as magazines at the stall – from 1985 onwards – we did really well, financially, *Wembley* being a three-day event by now. It was terrific and helped keep us afloat, actually."

What about magazine subscriptions – did you employ staff especially to deal with these?

BP: "Not exactly! I would accost women on the street once a month because we would have to deliver about 1,000 *CMP*s [for individual subscribers, i.e. not shops or newsagents] to every part of the globe and we had a couple of big tables. We'd put them out – until I got enough regulars – and I'd watch people going by. I'd say, 'Sweetheart, would you like to earn a tenner for about an hour's work?'

'Yeh.'

'There you are, then, just put the magazines in the packet – Dolly will show you how to do it.'

That's how we got the staff. We had to put the magazines in order of postal territories, so it needed about 100 different packets, using rubber bands and the Post Office said, 'You'll need some post bags.' So they delivered about two hundred of the bloody things! They were underneath every single rack, I think – about 10 years' supply they sent! The minimum number of subscribers was a thousand and when we started, we had 738 or something like that, but it was still much cheaper than doing it the other way, even though we were paying for a thousand. But, of course, we went up and up to 1,500."

How did you retain subscribers?

BP: "I bought this machine for a couple of thousand quid – very expensive – and it told us when the subscriptions were up. It told us months before, and, most importantly, it divided the subscribers into postal areas. We would put a form in the mag. I have subscribed to a number of magazines – *Variety* is the latest one – that never give you an offer to come back. So, what I used to do – again, thanks to this machine – is, once they [subscribers] were 3 months old and they hadn't renewed, I would send them a free copy and say, 'Look what you're missing' and all this sort of thing. And, of course, it didn't cost me anything because they were still among the 1,000 or whatever."

How did you obtain records?

BP: "Oh, from all over – members of the public would bring in second-hand albums and I'd make an offer. Dealers – we got the latest American imports from *Record Corner* in Balham – my friend, Dave Hastings. Then there was a van that came round, full of records and stuff, many of which were country. I visited them at their office in the East End of London one time. They had racks and racks of stuff and their cheapest price was 64 pence – for a sealed album. A trip to New York via Concorde was a 'one-off' – it wasn't a great place for wholesale. Nashville, where all the record companies are, was better."

Did you offer any special inducements to buyers?

BP: "Only our little 'trick.' If a customer had bought a dozen albums and I'd given 10% off, they'd never remember. So, if I had more albums than I needed by one particular artiste, I had a chair, about the size of the newspaper racks that we got from the Council. I'd fill it full of albums, then, if the customer ordered over 10 albums, I'd say, 'Do you see those records there? Well, help yourself to one.' If they bought 15 albums, then 'help yourself to two,' 20 albums 'three,' and all this sort of thing."

Did you attract any bulk buyers?

BP: "Well, we had this very nice guy come round with a huge, great lorry from Denmark and he was a member of this country music club and he would take orders from our latest list in *CMP* and he would order 120-130 albums. And you know what he was shipping over here? Plants – in pots!"

How often would he visit?

BP: "Not often enough! He'd come over about every six weeks or so – then, unfortunately, he got ill and I didn't see him again. I was going to go and join him one time for a visit but we never did get round to it."

So, custom came from far and wide?

BP: "Yes, from just about every county in Britain – as well as places like France, Holland, Spain, Germany and even Canada, USA, Singapore and Saudi Arabia!"

Didn't you occasionally have 'live' performances, in-store?

BP: "Although we had George Hamilton IV and surprise guest, Patsy Montana, at the opening, we didn't have any singing that time, but every subsequent time we did: George came again, Boxcar came, with Johnny Russell and his touring band, Billy Walker, Jonny Young, Rattlesnake Annie, Tony Griffin and many others."

Who else was involved in the running of the shop?

BP: "Eddie Pearson, the manager, was a great help, of course – the thing is, his job during the summer was teaching people how to windsurf in the south of France, and he said, 'I don't want to miss that job.'

So, I said, 'No, no, we'll just do it until such time…' Anyway, he never did go back, he stayed with me the whole time. He lived at Gravesend, so it was really good. Then I had a secretary, Margaret Lyon, who still lives around the corner…then there was Valerie George, who, with her partner, Lester, subsequently opened up her own shop [*Bud's Country Store*, 6mi/10km away in Penge, S.E. London, which continued operating beyond the millennium]."

Wasn't there once a robbery at the store?

BP: "Yes, and, funnily enough, it did me a favour. As I've said, the shop used to be a grocery store, and the glass front-door had the residue of previous posters and stickers all over it – not a pretty sight. And the burglar put a brick through it. Now, what we always did – what shop-keepers should always do – is take the bulk of the money but leave some cash in the till, so they don't get too upset and start trashing the place. But one annoying thing he did, as well as taking the money, he took the drawer it was in and it

217

was a bit of a nuisance getting a replacement – but he didn't steal any records. The police were called, we put in an insurance claim and got the money back, which enabled us to get the nice, new glass fitted to the front-door – within a couple of days, too. All very efficient."

As 1988 drew to a close, although now without radio or journalistic commitments, and – theoretically – with more time to devote to shop business, there was no corresponding upsurge of interest or effort from the owner, who, having developed the enterprise purely out of a need for office space, felt no particular attachment to it. Perhaps also, no longer enjoying the high profile *CMP* editorship and *London Country* broadcasting afforded, he found custom starting to drop off.

Whatever the reasons, by May, 1989, the ads had stopped appearing in *CMP*, Bob, through ignoring summonses, had been declared bankrupt, his shop had been placed in the hands of the Official Receiver and KPM Financial Services were acting on his behalf.[102] A rather gloomy scenario – and yet, as ever, the 'failed' entrepreneur remained optimistic:-

BP: "I hadn't paid Corporation Tax and the part-time lady accountant I employed had disappeared with all the paperwork, so I was made bankrupt. However, taking the value of my house into consideration, I knew my assets greatly exceeded my liabilities. Then, with the court case

---

[102] Despite enquiries at the Official Receiver's Office, Bromley Council, KPM Financial Services and Bromley Crown Court, no records for this case have been traced. The fact that many organisations switched to a new, computerised database system around the turn of the millennium has not helped, nor, of course, Bob's own rather haphazard record-keeping.

coming up, it seemed the perfect time to go, leaving matters in the hands of KPM, who duly paid the fine – £10,000, I think – sending on the balance to me."

In July, 1989, ex-RCA A&R man, Shaun Greenfield, bought all the albums from Bob and the shop from the Official Receiver, at the same time making a goodwill payment to Bromley Council, while, three months later, the ads reappeared in *CMP*, still under the old title, 'Bob Powel's Country Music Store.' However, by January 1991, Greenfield, who lived some distance away and was beginning to tire of the daily commute, found he was making more profit from his mail order business, anyway, so sold the property once more. Today, a barber shop stands on the site.

Chapter 10

Country Sounds: 1989-90

Howlin' at the Moon ("Now, I can't tell the day from night...")[103]

Since his final *London Country* show on 1 October, 1988, Bob Powel's rich, distinctive tones had been missing from the airwaves. Now, as 1989 dawned, and with no offers coming in, he found himself in the unusual situation (for him) of having to apply for a position. Hearing that London's Capital Radio might be launching its own country show, he wrote into the station. However, before his application had even been processed, he learned that presenter Neil Coppendale was about to be dismissed from Radio Sussex show, *South Coast Country* (produced by *BCMA* founder and chairman, Jim Marshall), prompting an immediate, opportunistic telephone call to the programme director:-

---

[103] *Howlin' at the Moon.* Recorded at the same 16 March, 1951 session as *Hey, Good Lookin'* and *I Can't Help It (if I'm Still In Love With You)*, this self-composition provided Hank Williams with a No.3 country hit in 1951.

BP: "Hello, I'm Bob Powel of Radio London…"

PD: "Oh yes, I've heard of you."

BP: "Well, I understand you're looking for someone to do a country show."

PD: "Yes, we are."

BP: "Well, as you may know, Radio London has become GLR and they've let all their freelancers go, so I'm available, if you're interested."

PD: "Right, can you start Saturday?"

"It was as simple as that," said Bob (although, in fact, Jim Marshall had been first choice to replace his old presenter but declined). Of course, there remained the little matter of a 100mi/161km round trip to the seaside resort of Brighton, a few miles east of schoolboy stomping-ground, Littlehampton, but he had plans to deal with this. For now, what could he expect at his new home?

Radio Sussex, or Radio Brighton, to give it its original name, was, like Radio London, one of the first wave of BBC local radio stations that took to the air during the late 1960s. Broadcasting from Marlborough Place in the town, it officially opened on 14 February, 1968. Initially operating on 88.1 MHz VHF frequency only, the station later acquired a medium wave frequency of 202m and transferred to 95.3 MHz on VHF. In common with much of the BBC's early radio output, Radio Brighton broadcast only for limited daytime hours in its early years, relying on Radio 2 and Radio 4 for a sustaining service, but building to a full daytime service by the mid-1970s.

On 22 October, 1983, as part of the BBC's move to extend its local radio network across the UK, the station expanded further to include the entire county, in the process changing its name to Radio Sussex. After undergoing a further name-change in 1994, the station settled on its current name – BBC Sussex – in 2009. Famous presenters who began their career here include Des Lynam, Kate Adie and Gavin Hewitt.

Country Music People's February, 1989 edition announced the news as follows:-

"Bob Powel, for seventeen years the host of BBC Radio London's *London Country* programme, until Radio London became GLR last October, is back on the airwaves as the country DJ on BBC Radio Sussex programme, *Country Sounds*. Powel, happy to be back on the air once again, says, 'It's great being back with the BBC and I hope I will provide listeners to Radio Sussex as entertaining a programme as they have received in the past when Neil Coppendale hosted the show.'"

The item proceeds to list relevant wavebands together with the broadcast time: Saturdays between noon and 1pm. And so, early Saturday morning, 4 February 1989, the 'back-in-demand' DJ set off on the first of what would become regular, fortnightly commutes from his St. Pauls Cray home. 'Fortnightly' because he managed to secure an agreement whereby a pre-recorded show was followed by a 'live' one on the same day, although, in fact, this arrangement did not last long, as, being an early riser and invariably arriving when the station opened at 6am, he had usually finished his pre-recorded show by 7, giving him a two hour wait until he performed 'live' at 9. Soon, therefore, he began pre-recording both shows, allowing him the luxury of travelling home while listening to his own programme.[104]

---

[104] One day, having recorded his two programmes and enjoying breakfast in a seafront café before undertaking the homeward

Knowing that certain people in the area "would not be impressed" at his – "or probably any outsider's" – appointment, the new presenter then took an unusual step:-

BP: "I said to the programme director, 'I want you to do me one favour: I only come in on a Saturday, of course, so my mail will be there already. Would you, on a Friday, go through all my mail and have a read of it?' And, of all the mail received, I never once had an uncomplimentary letter. And then this petition came, signed by 38 million people – or under! – saying what a terrible programme it was, and all this sort of thing. And the programme director wrote back, saying, 'I've been reading all Mr. Powel's mail and we haven't had one complaint about him!'"

Has he any idea who organised the petition?

BP: "I have more than an idea – it was my predecessor, Neil Coppendale. And, as an addendum, the only other compliment – or comment of any kind – I received from the directors at the station came 18 months later, after I handed in my notice and was told, 'Oh, what a shame – you were brilliant!'"

In reply, Neil Coppendale states that his memory of the incident is hazy and "only rings a very distant bell."

journey, Bob heard his show being broadcast on the proprietor's radio and could not resist mentioning that it was his voice blaring out. However, the man refused to believe this until upcoming tracks could be correctly forecast, which, having the running order on him, the off-duty DJ was easily able to do.

However, he justifies any feelings of resentment he may have felt by pointing to the fact that he and Jim Marshall "had a very popular programme and had worked on it for buttons since persuading the then-management to air it 15 years previously." So, presumably, it must have been galling to see a non-local move in, especially if at a higher rate of pay. Disappointed as he must have been, the episode seemed to have no adverse effect on Coppendale's career, which subsequently included TV voiceover work, an interview with Tony Blair and FA Cup Soccer Final presentation.

As for his successor, he continued serving up the same recipe – though minus the impressive guest list. In fact, during his 18-month stint at the station, he managed to attract just two stars: Hank Thompson and Jean Shepard, who, touring together at the time, appeared on the same show. Was the new host given a free hand in choosing material? "Absolutely." He also self-produced, which, in view of his special recording/travel arrangements, made life considerably simpler.

Two *Country Sounds* shows survive on tape. The first of these dates from 7 April, 1990, and among the artistes featured are home-grown talents, Mick Flavin, Poacher and Little Ginny, alongside old favourites such as Don Reno (& Bill Harrell), Hank Snow, Grandpa Jones, Bobby Bare, Hank Williams, Hylo Brown, Tommy Collins, Wilf Carter and Roy Acuff. So, no concession to contemporary 'crossover' music here!

Eventually, 11 August, 1990, the day of the final *Country Sounds* show, arrived. This features exclusively mono 45 recordings, and, after opening with Lefty Frizzell's *A Hobo's Pride*, the host makes the following announcement:-

"Well, welcome again from yours truly, Bob Powel, to *Country Sounds* – a good hour of country music every

Saturday. But this is quite a sad programme for me, really – great news for you, but bad news for me, because I'm leaving. I've got a few other things to do, and, just coming down – I live in Orpington, Kent – it's a long way, and I really enjoyed my 18 months, but eventually decided it was time to pack it in, after great fun. So, sadly, this is going to be my very last programme."

He then introduces his successor, Jim Marshall (now free and willing to take over), who vows to continue "the mixture as before." Their ensuing banter includes the following:-

JM: "I have fond memories of…I think it was called 'The Country Guitar' – there used to be a coffee bar opposite the Dominion cinema in Tottenham Court Road, central London. And we were there, and I remember you were very enthusiastic about a place that you were going to take us to, and you took a crowd of us to this – I think it was a café – and it was a real dump!"

BP: "Yeh, it was, wasn't it…"

JM: "I'll never forget that, Bob."

BP: (Laughing) "Well, you wanted me to pay – what did you expect?"

A letter printed in *CMP*'s September, 1990 issue reflected the feelings of many listeners at this time:-

"Dear sir,

May I, through your column, be permitted to express my regret at the news that Bob Powel is to leave our airwaves for pastures new. Bob's country music knowledge was without peer, and, to this day, his Radio London interviews with such luminaries as Hank Snow, Joe 'Red' Hayes and Tex Ritter remain a treasured source of historical documentation. In the early 1970's, his *London Country* programme opened up a whole new and exciting world for raw beginners like me for which I shall be eternally grateful."

– Stuart E. Oliver, London, SW4.

If the titles selected for *London Country*'s last show, two years earlier, seemed somehow relevant, they are equally so, now: *You're The Judge and Jury* (Warren Smith), *Killin' Time* (Kris Kristofferson), *They Laid Him in the Ground* (Homer & Jethro), *What Goes Up Always Comes Down* (Ray O'Daniel) – each seems to be making some sort of statement on the situation. It's also worth comparing the last three records played on this show with the first played on *London Country* (listed in footnote 24 of Chapter 1). Here, they comprise:-

Penny Wishes – Tommy Hunter

When I Get the Money Made – Mac Wiseman

Louisiana Swing – Schroeders Playboys

The first of these, dating from 1962, is a particularly poignant slice of country-pop, containing the line, "all my dreams aren't worth a penny anymore." *When I Get the Money Made*, is, by contrast, bright and optimistic:-

"A little mansion in the shade

And a pretty little maid

Will be mine when I get the money made."

Is it coincidental that both these songs mention money? The final track, *Louisiana Swing*, is a Cajun-style instrumental, featuring fiddle and accordion, set against a pronounced 2/4 beat. However, by this stage, the host's interests are moving away from 'swing' music – from western culture, generally – and taking him in an altogether more easterly direction: to Thailand.

Chapter 11

Thailand: 1990-2001

Ramblin' Man ("There's something over the hill that I've gotta see...")[105]

Since first harbouring, as an eleven-year-old in Quebec City, his dream of bringing country music to the masses, Bob Powel had behaved rather like a man possessed: writing, reviewing, planning, presenting, travelling, interviewing, meeting schedules and chasing deadlines – a never-ending cycle of hectic activity, all wrapped up in a burning desire to promote the music he loved. So much so that, by 1977, he felt the need to relax. The first signs of this came in January of that year, when, on completion of his initial *CMP* editorial stint, he undertook a trip to Thailand, along with friend, Dave Travis. How had the pair met?

---

[105] *Ramblin' Man.* Written and originally recorded by Hank Williams, this moody, minor-chord piece was covered in 1975 by Steve Young and included on his album, *Honky Tonk Man.* Bob recounted how, seated beside Conway Twitty on a tour bus one time, he happened to mention that this was his least favourite Hank Williams tune, prompting a non-stop rendering of it by the provocative performer for the journey's duration!

Although little-known beyond UK country music circles, Charterhouse-educated Travis' name crops up frequently in past issues of *CMP*, usually upon release of a new album (he has made twenty, to date) or when embarking on a tour of either the UK or continent, where, through time, he has achieved considerable popularity. A singer-songwriter/guitarist in the tradition of mid-sixties contemporaries, Bert Jansch and John Renbourn, he is as comfortable playing folk and rock & roll as country. Being a regular *LC* guest, he soon became friendly with its host.

It was after one such appearance that the idea of a foreign trip emerged, South Africa being the initial suggestion. This project fell through when the freelance, Texan pilot responsible for arranging the schedule proved to be "a bag of hot wind" – and they didn't fancy travelling by balloon! The singer then remembered a Thai-born schoolpal, Army captain, Visnu Conchary. Having moved back to his home country, he was able to recommend the best deals available, especially since his wife worked for Thai Airways – and so the proposed venture became reality, January, 1977's *CMP* referring to it in the *Tickertape* section, as follows:-

"Bob Powel and Dave Travis holidaying in Bangkok during early January. Is Powel seeking out an exclusive or Travis finding a new market for his material?"

Neither was true, of course – they were merely relaxing, and, in the former's case, at least, testing the waters, albeit subconsciously. This first visit (during which they stayed at the 'Indra' Hotel) left no abiding impressions – apart from the lightning speed with which made-to-measure outfits could be produced by local Chinese tailors, a service Bob used frequently in the future. Their second trip two years later, however, was both longer (six weeks) and more varied. Starting off in Bangkok, the pair took the train to Kuala Lumpur via Penang, where they met Dr. Lee (a *CMP* subscriber whose name and address had been noted by the ex-editor prior to departure). While in Malaysia, they had at least one strange encounter...

Visiting a local zoo, the pair noticed a pretty young girl trailing around an orang-utan (perhaps seeking its cage?). Later, relaxing in a restaurant, they found themselves in close proximity to the unlikely duo, prompting the slim, suave partner to charm the fairer of the two, leaving his bemused companion staring into the eyes of her hairy companion. It wasn't love at first sight – in fact, each seemed remarkably unimpressed with the other. Still, at least Bob escaped with his dignity – and everything else – intact!

Boarding the *Raj Brooke* [106] in Singapore, they then sailed across the South China Sea to Brunei, in the process meeting some interesting fellow passengers, including "a very nice Australian couple, a bald-headed, retired Californian professor called Fred who taught us the 'Uno' card game and a Chinese dockside worker, who, having seen the boat pass by regularly, decided to sample life aboard." From this gentleman, the English tourists discovered a little of the art of haggling...

BP: "Dave decided he wanted a mah-jong set. I wasn't familiar with the way they conducted bargaining in this part of the world. Well, Dave got into a long discussion with this guy about the mah-jong set. I've no idea of the prices, so I'll estimate: the Chinese wanted, say, 50 dollars

---

[106] The *Raj Brooke* was named after Yorkshire-born military officer and explorer, John Weston Brooke (1880-1908), murdered by the Yi people in the independent Lolo region of Tibet, while leading a geographical expedition.

for it and Dave said 20 dollars – and it kept going on like this for ages, until it ended up knocked down – or up – to 34 dollars. Neither would budge beyond this point, so they both withdrew. Then, as Dave was walking with me, he said, 'Do you know what, that wasn't a bad price – I think I'll go and get it.'

"Well, the guy wouldn't sell it to him – he wouldn't even negotiate with him! So, I had to go and start negotiating. Never got it for 34 dollars, of course, got about 36. The moral is: if you're going to buy it, buy it, if you're not going to buy it, don't buy it."

Summing up the trip, he said, "We had a real nice time – five or ten days on a boat, train all over the place...Dave was a great museum-goer, which I wasn't, but it was fine." After this second trip, Bob continued visiting the country alone, even buying a house in Pattaya suburb, Soi Watom, where he lived with a girlfriend for a time. Although this is probably the closest he came to marrying,[107] it is not a period of which he had fond memories – in fact, he described it as "a bit of a disaster," the girl's strong family ties apparently overcoming any love the couple may have felt for each other.

The house itself proved useful for storing items from his Broomwood Road residence, the articles being brought over in batches each time he visited. How many trips did he make before departing for good?

BP: "Enough to convince Dolly I was never actually

---

[107] Bob's last landlord claimed that, when taking the flat, Bob described himself as divorced, and there have apparently been similar rumours in country circles for years. No such declaration was made to this author, however. Perhaps some sort of local ceremony was carried out.

going to go! I'd get a couple of second-hand suitcases from charity shops, fill them full of stuff, go out to Thailand – to the villa – and come back basically empty-handed, without the suitcases. I did that about three, four or five times – the last time on a one-way ticket."

Was there anything left in your house by the time you'd finished?

BP: "A bloody ton of stuff! Colin Maitland [actor friend] got rid of some of the more valuable items – expensive books of Dad's, this sort of thing. In fact, he ended up owing me a hundred quid, which he paid me the moment I came back…very useful…but, oh, I left an absolute load, and I basically said to Dolly, 'Help yourself.'"

Then there was a garage, I believe?

BP: "Yes, with a car, which I couldn't sell on account of the bankruptcy business – as far as I know, the car's still there!"

Where was the garage?

BP: "Round the back of St. Mary Cray station somewhere. I hired it from the council, so they've obviously repossessed it by now. That's where I had all the *CMP*s – about 10,000 of them! One of the few survivors from it is a painting, *Night Mists*, by 20th century British artiste, Montague Dawson, valued at several hundred pounds, that Dolly's daughter kept in her garage for me – it's now hanging on my study wall."

While in Thailand, did you ever think of the garage?

BP: "No, no, no! What could I want from it? The car was no good to me – it hadn't been used for years. There was nothing particularly personal there, things like that I kept at the house. I even forgot I'd given clothes to a friend [Del Grace], so when I returned from Thailand, it was like being given a huge Christmas box [actually two full suitcases] of all the clothes I wanted!"

And so, finally, in August, 1990, with his last *Country Sounds* show behind him and the CMP Shop court case ahead, Bob Powel departed England's green and pleasant land for pastures – and pleasures – new. But what sort of country was he choosing?

Bordered to the north by Burma and Laos, to the east by Laos and Cambodia, to the south by the Gulf of Thailand and Malaysia, and to the west by the Andaman Sea and the southern extremity of Burma, Thailand is a constituted monarchy headed by King Rama IX, the world's longest-serving (since 1946) current head of state and the longest-reigning monarch in Thai history.

It is the world's 51st-largest country in terms of area (slightly larger than Spain) and the 20th most populous, with around 64,000,000 people, 80% of whom are ethnically Tai and 14% Thai-Chinese. Additionally, there are approximately 2.2 million legal and illegal immigrants, plus a number of expatriates from developed countries. The official language is Thai and the primary religion (95%) Buddhist, of the Theravada tradition.

Historically, there is evidence of human habitation dating back 40,000 years but the heavy influence of Indian culture and religion evident today commenced only around the first century. Despite much turbulence and conquest in the intervening years (a third of the population of some areas of the country were slaves between the 17th and 19th centuries), Thailand remains the only south-east Asia nation never to have been colonized.

Politically, the country operates within the framework of a constitutional monarchy whereby the Prime Minister is head of government and a hereditary monarch head of state, this system being inaugurated in 1932, when, following a bloodless coup, a 'Draft Constitution' created the first legislature, leading to elections, despite which subsequent years (up to 1972) were dominated by military dictatorships. Eventually, in the 1980s, a stable prosperity and democracy emerged, although there has recently been an upsurge in violent protests by both anti-government ('red shirts') and pro-government ('yellow shirts') supporters (87 died and 1,378 were injured in clashes in 2010).

Geographically, Thailand contains several distinct regions: the north of the country is the mountainous area of the Thai highlands, the highest point being 8,415ft/2,565m above sea level, the centre is dominated by the mainly flat Chao Phraya river valley, which runs into the Gulf of Thailand, while the southern region (including both Pattaya and the capital, Bangkok) consists of the narrow Kralsthmus that widens into the Malay Peninsula. The Chao Phraya and Mekong River are the sustainable resource of rural Thailand, while the Gulf of Thailand contributes to the tourism sector, owing to its clear, shallow waters along the coasts in the southern region and the Kralsthmus – it is also an industrial centre containing the country's main port.

The Andaman Sea is regarded as Thailand's most precious natural resource, as it hosts the popular and luxurious resorts of Phuket, Krabi, Ranong, Phang Nga and Trang and their lush islands. The local climate is tropical and characterised by monsoons: there is a rainy, warm and cloudy southwest monsoon from mid-May to September and a dry, cool northeast monsoon from November to mid-March. The southern isthmus is always hot and humid.

Thailand is an emerging economy heavily dependent on exports, chief among which are rice (the largest in the world), textiles, footwear, fishery products, rubber, jewellery, cars, computers, and electrical appliances. Tourism makes up 6% of the economy, with prostitution and sex tourism forming a substantial proportion of this, the chief reasons for which are cultural milieu, poverty, and the lure of money. One report published in 2003 estimated the trade at $4.3 billion per year – or 3% of the Thai economy (other sources rank it higher), while recent research found that prostitution in Thailand between 1993 and 1995 accounted for 2.7% of GDP. With a GDP worth $602 billion, the country is the second largest economy in south-east Asia (after Indonesia) and the 4th richest behind Singapore, Brunei and Malaysia.

Though the official language of Thailand – spoken throughout the land – is Thai, the country is host to several other minority languages, the largest of which is the Lao dialect of Isan, spoken in the north-eastern provinces. Numerous tribal languages are also spoken. English is a mandatory school subject but the number of fluent speakers remains low, especially outside the cities.

Thailand may seem a strange choice of venue, so what was Bob's prime motivation in moving there?

BP: "I fell in love with it when I went with Dave Travis to start with…I loved the people – the fact that they liked fat people didn't do any harm, either![108] And it was a very

---

[108] This has its origins in the traditional reverence shown towards the 'fat Buddha', a laughing, jolly Bodhisattva (Buddha-

cheap place to live then, compared to here."

What were the main obstacles?

BP: "Well, firstly, when considering moving to Thailand for good, there's one thing to bear in mind: you CANNOT move there for good! It's such a long rigmarole, you need to have a load of money to invest in the country, and all this sort of thing. So, you have to do what we 'plebs' did: you simply go and don't come back, i.e. you get a double-entry tourist's visa – obtained in Knightsbridge, London, before you go. Then, after three months, you have to leave the country and come back. And the cheapest way of doing this – and, in my opinion, by far the most enjoyable – is to travel by train, which leaves every weekday at 3pm from Hua Lamphong station, Bangkok. For £8 or £9 sterling, you get a nice little bottom bunk and you sleep – I did, anyway – very comfortably, though it's the one time I'd take a sleeping pill, to be fair."

How long did the journey take?

BP: "We'd arrive at the [Malaysian] border about 9am the following morning – so, 18 hours. If this was the 'first' run [i.e. a quick IN/OUT trip], I'd get off there, at Alor Setar, just inside the border. I'd still have quite a bit of stuff, so would slip the porter a fiver to lock my

---

to-be) of ancient Chinese culture called, Pu-Tai. In Asia, generally, chubbiness is a sign of wealth (i.e. you have enough to eat) and can also symbolise spiritual wealth. It is regarded as lucky to rub the fat Buddha's tummy, but one would not be advised to touch a statue of 'Siddhatta' (the thin Buddha).

belongings into the top bunk, for safekeeping. Then I'd just go shopping for three or four hours – and you can buy a lot of stuff in Malaysia. In Thailand, even pears are 80% duty, whereas in these two big Malaysian supermarkets, you can get all sorts of silly little items – like Tesco gravy granules, and this sort of thing that you couldn't get for love or money in Thailand. After this, I make the return journey to Hua Lamphong."

Was it a safe journey?

BP: "We never had any trouble but the train had been attacked by Muslims in past years – that's why we always had a Thai armed guard on board."

If embarking on a 'second' visa-run (i.e. 3 months later), he would remain on the train for a further three-hour ride into the English-sounding town of Butterworth, followed by a boat trip to Georgetown, on the island of Penang, remaining here for three nights (usually Sunday to Wednesday morning), by which time his visa renewal application would have been processed:-

BP: "This requirement led to a whole new industry in Penang. You'd go there and you'd see all these book stalls, but they made very little money out of books! What happened was that someone like me would turn up on a Monday. I'd go to the same guy every time, give him my passport, then he gets a few together, his motorcyclist delivers them to the Embassy, then, three days later, about an hour and a half before the train departs, we'd get them back."

Was this legitimate?

BP: "Well, let's put it this way: the authorities knew what was going on, you needed to go through immigration initially, that is, check in and produce your passport, etc., but no one stopped it."

Did you make the visa-run alone?

BP: "Usually, yes, but more often than not, you'd meet somebody on the train you knew. Then, staying in the same place [in Georgetown] each time, I'd need to hire a cab really quick because it was by far the best and most reasonably priced accommodation, and by the time I'd walked there, it would have gone."

Although the 'visa-run' procedure sounds like an inconvenient ordeal, the expat claims to have enjoyed the change of environment, unfamiliar scenery, opportunity to sample better-quality shops and restaurants (he is not a Thai food lover), and the company of fellow passengers. How did he spend his time in Georgetown?

BP: "Mainly shopping, or browsing. There was this building housing a huge market about 15 minutes' walk from my hotel. It stretched out for miles at the back – you could easily get lost in it. There was an escalator that never worked throughout my time, so you walked up to the floors. The first floor contained all food, the second was clothes, but then, on the third floor, right at the back, there were about a dozen book-stalls run by these Muslim guys. A lot of the books had been there for years – all paperbacks with the prices on them, dead cheap…I read a heck of a lot in those days. You just had to avoid Fridays, when they were at prayer."

And, naturally, you sampled the food there?

BP: "Absolutely – and much preferred it to Thai food. Malaysian food is basically Indian food – meat kormas, this sort of thing. And there was a fantastic place called the Taj Mahal, which was very un-Taj Mahal-ish, I tell you! Very much a workers' type of thing, but fantastic food. Then we'd go to a different place for breakfast, have maybe English. Yeh, I enjoyed Penang very much. So, going on the visa-run wasn't a penalty for me, it was a joy."

So, in which part of Thailand did you actually live?

BP: "In Pattaya, a place called Pattaya Klang."

Situated 62mi/100km south east of capital, Bangkok, on the Gulf of Thailand's east coast, Pattaya became popular with American servicemen during the Vietnam War. Having previously been a small fishing village, it subsequently thrived as a tourist destination, many ex-servicemen returning in the eighties and nineties to run establishments in which they'd previously spent their dollars. Today, at least half the bars and restaurants in the city are Western-run. As for inhabitants, there were 104,000 registered dwellers in 2007, but, including non-registered residents and those who work but don't live in the area, the population numbers around 300,000 at any given time (some estimates place the figure at half a million). It is Thailand's second most visited city, after Bangkok.

The *Rough Guide to Thailand* (publ. 2012) sums up the city thus:-

"With its streets full of high-rise hotels and hustlers on every corner, Pattaya is the epitome of exploitative tourism gone mad…the city swarms with male and female prostitutes, spiced up by Thailand's largest population of transvestites (katoeys)," while the beach is described as "the noisiest, most unsightly zone of the resort, crowded with yachts and tour boats, fringed by a sliver of sand and a paved beach front walkway."

The entry concludes:-

"More recently, there has been an influx of criminal gangs from Germany, Russia and Japan, who reportedly find Pattaya a convenient centre for running their rackets in passport and credit-card fraud, as well as child pornography and prostitution; expat murders are a regular news item in the *Pattaya Mail*."

All of which, to an outsider, seems rather like a vision of Hell on earth, but is it really as ugly as it sounds? I never got a chance to put this question to Bob, but, from past conversations, I know that he seemed to enjoy the commotion and general excitement of the place. He communicated as much – and more – to colleague, David Allan:-

"He never used to have too much success with the ladies, although always charming and polite with them. But he found that in Thailand, they appreciated the more 'rotund' figure, shall we say, and ended up living with about three of them on a ranch, I believe. He went from thinking of nothing but country music to the other extreme. Tom T. Hall was going to write a song about it!"

So, where exactly did he make his home in this overcrowded place?

BP: "I initially rented a house where, for some reason, they wouldn't allow me any electricity, so after about six months, I found out about this house through a friend of Walter, who then became my neighbour. This place was cheaper, anyway – and very nice. As you went in, there was one big area and I had my little cooking stove with a gas container and a refrigerator nearby, plus the Thai toilet [basically, a hole in the ground] to one side.

"There was no upstairs, of course. Then, outside [rear], there was an open area where I had the washing machine – I couldn't actually be overlooked here. Then I had my office, plus a bedroom, which incorporated another, more conventional sit-down toilet, a couple of metres from my bed. It was also the only place with an air conditioner, which, to begin with, I used all the time. Later, I would only put it on for an hour at night, maybe go into the office for a while, come back and it would be cool enough. But I would have two fans on throughout the night, then I would sleep during the afternoon with the air conditioner on, but at nights, you didn't need it."

Describe a typical day:

BP: "I leave the house at about 6.30am, go through a little gate and cut across the side of a football field (unless wishing to go the long way, in which case, I walk around it). This takes me to the main road, where it's possible to hire taxis. It's also where the FOODLAND supermarket is located. On weekdays, I meet an Englishman (whose name I forget) and an American, Colby Haggard (no relation to Merle!), from Texas, and we have breakfast together. Being the best time of day, weather-wise, I stay out, maybe get some shopping, after which I come back, say between 9 and 9.30, when it starts to get hot. I then generally don't go out again until evening time."

You'd stay inside the house throughout this time?

BP: "No, usually outside. There was a large, overhanging wooden canopy at the front of the property under which I'd have a desk and chair. You'd buy a pack of these little, curved acrylic devices for about 25p, which you separated before attaching to a piece of metal and lighting – each lasted three hours and kept the mosquitoes away."

Was there a garden?

BP: "Only at the front, consisting of, basically, a banana tree (which I planted myself) and a palm tree, but I had to keep cutting back the former as it secreted a sticky substance that got on my clothes, so the palm tree provided most shade and seclusion."

How about the local area – was this noisy and crowded?

BP: "Well, there were many people about, because Katoeys (lady-men) lived on the block, though we didn't have a lot to do with each other. The thing is, the rent was

£40 per month – very cheap, even back then, yet a lot of money for locals, so only the top Katoeys could afford it. There were these very big shows, like the 'Alcazar' show, and these were the performers."

Was there much crime?

BP: "An expat neighbour, Thelma, was robbed several times because the back of her property was like a jungle – easy to break into – whereas there were houses the other side of me and I never did get broken into. The other good thing: the Katoeys would come back from their show about midnight, and stay outside gossiping until four or five in the morning. Someone said, 'If you sign a petition, they'll go away.' But I replied, 'Let them stay, because they're keeping the thieves away!'"

How about the general lifestyle?

BP: "I must confess, I never realised what a big difference there would be between visiting the country and living there. It's a whole different mind-set. Once you get into that mind-set, you're fine. I mean, while tourists go around at three o'clock in the afternoon, I'm at home with my air conditioning on, because that's a hot time of day."

Was the heat a problem, then?

BP: "Not really, despite my reply to Dolly's letter informing me of the 76ᵒF (24ᵒC) temperature in England: 'We haven't had weather that cold since I arrived here two years ago!' It was never unbearably hot – except during the hot season, which is why we loved the monsoons, because they ended the hot season. Although in films, they may appear to go on for 12 months, they actually last for just three – where I was, anyway."

You did not use your own car, so was travelling a problem?

BP: "Absolutely not! At the lower end of the scale, there are rickshaws, which operate in Malaysia but not Pattaya or Bangkok. To be honest, I only got one once – the guy kept bumping into things and didn't seem to know where he was going! Next up would be tuk-tuks, which operated in Bangkok, but not in Pattaya, or Georgetown, as far as I remember. It's a cheap mode of transport, which I used until metered taxis came in, outdoing the old, clapped-out licensed cabs that had previously been making a fortune by screwing tourists. From then on, I used nothing but metered taxis.

"Motor-cycle taxis are very popular throughout Thailand, but I know nothing about them – I don't have the figure – but you just sit behind the rider, rather precariously, in some instances.[109] In Pattaya, I used, almost exclusively, pick-up trucks, which are not nearly as horrendous as they sound. With stairs at the rear of the vehicle, you sit 'up-top.' They're hired as either a bus or taxi. For a 'straight-ahead' trip, you just put out your hand, and in my day that would be 10 baht. Alternatively, you point in a certain direction, but it's still considered a bus ride at the same price. However, if you want to go to a

---

[109] Bob recalled one particularly steep hill area of Penang that bicycle vendors would negotiate with the aid of motor-bike riders, the technique being that they (the bike riders) would place a hand on the cyclists' backs and carry them up alongside them. "An amazing sight," he said.

specific place, then you speak to the driver and it's treated like a cab, but still reasonably priced."

How about 'haggling' – was this commonplace?

BP: "To be honest, most of the stuff we bought was in supermarkets – it's only when you went to a street market this happened. And then the procedure is quite straightforward, as illustrated by the 'Dave Travis' incident: when they say '50 baht' or whatever, you say '20,' and you know you'll end up paying thirty something. You just do it, but, to be honest, it was a very small part of our life."

Were you ever recognised by *London Country* fans?

BP: "Yes, three or four times. Once, on the 'Visa-Run' train, a passenger in the seat opposite instigated the following conversation:-

Passenger: 'Excuse me, did you ever work for Radio London?'

BP: 'Yes, I did, for many years.'

Passenger: 'You presented the Country show, didn't you?'

BP: 'Yes.'

Passenger: 'Well, I don't like country music, but I kept tuned to Radio London and I recognise your voice!'

"Then, a part-Indian fan who lived in England but who happened to be in Thailand recognised me and requested an interview, to which I consented. The article was supposedly submitted to *Country Music People*." [Though editor Craig Baguley claims never to have received it].

What about the rumour of your death?

BP: "The first I learned of it was upon receipt of a letter from Craig Baguley which said, basically: 'Are you dead?' He'd heard a rumour, apparently. This was followed by a couple of similar letters. I responded by quoting Mark Twain: 'Reports of my death have been greatly exaggerated.'"

Have you any idea how it started?

BP: "Well, there were a lot of local drug-related murders – one in particular involving a poor Canadian kid who reportedly died from natural causes but when his body was returned home to Canada, they found his tongue had been cut out."

What about some of the characters you became friendly with?

BP: "There was Walter [a neighbour, two doors away], through whom I got this house. Firstly, it must be said he was the biggest liar in the world – Walter Mitty, I called him. When he died, we had to go through his stuff, and only then discovered he was married with a kid, which he denied he ever had. There was also a picture of him in Russian uniform…but his biggest lie was that he was born in Toronto sometime around 1920, then joined the Canadian Army before travelling to England and switching to the British Army. So I said, 'You must have seen a lot of the 'Leafs' [Maple Leafs, ice hockey team], then.' And he hadn't the slightest idea what I was talking about – well, that's like living in London and not knowing who Arsenal and Tottenham combined are!

"And it turned out that he went to England when he was five with his mother, after she divorced her husband. What we think is that he never fought. Because he was over in Canada, he was never on the radar to be called up, and I think he wriggled around and managed to succeed in not joining any of the services, though he claimed to be an officer. What he did do, after the war, was join the NAAFI, looking after clubs in Berlin for British officers, that sort of thing…"

But you remained friends?

BP: "Well, we fell out a few times. Once, when we weren't talking, I came across a book by Oscar Levant I knew he'd like, so bought it for him – and we were friends again. He was the most difficult man in the world, but then, when he became really ill with emphysema and needed me, I looked after him for two years, until he died in hospital – three of us even clubbed together after his death to pay off his debts. The postscript to this story is that his married son came over for his funeral and promptly fell in love with a go-go dancer – but don't ask me how the 'romance' turned out because I steered well clear of it all!"

Other characters?

BP: "Well, there was another neighbour, Thelma, not the most charming lady in the world – a loud, abrasive Australian with a toy-boy, police sergeant lover, yet with plenty to say about the morals of others! Then there was this retired American Army sergeant, a scholar of history, with very right-wing views, who may or may not converse with you, depending on his mood. There was also another American, whose father had been No.2 animator at Columbia Pictures back in the 40s and 50s, but who never made his own mark in movies. He used to sell dodgy film reels under the title *De Lorentis* (deliberately misspelt) *Films*. We got along reasonably well, though he was a bit of a bull-shitter, to be honest."

Around the mid-nineties, the Thai government started making life difficult for their not-so-welcome visitors, announcing that they must apply for a proper visa or leave the country. However, with Bob preparing to pack up, the situation suddenly changed…

After experiencing the world's highest economic growth rate from 1985 to 1996 – averaging 12.4% annually – Thailand, in 1997, suffered increased pressure on its currency, the baht, leading to flotation. The subsequent (January 1998) low point of 56 baht to the dollar (from a consistent 25) triggered the Asian financial crisis, which, in turn, caused the authorities to reverse their earlier decision, bearing in mind the economic repercussions of repatriation. Nevertheless, within three years, the reprieved and relieved expat *would* be homeward bound – but not as a result of any government ruling. It was much more pragmatic than that: quite simply, his money had run out…

BP: "I thought I would die 5 years or so into my Thailand retreat and that would be it. I didn't count on surviving into my 70s, let alone returning to England!"

Even allowing for his unexpected longevity, Bob might have been able to remain in his exotic locale for life, but for two unforeseen occurrences:-

1.   When discussing the Soi Watom 'affair' with me, he hinted that, as well as a partner, a considerable sum of money was lost into the bargain, making a dent in his already shaky finances.

2.   In 2001, he endured a frightening bout of concussion in a Thai hotel room, with no recollection of the circumstances. The subsequent hospital bill precipitated his return to England, with financial assistance from the British Embassy.

And so, the freewheeling expat was forced to return to the land of his birth – but what sort of reception would he find there?

Chapter 12

Homecoming: 2002-2014

"Boomerang"[110]

Sidcup is a town of around 60,000 inhabitants situated within the London Borough of Bexley, 11mi/18km south-east of central London, its name (first recorded in 1254) deriving from Cetecopp, meaning flat-topped hill.

Among its landmarks are a hospital, leisure centre, rugby club and two colleges – *Bird College* (music and dance, named after former resident, Doreen Bird) and *Rose Bruford* (drama, named after its founder, in 1951). There are also a number of manor houses, including *Frognal House*, the birthplace and residence of Thomas Townsend, 1st Viscount Sydney, after whom Sydney, Australia is named (this is now converted for use as residential and nursing accommodation), *Lamorbey House* (occupied by *Rose Bruford* students – referred to in Chapter 1, footnote 7) and *Manor House*, a Georgian listed building currently used as a Registry Office. Additionally, there are several areas of green space, notably 250-acre Footscray Meadows, incorporating one of the district's most identifiable

---

[110] *Boomerang.* For background information on this song, see Chapter 1, Footnote 17.

features, Five Arches Bridge that crosses the River Cray.

The town is mentioned in two well-known plays and their film adaptations: Noel Coward's *Relative Values* and Harold Pinter's *The Caretaker*. Also, in early episodes of classic BBC1 sitcom, *Porridge*, starring Ronnie Barker, Brian Glover's character, Cyril Heslop, mentions that his wife's sister, Gwendoline, lives there.

Famous people connected with the area include:-

- Sir Edward Heath, who represented the constituency as a Member of Parliament for many years, serving as Prime Minister from 1970-74.
- Steve Backley, Olympic javelin silver medallist, born in Sidcup, currently living in nearby Chislehurst.
- Gary Bushell, journalist and author, currently lives in Sidcup.
- Tommy Connors, songwriter (*Lili Marlene, I Saw Mommy Kissing Santa Claus*), lived in Sidcup.
- John Paul Jones, Led Zeppelin bass guitarist, born in Sidcup.
- Rob Knox, actor, murdered in Sidcup, 2008.
- John Regis, Olympic athlete and world indoor sprint champion, lived in Sidcup.
- Dick Taylor, founder member of Pretty Things and early Rolling Stones bass guitarist, schooled in Sidcup.

Although legend states that world-famous, veteran rock 'n' rollers Mick Jagger and Keith Richard first agreed to form the Rolling Stones after meeting on a platform at Sidcup railway station, it's more likely the encounter happened (purportedly on 17 October, 1961) either on the train itself or a couple of stops down the line at Dartford. (Perhaps the fact that Keith was on his way to Sidcup Art

College confused the issue.)

The town is located 4mi/6km from Bob's birthplace, Bickley, 10mi/16km from his adolescent home in Sevenoaks and 2mi/3km from 70s/80s dwelling, Broomwood Road, St. Pauls Cray, meaning that, on arrival here at the tail end of December, 2001, he found himself back on very familiar territory.

Unsurprisingly, the returning exile, with just £40 in his pocket, received no red carpet treatment from the land where he made his name – indeed, he was reduced to seeking favours from friends unseen and uncontacted in years. Many gave him the cold shoulder, but then, people move on and don't always appreciate faces from the past reappearing in their lives, especially when the person concerned put 6,000mi/9,600km of space between them in the first place. However, some responded kindly: neighbour Dolly Waterton put him up for a few nights, her son, Rob, repeating the gesture at his Sussex pub – on this occasion, for 10 days.

By this stage, thanks to cashing in his father's War Bond certificates, and several loans, the itinerant DJ had managed to gather together sufficient funds to rent a room at the home of friend and businessman, Del Grace. However, the arrangement lasted only a month before he was moving on again – this time to a small flat above the Tudor Café in Maidstone Road, just a stone's throw from where *CMP* used to be printed in Cray Road. An insight into his lifestyle at this time is provided by Jon Philibert, who kept a diary. The entry for Tuesday, 23 July, 2002, reads:-

"I leave half an hour early at 5pm and make my way…to *CMP* HQ. Julie has already gone home and it is just Craig and I to meet Bob Powel. Eventually, we get to his old stomping-ground of Footscray and Craig finds

Bob's street. I stay in Craig's SUV while he goes over the road and calls for Bob. Through the back window, I can see Bob and we smilingly greet one another – outwardly (and there is not a lot of outward). He doesn't seem to have changed at all, the same thing he tells me.

"We find the Indian restaurant about a mile away – apparently a recommendation of Craig's friend, Bruce. There is one other diner when we get there and we settle in. We order and as we wait for the food to arrive, Bob tells us a little of his current lifestyle. It is exactly diametrically opposite to his previous lavish, consumerist, material way of living he had before he went to Thailand. He is on the dole and really on his uppers, living on about £6.50 per day. It is rather sad to hear how he is struggling, yet he says it is a discipline he quite enjoys. His eyes light up with almost religious fervour when he speaks about the new simplicity. However, stories of coupons, two-for-one blueberries from Tesco and second-hand charity shop stuff finally gets to Craig, and he guffaws, 'How the mighty have fallen,' though this is not malicious and taken in good heart…At the end of the meal, Bob lurches off to the loo and I suggest that Craig and I pick up the tab. He agrees, although I'm not sure his heart is 100% in it. Bob, however, is genuinely grateful – I tell him he probably bought me a meal or two 'when times were better.' We drive back to his lodgings – not the first place we picked him up from and I wasn't quite sure what was going on there – entering it from the back, an alley with no lights, with Bob imploring Craig not to drive off until he was safely up the stairs, using the car's headlights to guide him.

"Craig drives me home, though we say fairly little, as we are both tired. Interesting evening."

Not much is known of the subsequent five year-period, except that Bob continued to keep in touch with old friends, even applying for a few jobs, all while maintaining a low profile. One lesson learned fairly rapidly was to phrase his sentences differently – he realised this when, informing people he'd "been away for 10 years," he began receiving very odd looks! Then, in February, 2007, he uprooted once again, for the last time.

This move, bringing him even closer to *CMP*'s ex-printing works in Cray Road, afforded him the luxury of a garden. The property itself, 31 Amberley Court, was a pleasant-looking ground-floor maisonette, one of around 30 similar dwellings situated in a quiet close at the foot of Sidcup Hill, his occupying a corner position and flanked by tall conifer trees to one side.

After visiting singing cowboy Rex Allen in the late 1980s, Bob had imagined living in similar surroundings – a comfortable ranch in an attractive rural setting. Well, Sidcup is not Tucson, and a humble ground floor maisonette no ranch, but if his reduced circumstances bothered him, he didn't acknowledge it, as he repeated to me frequently: "I grew up in some grandeur and understand what that lifestyle entails, so I could care less about it, now." And, just as he coped with being away from home, family and friends at boarding school, so also he adjusted to the new situation without fuss or complaint.

Increased immobility blighted these later years, but the computer provided a lifeline, enabling him to keep in touch with friends and colleagues around the world. Additionally, to fill his leisure time, he, although living close to a social club that featured regular 'country music' evenings, preferred to download from the internet obscure recordings of (invariably) country artistes, usually dating from his favourite era, the 1950s. Of 'non-country' artistes, he liked Bing Crosby, Dean Martin and Edith Piaf best – these were all 'hoarded' for future use at some unspecified date, along with thousands of movies. Here, he was far more eclectic than in his musical tastes and a list of favourite actors and actresses would probably fill this page – Cary Grant, David Niven, Alastair Sim, William Powell,

Myrna Loy, to name just a few – plus any number of obscure character actors, who held a special interest.

As for comedians, Bob Hope, Milton Berle, Victor Borge and Jack Benny (a great favourite) could all bring a smile to his face, as could British funny men Ronnie Barker ("absolutely brilliant"), Morecambe & Wise, Kenneth Williams (in 'Rambling Syd Rumpo' mode only), Billy Dainty, Harry Secombe, and many more. (Within country music, of course, old favourites Homer & Jethro reigned supreme). A list of favourite TV programmes would be too long to reproduce, but quiz shows, *Pointless* and *Would I Lie To You?* ranked highly. 'Online' versions of solitaire, roulette and horse-race betting (small stakes only) all helped alleviate those periods when his favourite sport was out of season...

Baseball was not always his No.1 sporting passion. An avid ice hockey fan from childhood, Bob felt the game did not translate well to a television sport because of difficulty in following the puck. The many trips made to Nashville over the years converted him to baseball – just seeing it on TV, or, less frequently, in person. Only once did he attend a match with a country star, when, accompanied by Allen Reynolds and son, he watched Nashville Sounds play (marred only slightly by the boy's constant questioning – well, there are a lot of rules). Being a son of Quebec, Montreal Expos[111] were for many years his favourite team. However, when the club moved to Washington DC after season 2004 (becoming Washington Nationals), he began following Canada's only other major league baseball team,

---

[111] Major League baseball team formed in 1969. They were named after the *Expo 67* World's Fair held in the city, the name being chosen as it is the same in French and English, keeping speakers of both languages happy. Won East division title 1981 and were well ahead in 1994 when a players' strike wiped out last 8 weeks of the season.

Toronto Blue Jays.[112] In later years, he was never happier than when propped up in bed, every convenience known to man (and some unknown) within easy reaching distance, watching a major league baseball match on TV ('Snub' Pollard[113] would have been proud of him!) And this is invariably how you would have found him on any given evening between April and October, with the game in-season.

Bob was a dedicated nature lover and, although having only a small garden, thanks to generous feeding on his part, it served as a mini-wildlife sanctuary for birds, foxes, squirrels and frogs – plus Georgia the (neighbour's) black cat, with whom he had a love-hate relationship (owing to her habit of preying on birds and fish). All came and went freely, attracted by the pond and bird-bath/feeding-table, invariably well-stocked with fat balls, halved coconuts and bird seed. Not wishing to miss any of the activity, he rigged up a camera to capture every second – the slightest movement and his gaze was diverted from the Toronto Blue Jays on 'screen one' (TV) to the Sidcup blue tits on 'screen two!'

A lifelong teetotaller and non-smoker of tobacco or

---

[112] Major League baseball team located in Toronto, Ontario, founded 1977, members of American League. Named after bird of the same name – plus, blue is the colour of the city's two other professional sports teams, Maple Leafs (ice hockey) and Argonauts (American football). Currently (2015) only MLB team outside US. World Series Title: 1992, 1993. Eastern Title: 1985, 1989, 1991, 1992 1993.

[113] 'Snub' Pollard – Australian-born 'silent movie' star (real name Harry Frazer). The reference concerns his 1923 silent classic, *It's a Gift*, in which he employs all sorts of labour-saving gadgets to make life easier for himself, including a breakfast-cooking device (operable from bed, of course) and car that runs by magnet! Although making the transition to 'talkies', he never rose above bit-parts.

anything else, this was compensated by his love of food, a favourite dish being Parma ham served with slices of melon, closely followed by stilton cheese with water biscuits – all washed down with large gulps of Diet Coke! For his last meal on earth, however, he once claimed he would opt for something a little different: corn on the cob, with fresh blueberries for dessert. His funeral directions were equally straightforward – and blunt: "Just dig a hole in the garden and bung me in it, to the accompaniment of any music – except *Golden Guitar* by Bill Anderson!" (Well, he got one out of two).

When it came to sweeter delicacies, Bob freely admitted to being an incurable chocaholic: "If you were to let me loose with a million pounds and dare me not to spend it, I could manage to restrain myself quite easily, but put me in a room full of chocolate and I'm not sure I could last out a day!" Consequently, if you had opened almost any drawer in his house, you'd have been confronted with boxes of the stuff. In light of all this, it's hardly surprising he had some fairly serious medical conditions – he took 15 tablets a day, to help cope with conditions such as hypertension, poor blood circulation, stomach ulcer, leg cramps, hay fever and any number of other allergies.

In 2009, his health deteriorated to the extent that he had difficulty in breathing, resulting in a recommendation for major heart surgery. And so it was that, on 10 April that year, Bob entered St. Thomas's Hospital, London, for an aortic heart valve replacement operation. Thankfully, this proved successful, although only after an incredible 'post-op' period of 56 hours in a coma. He followed up this traumatic experience with a 4-week spell in a convalescent home in Herne Bay. Subsequently, although gaining a large scar on his chest and increased medication, he made a full recovery.

Bob had no strong political convictions – nevertheless, I asked him once how he generally voted.

BP: "Well, I used to vote Conservative, and I voted for – to my undying shame – Margaret Thatcher. But what did it for me was the Falklands War. People forget that the reason the Argentinians had the courage to invade was because she scrapped *HMS Endurance*, the only battleship the Falklands had, so I hold her responsible for the lives that were lost."

So, which party did you switch to?

"I voted for Blair, and then the Liberal Democrats last time."

As for religion, it was a subject we rarely discussed. For one thing, I knew his anti-Catholic (my faith) views, he having once quoted examples of how the Church in Canada had abused its power. Although he described himself as "agnostic", he was first and foremost a humanist, someone who recognised the good in others, without necessarily acknowledging the God behind their actions.

I'm not sure if Bob truly respected human beings for anything other than the talent they possessed, but I do recall his once expressing a certain admiration for ex-TV producer turned painter/mystic, Jack Good, best known for the pioneering 1950s UK teenage pop shows, *6.5 Special* and *Oh Boy*. And there are parallels between the two men: early retirement from the entertainment profession, followed by a period spent living abroad (Good lived reclusively in New Mexico for a number of years), before a return to the UK, in relative obscurity. Good famously depicted TV as the Devil in one of his paintings. While I don't think Bob felt that way about radio, it was always fairly obvious where his heart lay.

In his more fanciful moments, Bob liked to imagine living aboard the 44,000-ton cruise ship, *The World.* Launched in March, 2002 and operated by ResidenSea, headquartered in Miramar, Florida, the ship serves as a residential community owned by its residents, who number between 100 and 300 (excluding guests), representing about 40 different countries. They live on board as the ship travels the globe, staying in most ports from two to five days. Some reside permanently, while others visit periodically throughout the year. Boasting 12 decks and employing 250 crew members, its facilities include 6 restaurants, a grocery store, delicatessen, boutique, golf simulator, putting green, full-sized tennis court, jogging track, gym, movie theatre and library. Understandably, Bob felt that this luxurious existence might suit him rather nicely. He never made it, of course, but then as the price for one studio unit is in the region of $600,000, he hardly had a chance.

Was he star-struck? In the early years, I think definitely so. However, he claimed that, "once I got to meet the legends behind the music, I completely forgot who I was speaking to and their reputations meant nothing." Perhaps, but, the fact is, stars' names were never far from his lips, and the following chapter provides some insight into his relationship with these gifted individuals whose world he shared.

Chapter 13

Stardom

Don't Let the Stars Get in Your Eyes ("Don't let the moon break your heart...")[114]

As a dedicated journalist and radio host, Bob had the opportunity to meet literally hundreds of country stars over the years – meet, interview, and, even, on occasion, stay with them. Perhaps the greatest of all – and certainly one of his favourites – was legendary 'singing cowboy', Tex Ritter. Born Woodward Maurice, on 12 January 1905, in Murvaul, Texas, to German-American James Everett and Martha Elizabeth (nee Matthews), Ritter, having briefly studied law at the University of Texas, became a weekly featured singer at radio KPRC, Houston in 1928, soon thereafter moving to New York, where he participated in various stage and radio productions and cut several records before relocating to Los Angeles. Here, he

---

[114] *Don't Let the Stars Get in Your* Eyes. As well as providing a transatlantic No.1 pop hit for Perry Como in 1952, this country standard achieved Top 10 country chart status for no fewer than four different artistes that same year: Skeets McDonald (No.1), Slim Willet (No.1), Ray Price (No.4) and Red Foley (No.8). Other performers to have recorded versions include: Johnnie & Jack, Slim Whitman, Boxcar Willie and Jerry Lee Lewis.

embarked on a series of westerns (over 70, between 1936 and 1948). In 1942, he signed to Capitol Records, leading to numerous hit singles. A founder member of the *Country Music Association*, he was elected to its *Hall of Fame* in 1964 and also has a star on the *Hollywood Walk of Fame*. In 1970, he surprised many people by entering Tennessee's Republican primary election for the United States Senate (losing to Bill Brock).[115]

A fan from childhood, Bob claimed to have subsequently enjoyed a father-son relationship with his hero – a claim made by at least two other country music media people: American DJ Ralph Emery and Bob's own friend and colleague, Tony Byworth. Although hardly seeming likely, if anyone could fill the paternal role for multiple individuals, then it would be the larger-than-life Texan. As a house guest with the Ritters for several weeks in 1972,[116] adopted son No.1 was privileged to observe the superstar up close – not that there was anything particularly 'starry' or extravagant about the man.[117] Nevertheless, he proved a fascinating subject, especially,

---

[115] Accused of being too traditional in his outlook, Tex once imparted this piece of German philosophy to his (then ultra-liberal) children: "He who is young and is not liberal has no heart; he who is old and is not conservative has no brains."

[116] During this stay, Bob suffered the indignity of being locked out of the house! Arriving back late one night and receiving no answer, he ended up sleeping in his car. Although Tex's kind-hearted but rather forgetful wife, Dorothy, was full of apologies the next morning, their guest decided to book into a motel for the remainder of his Nashville visit – just in case...

[117] There is a story, related by Brian Golbey, of how Tex was spotted by a fan as he sat in Nashville's *Linebaughs* café. Getting excited, this dedicated follower of celebrity began rattling off a list of the many other Hollywood stars he had encountered, at the end of which the expressionless Ritter commented drily: "Well, the only one you need to see now is Rin-Tin-Tin and you'll have the full set!"

his guest felt, first thing in the morning, when, hair rumpled and seemingly half-asleep, he would shuffle in to breakfast, occasionally delivering terse, grumpy, responses which, when properly digested, revealed a wit as sharp as any early morning razor! As for social occasions, with wife Dorothy beside him, the couple presented a formidable, often humorous double-act, as he introduced her thus:-

"This is my wife, Dorothy – I couldn't do without her-"

Dorothy (interrupting) "-but he'd like to try."

Tex (as if enjoying the thought) "But I'd like to try…"

In fact, they remained married right up until Tex's death on 2 January, 1974, from a heart attack suffered while visiting band member Jack Watkins in prison. (Watkins, once married to singer, Connie Smith, was accused of failing to pay maintenance to an ex-wife – not Smith).

To long-time Bob Wills vocalist Laura Lee McBride, guesting on *London Country* in 1979, the host confessed to knowing "a hundred Tex Ritter stories – most of which we cannot say here, though if you get me drunk, you dear listeners, I might tell them to you all." Thankfully, two have surfaced without discernible alcoholic consumption on his part, the first imparted to the aforementioned Mr. Emery, a *London Country* guest in 1978:-

"Some years ago – it seems to have passed, now – there was a trend in Nashville for women to wear their hair in beehive style (which Barbi Benton described rather well as 'early waitress'). Well, at the *Convention* around then, I bumped into Anne Murray. I thought she looked terrific and told her so. 'Thank you,' she replied, 'but I've got less hair than the rest of the girls. Sharing a room with around five of them, I was nearly asphyxiated by the hairspray!' Now, I happened to be staying with Tex at the time and, after I repeated the story, he shot back: 'Tell her if she'd been sharing a dressing room with the men, she *would* have been asphyxiated by the hairspray!'"

The second involved a concert appearance at which a fan called out for the old Marty Robbins number, *El Paso*. Without batting an eyelid, the masterly performer responded: 'Buddy, I've recorded 2,400 tunes – and, once I've learned them, I'll learn *El Paso!*'

Actually, there are two further Tex Ritter stories, albeit ones in which the star played only a passive role. The first involves ex-record dealer (now sheet-music collector) Dave Turner, who, about to submit an original composition to his hero (with a view to recording) during lunch at 1970's *Wembley Festival*, was advised to hold off until Ritter had finished his meal. Meanwhile, from out of nowhere, a 'man-with-a-mic' appeared to conduct an interview – and Dave's chance was gone. However, he's forgiven his friend, Bob Powel, who was only doing his job – with customary excess zeal!

The other, as related by Goff Greenwood, occurred while the *BCMA* co-founder was staying in Nashville in the mid-70s. Awakened in the early hours of the morning by fellow-guest Bob Powel, he was suddenly given the sort of invitation most music fans would jump at: "Goff, get yourself ready, we're going to meet Elvis at Graceland. Tex Ritter is taking us – you and me!" If, however, the 'intruder' expected equal enthusiasm in return, he was disappointed, as Greenwood explains:-

"I knew Tex's fondness for the old chuck wagon. We'd be stopping a lot for grub and the Nashville to Memphis mileage is considerable – Cadillac or not. Also, what would we say to Elvis? 'I like your Sun records, man.' Added to which, I had arranged to meet Waylon Jennings, followed by a full dance with Ray Price & Cherokee Cowboys – definitely more preferable, to my mind."

Though he put his case "diplomatically," Greenwood claims his ever-keen buddy was "incensed" at missing out on this once-in-a-lifetime opportunity, an assertion that must be accepted, since the incident was never mentioned by Bob to me during his lifetime.

Although the majority of Tex's appearances came in western movies of the 30s and 40s, it is for his recording of the song, *High Noon* in the 1952 film of the same name (in which he did not appear), that he is most well-known, and for which he won an Oscar.[118] In that same early 50s period, another singing star with a similar first name was just beginning to make his mark in westerns. Known as the 'Arizona Cowboy', Rex Allen, like Tex, achieved Hollywood fame by portraying the clean-cut, God-fearing American hero of the wild West, who wore a Stetson hat, loved his faithful horse (Koko) and had a loyal buddy who shared his adventures. As a singer, his biggest successes were *Crying in the Chapel* (later covered by Elvis), No.4 country/No.8 US pop in 1953 and *Don't Go Near the Indians*, No.2 country/No.17 US pop in 1962. Again like Ritter, he was awarded a star on the Hollywood Walk of Fame for his contributions to the motion picture industry, while, in later years, he narrated a variety of films, most notably Walt Disney's *The Incredible Journey* (1963), possibly the greatest ever animal adventure. He also invested shrewdly in Disney stock.

---

[118] His choice to perform this classic song prompted the jokingly derogative response from Dorothy: "Frankie Laine was out of town!"

Among Bob's many interviews – nearly all of which were conducted one-on-one and face-to-face – that with Rex Allen stood out in his memory. The long-awaited opportunity to meet him arose when, having use of an office at Allen Reynolds' Nashville publishing company in the late 1980s, he learned that Reynolds' accountant, a beautiful lady named Terrell Tye (now sadly deceased), was the former wife of Rex's son, Curt, and, luckily, still on friendly terms with her ex-father-in-law. She must also have taken a liking to this keen, young English-Canadian, for, no sooner had he requested it than an interview was arranged.

Never having been to Arizona before, Bob, on the journey to Rex's home outside Tucson, felt as though he were in a western movie himself – sun beating down, parched desert landscape dotted with cacti as far as the eye could see and a confrontation between, in effect, two strangers – though it would not end in a shoot-out! (In fact, he almost never made it, owing to several hair-raising, 'cliff-edge' moments during "the most terrifying car ride I've ever had in my life"). Eventually, arriving at Rex's home, 'Lone Steer' ranch – so named because there was just one steer in residence[119] – he surveyed his surroundings with a degree of awe, admitting to Allen, "This is where I'd like to live." Instead, he had to content himself with the next best thing, which, in many ways, represented the fulfilment of a childhood fantasy: meeting a western hero admired from afar, the trip through prairie country, ranch standing stately amid rugged terrain and, best of all, the 'hero' looking and acting the part. As such, the encounter was rather different from his initial meeting

---

[119] Rex, who in his younger days worked as a cowhand and rodeo contestant, liked to practise his roping skills on a mechanical bull kept at his ranch. When asked why he didn't use the real animal, he replied, "Are you kidding? I leave that son-of-a-bitch alone!"

with another boyhood idol, Tommy Collins (see Chapter 8, Footnote 96).

Despite living alone, Rex did not seem lonely. On the contrary, the 69-year-old – named Arizona's 'Man Of the Year' in 1966 – possessed an air of contentment that perhaps only those nearing the end of a life well-lived are granted and his interviewer felt this was how all cowboys, whether real or mythical, should spend their final days (if not having been gunned down in their prime). He sensed an affinity with the soft-spoken individual – less famous than Roy Rogers or Gene Autry[120] but arguably tougher than either. In Bob's words, they "got along," and the one-hour scheduled interview stretched to a seven-hour social occasion before they finally went their separate ways, never to meet again. (As a footnote, Rex died exactly ten years after this interview, on 17th December, 1999, when, suffering a massive coronary, he collapsed in the driveway of his home, unfortunately incurring additional injuries when his caretaker accidentally ran over him in the driveway).

Dolly Parton, in many ways, represents the antithesis of the rugged, wayfaring cowboy of American mythology, yet she can easily match the Tex Ritters and Rex Allens in terms of world acclaim – and outdo the two combined in wealth. From a journalistic viewpoint, however, global superstardom has its drawbacks and a one-on-one interview proved impossible to arrange. Bob, therefore, had to content himself with being part of a large group of journalists at an official press conference. Nevertheless,

---

[120] Jimmy Wakely, guesting on *London Country*'s 'Western' show, broadcast 17 December 1977 (but recorded a year earlier), provided an amusing anecdote of the difference between these two great 'singing cowboy' stars: "They'd both make ideal neighbours," he says. "Roy Rogers, if your kitchen sink failed, would fix it for you. Gene Autry, on the other hand, would claim not to have the time – instead, he'd *buy* you one!"

with just one question, he was able to lift the veil of secrecy surrounding reclusive husband, Carl Dean – someone who, up to that point, no one, not even the notoriously persistent paparazzi, had been able to photograph.

Having brushed aside a previous question on this subject, the famously well-endowed blonde is in no mood to yield, but the canny Canadian, having done his homework, adopts a more subtle approach:-

"Dolly, who's the young man pictured on the front cover of your solo album, *My Blue Ridge Mountain Boy*?"[121]

The normally self-assured glamour-girl is wrong-footed and can only exclaim in disbelief:-

"How did you know *that*…?"

"Know *what*, Dolly," responds Bob, innocently.

Cover blown (literally), Mrs. Carl Dean has no option but to confess all:-

"Well, I must admit, that *is* my husband."

The news is duly reported in the tabloids the following

---

[121] *My Blue Ridge Mountain Boy*, issued on the RCA label in September, 1969, is Dolly's fourth solo album and, as the only one of her recordings never to have been issued on CD, the most sought-after. Despite reaching No.6 on the country album chart and containing some well-known tunes, including *Daddy* and Elvis's *In The Ghetto*, it failed to yield any hit singles.

day. Additionally, the details are subsequently confirmed in a *Country Music Television* interview with singer Patty Loveless some years later. Today, of course, one has only to tap in relevant details on a computer keyboard to view all the photos one wishes of the supposedly camera-shy Mr. Dean.

Bob delighted in catching people out with his quick wit – and the bigger the name, the more he enjoyed it – as on the occasion he met up with singer-songwriter and host of (American) TV's long-running *Hee Haw* show, Roy Clark, who apparently prided himself on having an exceptional memory. Clark greeted his friend brightly, "Howdy, Bob – last time I saw you was in Saginaw [or wherever]."

"Really?" came the response, "that's funny, the last time I saw you was in Montreal!"

"Montreal?" queried Clark.

"Sure," said Bob, "I was taking a shower and you were on *Hee Haw!*"

Being in the media business, Bob needed to get along with everyone he encountered, especially the stars themselves. However, while obviously not deliberately aiming to upset anyone, his natural tendency to be open and forthright did, on occasion, cause a degree of friction. An early example might be his tackling of Buck Owens (*CMP*, June, 1970), following the star's withdrawal from a British tour. Later, in November 1985's *CMP*, Bob, via *Powel's Page* – reproduced in full below – illustrates the point, citing examples where five particular country performers had to accept that, whatever the consequences, honesty must take priority:-

"You have a great job, doing for pay what we pay to do, some say, and I can't really argue with that. Not many people have the luck to turn their hobby into a full-time job. What makes country music such a great business to be in is that the great majority of the people are so nice, from the band members to the managers to the stars. I have friends in all three categories, and even though most can hardly be described as bosom pals, nearly all the artistes I have met are delightful people. Mind you, I have had the odd disagreement: during my first stint as *CMP*'s editor, I did an interview with Canadian Ray Griff, who wrote the song, *Canadian Pacific*. He was most upset that I concentrated on his friendship with Jim Reeves and was even more upset when I printed his letter and stated in my reply that the reason I did not print that much about Ray Griff himself was because he was (and sadly still is) totally unknown over here. That does not stop me playing his records on my radio show as he is a talented fellow. The fact that he has all but disappeared now upsets rather than pleases me. Perhaps his attitude didn't help but he is a superb writer and a very fine singer.

"One slight problem going on at the moment concerns a superstar that normally I get along with very well. I have known Conway Twitty for years and he has always gone out of his way to be helpful. I have managed to get interviews with him when representatives of much larger publications have tried and failed. For instance, this Easter, after completing his performance when he had a serious throat problem and was feeling like death, he got up early the following morning to appear on my radio show for an hour and a half. In his eyes, I guess it looked like I repaid his helpfulness by printing a letter about him that accused him of drinking. The letter in question by reader G.A. Palmer, in the June issue, heavily criticised Conway's performance and some people have read into the letter an inference that Conway was drunk. Firstly, it was pointed out to me, not by Conway directly but from someone close to him, that I should have mentioned his sore throat. I disagree with that, as Conway himself didn't mention it on stage – in other words, he was quite content to let his performance speak for itself, and I thought, as he did that, so should I. The second point is less clear-cut. Mr. Palmer's statement in his letter didn't strike me as an allegation that Conway was drunk. If it had, that would have gone in, because I have known Conway since 1969 and I happen to know that he is a teetotaller. I still do not read that inference into the letter, but some of Conway's fans and friends did, so a little coolness awaits me, possibly, next time I see him, but as Conway is a very nice and reasonable guy, I'm sure we will soon be friendly again.

"An earlier example was when Tom T. Hall got so upset with me he even had a go at me in his autobiography.[122] Now, at the time, Tom was my favourite living singer (he is not all that far down the list, now), so it comes as a shock when your favourite has a go at you in his book. I felt Tom's ire when I started to criticise his records in my record reviews. Every journalist worth his salt will totally disregard any friendship he has when it comes to giving an opinion. I just felt Tom's records at the time (this was the mid-seventies) were not up to the standard of his brilliant early ones, and it was my duty to say so. I've done that since, too. George Hamilton IV, who is everybody's friend, made a point of my programme getting the very first radio play of his latest single at the time. On air, he asked my opinion, and on air, I told him. George naturally took it like a gent. I hasten to add there are a lot of his records I like – that wasn't one of them.

"Jim Glaser made the same mistake in 1984, when he, like Conway, went out of his way to do my radio

---

[122] *The Storyteller's Nashville* by Tom T. Hall (published by Doubleday, 1979). In the relevant passage, Hall complains that "after spending time with me and getting to know me better, he [Bob] wrote some very unflattering reviews about my music. (Familiarity breeds contempt)." Bob's typewritten response to Tom T. is included in the illustrations section of this book.

programme and then asked my opinion of his album. When you think how many hits that came from *The Man in the Mirror*[123] on a commercial basis, at least I was proved to be wrong. Jim took it like the friend he is. Later, back at the hotel, drinking with the likes of Lee Greenwood, Ray Pillow and David Frizzell, he announces to everybody: 'See this guy? Because he is an old friend, I curtailed a sight-seeing trip to do his show, and how does he repay me – by telling everyone he doesn't like my album!'[124] He said that with a twinkle in his eye and, happily, like Tom T., George and, I'm sure, Conway, we are still mates!

"Yes, it is a fun business, but you sometimes do upset people by telling the truth, but I feel that I should never lie or even disguise my opinion. In the long run, it would be doing the artiste a disservice and it would also make life just that much duller. It also would not be fair to you, the readers. Not only that, but soon you would realise that some artistes are getting a favoured treatment and my publication and myself would lose its credibility, and that would be fatal."

Another star Bob managed to upset, albeit in a light-hearted way, was singer, Garth Brooks. Invited by Garth's then-publicist, Tony Byworth, to interview the up-coming performer, he happened to be in the studio when Brooks laid down tracks, including *I Know One*, for his debut album and couldn't resist mentioning that the song had previously been recorded by Jim Reeves – a fact unknown to the singer, who immediately tackled producer, Allen Reynolds:-

---

[123] *Man in the Mirror*, issued on the Noble Vision label, reached No.16 on the country album chart in 1983.

[124] Bob's response to this remark (not mentioned in his article) was: "You forgot to mention something, Jim – you asked my opinion."

GB: "You didn't tell me this had been recorded by Jim Reeves."

AR: (Awkwardly): "Oh, didn't I…I thought I did…"

At this point, feeling he had not caused quite enough mischief, Mr. P. followed up with:-

BP: "Of course, more recently, Charley Pride covered it…"

GB: (Incredulously) "*What*?!"

In the event, Brooks went ahead and recorded the song, which duly appeared as track 10 on his eponymously titled debut, released in 1989 – and producer Reynolds continued talking to his friend, Bob Powel.

Still, many stars have cause to be grateful to the publicity-generating DJ – and not just in a professional sense: Steve Young, for one. The Georgian-born singer-songwriter, whose composition, *Seven Bridges Road*, was recorded by the Eagles on their 1980 *Live* album, had just appeared on *London Country* when he found himself being treated by the radio host to a day-long tour of England's capital city. At this time, due in no small measure to the effects of drink, the singer was considerably overweight.

The day passed pleasantly enough, but was not thought of much again by the DJ – until, some years later, along with Glaser Brother, Chuck, he happened to visit a coffee club in Austin, Texas, where Young was due to perform. Seeing a slightly built guitarist take the stage, he enquired of the organiser when the main star was due to appear. "That's *him*!" came the reply. Speaking after the gig, Young confessed that the unscheduled outing years earlier had proved to be a watershed in his life, as he had planned a very different type of tour that day – one incorporating local boozers. However, managing to stay sober for 24 hours provided the impetus he needed to quit for good, the weight loss being visible proof of his success. (His host must have been quite an impressive tour guide, as Faron Young fiddler, Ernie Reed, recalls being treated, along with another band member, Dave Hall, to a similar tour in 1969, viewing "the sights that no one would normally get to see," adding, "45 years later, I still remember that trip.")

But how about stardom on Robert Powel's own account? Did opportunity ever come knocking for him? The answer is 'yes.' Twice, in fact – both in his formative years, the first arriving at the tender age of 5, when, being the cutest, most loveable child in town, he was chosen to play the rear end of a furry caterpillar. The setting: St. Michael's Church hall, Sillery. The anticipation: enormous. Everything, in fact, was set for a grand evening's entertainment, the only problem being that, mid-performance, the rear end of the caterpillar started spilling its load, the inhabitant's wriggling attempts at re-entering causing hysterics among cast and audience alike.

Perhaps because of these unscheduled gymnastics, his second role, as Frosty the Snowman in a Christmas panto, involved no movement at all – and no talking. The only requirement, in fact, apart from allowing himself to be covered in balls of cotton wool, was to stand perfectly still while the other children danced and sang around him. He managed to achieve this and surely made a fine Frosty, but no agents happened to be in the audience that night, and young Bobby's acting career melted away as quickly as it had begun. That's the trouble with peaking at the age of 5 – it's all downhill from then on…

However, the experience wasn't wasted, and he became quite adept at observing others perform and then reporting it – in the process, achieving a modest degree of fame. Not that he would have concurred – in fact, in terms of celebrity, he rated himself "not so much a 'D' list as 'Z' minus," a belief reinforced by his experiences at the *Wembley Festival*, where, signing autographs for eager fans, he would catch sight of them afterwards scrutinising his handwriting for clues to the writer's identity!

Nevertheless, it was occasionally brought home to him that some people, at least, regarded him as one of the privileged few, an example being when his Aunt Molly in Canada met a young country fan at a party, and, seeking common ground, mentioned her nephew's involvement in the business. On quoting his name, the fan responded incredulously, "You know *Bob Powell*!!" Which, naturally, came as quite a surprise to a family member so far removed from both London and country music, generally. On another occasion, a lady, obviously familiar with his work, approached him backstage at the *Opry*, expressing admiration. It turned out she was the Everly Bros.' mother, and the object of her adulation never did find out how she came to know of him.

Then there was Cliffie Stone. When introduced to the multi-faceted performer at a songwriter's convention, Bob discovered once again that his fame had preceded him. It transpired that Stone, while holidaying in England, had visited the *Cutty Sark* in Greenwich, London. There, he happened to sit down next to an avid country fan who suddenly turned to Stone and asked permission to tune his radio to *London Country*!

There are also instances of Brits abroad surprised to discover that their DJ friend was known and loved in foreign parts – like Stan Laundon, who, on a visit to Lafayette, Louisiana for the Festival Acadiens, happened to be relaxing in a local bar. On mentioning he was from England, the first question asked by a fellow patron (being unused to visitors from that part of the world) was, "Do you know Bob Powel?" Veteran UK country performer/frontman Frank Jennings had a similar experience while staying at a hotel near Utrecht, Holland, after spotting the globe-trotting DJ "strolling up the road like he owned the place," adding, "anybody who was anybody in country music back then knew Bob – knew him and respected him."

In fact, the 'faceless' radio presenter managed to acquire a reputation for being a scene-stealer, displayed to best effect during a brief spell early in his career, when he became known variously as the 'Demon with the Polaroid' or the 'Phantom Flasher' – a figure dreaded by all would-be posers and limelight-loving country stars. David Allan recalls: "He had this Polaroid camera and he'd get all these stars to pose, he'd take the picture, put the camera down and the flash would go off. This happened again and again!" Chet Atkins certainly did not appreciate his efforts, describing him bluntly as "a lousy photographer." However, in a November, 1969 article for *Opry* magazine, the 'Flasher', perhaps stung by Atkins' criticism, states proudly that "in his (Atkins) honour, I have purchased a brand new Polaroid camera, which, unlike my previous, slightly antiquated model, actually works!" Subsequently, on *London Country*'s 24 March, 1979 show, he feels sufficiently confident to gently deride the photographic skills of guest Jim Glaser, who happens to own a – very expensive – Hasselblad!

Despite the many country legends interviewed and friendships formed over the years, the one thing that impressed *musicians* most was the fact that Bob attended Albert Lee's *Country Boy* session. This came about in late 1970, when, following a Tumbleweeds concert, bass player Dave Peacock invited him to a Head, Hands & Feet session at which the track was recorded. While finding the occasion enjoyable, Bob did not pretend to have appreciated its significance at the time. (The recording surfaced on the group's eponymous debut album, issued in

1971, although the song has subsequently been re-recorded both by Albert and several others, including Ricky Skaggs, for whom it provided a No.1 country hit in 1985.)

Being primarily a fan, Bob (apart from those childhood flirtations) enjoyed little of the adulation accompanying stardom, but on one occasion, he was treated to a small sample. It happened at the home of country music, the *Grand Ole Opry*, where a backstage pass also entitled him to attend performances, if desired. One Friday night, spotting a seat in the front row – slap bang in the middle – he thought: "I'll sit here until I'm thrown off." Snapping away merrily with his camera, the first artiste to spot him was (he thinks) Jim Ed Brown, who introduced the reluctant 'celebrity' to the audience, obliging him to stand and take a bow. Shortly afterwards, good friend, Skeeter Davis, took the stage. The stars never watching each other's shows, she was unaware of what had taken place earlier and repeated Jim Ed's gesture, requiring our hero to once again face the spotlight, a little more self-consciously now. A third recognition from a performer brought an embarrassed shrug of the shoulders and hasty sit-down – but when the procedure was repeated a fourth time, although tempted to crawl under the seat, he instead stood there, rather sheepishly, able only to utter a profound "SORRY," to the audience – still, not everyone can say they took four bows at the *Opry*![125]

Bob's job brought with it plenty of travel, which he enjoyed. Deciding to take this a stage further and sample the ultimate in luxury, he booked a Concorde flight – on three separate occasions. The first, taken purely for pleasure, was paid for by himself, shortly after the prestigious airliner

---

[125] Bob believed the many visits made to the *Opry* over the years helped make him such a familiar figure among country performers – just sitting in the lounge between shows, communicating with people.

began commercial flights in 1976, and among his co-passengers on the trip were such luminaries as Yehudi Menuhin, Johnny Dankworth, Cleo Laine and Ray Ellington. This was a one-way only trip (to Washington – New York having imposed a ban), but because he had enjoyed the extra comfort involved, he decided to return on a first class flight, which, in the event, turned out to be a waste of money – little different to economy level, and certainly not in the same league as Concorde.

The second occasion was born of desperation. In New York with time running short and a show to do in London the following day, he received the devastating news that his flight had been cancelled, leading to an audacious suggestion of the supersonic alternative. Much frantic activity ensued before, finally obtaining a seat aboard Concorde at the very last minute (and at no extra cost), he, as in all the best movies, tore across the tarmac and scrambled aboard, with seconds to spare.

The third and final flight also proved the most enjoyable. Having paid £1,350 for his initial (one-way) venture, he, for the same price, now obtained not only a flight to New York but also a three-day stay at the *Waldorf Astoria* plus QE2 trip home, the motive on this occasion being to stock up with albums for the shop, any profit offsetting the cost (theoretically, at least). The date of this particular trip – 14 October 1987 – was easily remembered since it preceded by one day the Great Storm that struck the UK that year.

Chapter 14

Album Compilations

Kindly Keep it Country ("That's good enough for me...")[126]

In my *CMP* obituary for Bob (June, 2014), I neglected to mention his album compilations, an oversight of which he would undoubtedly have disapproved, for it was a task he not only took seriously, but enjoyed immensely.

By 1970, having established himself as a country music authority – and 'name' in journalism (though not yet radio) – he began to receive requests to provide liner notes for record releases, both individual albums and boxed sets, frequently being asked also to choose the relevant tracks – a labour of love for an enthusiast such as himself.

Never keeping a record of these assignments, it's impossible to know how many releases bear his name but, as he and colleague Tony Byworth (engaged in similar work) usually drew attention to the fact in their *CMP* album reviews (which were fairly comprehensive), the total

---

[126] *Kindly Keep It Country.* A No.48 country hit for co-writer Hank Thompson in 1973. A different, self-composed song with the same title provided Vince Gill with a No.33 country hit in 1998.

can be roughly estimated to be close to 100, of which he had managed to trace around half by the time of his death.

Bob once told me that, when choosing tracks for various artistes' compilations, the trick was to include as many well-known, popular titles as possible, regardless of whether or not they were original versions, the reason being that the casual buyer is more attracted to familiar song titles. Consequently, a feature of these issues is the preponderance of lesser-known versions of popular tunes.

The following lists record releases for which Bob supplied sleeve notes:-

* Track listing also chosen.

O No official acknowledgment on sleeve.

A – BOXED SETS

Title/ARTISTE	(Label/No.)	Discs(Tracks)	Year
Country Music's Golden Hit Parade /VARIOUS O	*(R. Digest, GMUS 6A)*	6 (96)	1976
150 Top Ten Country Hits/VARIOUS	*(R. Digest, GTEN-A-079)*	8 (150)	1981

(During his stay at a convalescent home in Herne Bay, Kent, following his 2009 heart operation, Bob, to his delight, discovered a copy of this in the library).

B – INDIVIDUAL ALBUMS

Title/ARTISTE	(Label/No.)	Discs(Tracks)	Year
Country Tonic /MEDICINE BOW	(Lucky LUS3009)	1(12)	1970
The old and the new /BRIAN GOLBEY	(Lucky LUS3010)	1(11)	1970
Johnny's Cash & Charley's Pride /MAC WISEMAN	(RCA LSA3210)	1(11)	1970
Famous Country Music Makers/G. HAMILTON IV	(RCA DPS2043)	2/(33)	1972
Golden Hour presents Country Music Greats/V.A.	(Golden Hour GH816)	1(24)	1972
King of the Ring /BRIAN MAXINE	(Starline SRS5140)	1(14)	1972
Reflections/TOM T. HALL	(Mercury 6338 194)	1(14)	1972
Int'l Ambassador of C. Music /G. HAMILTON IV	(RCA-LSP-4826)	1(10)	1973
Famous Country Music Makers/ VERNON OXFORD	(RCA DPS2045)	2(27)	1973
For the good times/V.A.*	(Nashville Int. NAL5008)	1(16)	1973

Country Comedy /HOMER & JETHRO*	*(RCA LSA3172)*	1(14)	1973

(Being a huge Homer & Jethro fan, of all his compilation albums, this is the one Bob treasured most, but unfortunately, he was never able to track down a copy in later years, though he almost certainly would have had one originally.)

Title/ARTISTE	(Label/No.)	Discs(Tracks)	Year
Best of, vol. 2/GEORGE HAMILTON IV	*(RCA LFLI7504)*	1(14)	1974
Canadian Country /V. A.ᴼ	*(RCA LSA3208)*	1(16)	1974
Famous Country Music Makers /HANK LOCKLIN*	*(RCA DPS2060)*	2(32)	1975
Famous Country Music Makers /CHET ATKINS	*(RCA DPS2063)*	2(32)	1976
(Liner-note duties shared with Roger Camden)			
25 years of Top Ten Country Hits/V. A.*	*(RCA LSA3263/4)*	2(25)	1976
The Versatile /SKEETER DAVIS*	*(RCA LSA3269)*	1(16)	1976
Famous Country Music Makers /CONNIE SMITH*	*(RCA PL42000)*	2(32)	1977

Sing the songs of Harlan Howard /V. A.*	(RCA PL42012)	1(16)	1977

(This album caused Bob some embarrassment, as, after compiling it, he discovered that one of the tracks, "A Thing Called Sadness," was written not by Harlan Howard but by his fellow Acuff-Rose songwriter, Chuck Howard, a mistake easily made since Acuff-Rose's catalogue lists writers by surname only. Harlan apparently took the error in good humour, calling out to his namesake whenever they met: "You've got a song on an album you shouldn't have!")

Title/ARTISTE	(Label/No.)	Discs(Tracks)	Year
Best of/CHARLEY PRIDE	(RCA PL42014)	1(12)	1977
Hits of/HANK SNOW	(RCA PL42175)	1(14)	1977
Hits of/WAYLON JENNINGS	(RCA PL42211)	1(13)	1977
Tribute to Hank Williams/V. A.*	(RCA PL42281(2))	2(30)	1977
This Is/LORETTA LYNN*	(Music For Pleasure MFP50329)	1(14)	1977
16 No.1 Country Hits/V. A.*	CBS Embassy 31456)	1(16)	1977
Radio London Tapes /BRIAN GOLBEY	(Waterfall TAD001)	1(12)	1977
(Tracks include 'Uncle Coosie')			

No.1 Country Hits /BUCK OWENS	*(Music For Pleasure MFP50357)*	1(12)	1978
The great MERLE HAGGARD sings*	*(Music For Pleasure MFP50392)*	1(14)	1978
Int'l Festival of Country Music /V. A.*	*(RCA PLA2407(2))*	2(32)	1978
Hits of/RONNIE MILSAP	*(RCA- PLA2429)*	1(14)	1978
Best of Music Country America vol. 3/V. A.	*(MCA MCF2829)*	1(20)	1978
Famous Country Music Makers /BOBBY BARE*	*(RCA PLA2958(2))*	2(40)	1979
20 Golden Country Instrumentals/V. A.	*(R. Digest RDS9660)*	1(20)	1979
Country Line Special/V. A.*	*(Music For Pleasure MFP50427)*	1(12)	1979
Tribute to Hank Williams /DRIFTING COWBOYS	*(Standing Stone- SSDC1234)*	2(20)	1979
(It's uncertain whether Bob chose the tracks for this.)			
?/WILF CARTER	*(RCA PLA0518)*	1(16)	1980
(Album withdrawn on release)			
16 No.1 Country Hits vol.2/V. A.*	*(CBS Embassy 31805)*	1(16)	1980

Side by Side/V. A.*	*(CBS Embassy 31812)*	1(16)	1980
Instrumental Country vol. 2/V. A.	*(CBS Embassy 31861)*	1(16)	1980
Nashville's Finest Hour/V. A.*	*(RCA PL43207)*	1(23)	1980
For the good times/BILLIE JO SPEARS	*(Music For Pleasure MFP50515)*	1(14)	1981
Keep on truckin' /V. A.*	*(RCA Int'l INTS5076)*	1(20)	1981
Hey! Where ya' goin' /FRANKIE MILLER	*(Bear Family BFX15082)*		1982

(One reason Bob enjoyed compiling albums so much was that he could indulge his tastes to a certain degree. Frankie Miller, an obscure 1950s country/rockabilly singer who once recorded for Starday, is a case in point. Bob certainly never managed to locate this album just as I haven't managed to trace track details).

Title/ARTISTE	(Label/No.)	Discs(Tracks)	Year
20 of the best/PORTER WAGONER	*(RCA INTS5197)*	1(20)	1982
Capitol Country Gems/V. A.*	*(Music For Pleasure MFP50550)*	1(14)	1982
Wild 'n' Cajun /JIMMY C. NEWMAN	*(RCA London PL70437)*	1(11)	1984

In the pines /DOC WATSON	*(Sundown SDLP1012)*	1(12)	1984
Mr. Entertainer /JOHNNY RUSSELL	*(RCA NL9000)*	1(16)	1987
John's been shuckin' my corn /ONIE WHEELER	*(I & B IB1001)*	1(10)	?
Duets, country style/V. A.	*(R. Digest RDS9157)*	1(18)	?

Chapter 15

Conclusion

Sunset Years of Life ("Not one moment of regret...")[127]

How will Bob Powel's contribution to (UK) country music be assessed in years to come? And what will be his legacy? There has been recognition over the years: the 'Mervyn Conn Award' for the person who contributed most to country music in Britain during 1972, US *Billboard* magazine's 'Country Music Media Award' (on behalf of *CMP*) in 1975, and *Country Music Association (GB)* 'Outstanding Achievement Awards' in 1975 and 1988. There may have been others, but he kept neither a record (these were discovered by chance in old editions of *CMP*) nor actual trophies, which may seem rather strange, offensive even, to the people/organisations who presented them. However, quite apart from storage problems during his Thailand stay, he did not appear to value such things very highly, preferring to let the work speak for itself. (Might a certain embarrassment over those early career progressions also have been a factor?)

Impresario Mervyn Conn, in his book, *Mr. Music*

---

[127] *Sunset Years of Life* – Written and originally recorded by Red Hayes. For further comment, refer Chapter 6.

Man,[128] claims much credit for the impact of his *Wembley Festivals*, held from 1969 to 1991 (+ 2012): "Before (them), the image of country music was all about hillbillies sitting on bales of hay and straw hats and dungarees and the music was completely overshadowed by rock and roll. Within a year of starting, I had turned this on its head and country became a massive industry as a result." A bold statement, but who am I to argue? I would, though, venture to suggest that Bob's role in spreading the gospel in this country via radio and the printed page was at least as effective, if more subtly so.

Regarding professional recognition, having taken every advantage of situations that fell in his favour before making an early exit from the industry that had been good to him, he probably did himself no favours. And yet it's hard not to sympathise with the genuine, accessible-to-the-end music lover who lived his final years practically in penury while the many country stars whose careers he boosted, often at his own expense, reaped the benefits of success in their gold-plated, out-of-reach *Mansions on the Hill*.[129]

Could Bob have performed DJ duties within the current musical climate, one wonders? Well, age should have presented no barrier – if Jimmy Young can continue broadcasting up to the age of 81, David Jacobs to 87 and Brian Matthew (86 and still going strong), then, why not

---

[128] *Mr. Music Man – My Life in Showbiz*. Mervyn Conn with Andrew Crofts. Published by Tonto Books Limited 2010. Copyright © Mervyn Conn and Andrew Crofts 2010.

[129] *Mansion on the Hill* – Hank Williams (co-writer with Fred Rose) reached No.12 in the country charts in 1949 with this ballad, subsequently recorded by dozens of artistes, including Charley Pride, Glen Campbell, George Jones, Emmylou Harris, June Webb, Michael Murphy and Ray Price, the last three-named charting in 1958, 1976 and 1977, respectively.

Bob Powel at 72? Whether a place could have been found within the industry for his brand of merry mayhem is another matter. Bearing in mind the current obsession with 'crossover' music, he may have felt obliged to compromise, or broaden, his tastes. In fact, he was quite dismissive of the trend towards 'all-in' music, especially when artiste-led, as he explained:-

BP: "Bill Anderson told me once that the four (Anderson-composed) songs included on Dean Martin's country album received more radio plays than his last 20 albums combined! And, of course, they (the artistes) want to get into that, but the idea of not splitting the music into separate categories means that every radio station would be the same. They'll start with Rachmaninoff, then go to light opera, then go to Louis Armstrong, then to Bill Anderson…it wouldn't work, but the artistes dream of that situation."

There's no doubt Bob was generally satisfied with the way his career panned out – but could it have been better? Were there areas of his ability he failed to exploit? One of his strengths lay in holding strong opinions and having the courage to air them. David Allan, recalling his *CMP* days, says, "He was very opinionated but that was good because it made the magazine individual."

However, an equally forthright approach with performers was not always appreciated, Bill Anderson's 'song narrations' episode being a case in point. Don Williams seemed similarly unimpressed when urged by the DJ to revive early composition, *You Have A Star* (*LC*, 8 May, 1983), while further examples of unfavourable responses are given in his November, 1985 *CMP* article (Chapter 13). Others proved more accommodating: Hank Snow welcomed his thoughts on whether he (Snow) should quit RCA for a new label, and a recommendation to Tex Ritter, made on behalf of Texan-born songwriter Billy Joe Shaver, resulted in Ritter recording Shaver's *Willy, the Wandering Gypsy and Me.*

Exploring different avenues, Bob, early in his career, flirted with artiste management, both the Jonny Young Four and singer/musician, Brian Golbey, coming under his wing. Neither lasted long, as, by his own admission, "it just wasn't me." Likewise, despite attending countless sessions over the years, he never sought involvement in the production process, content merely to observe. As for the two co-compositions, *Tadoussac, You're Calling* and *Uncle Coosie*, he claimed modestly that his contribution consisted purely of "providing background information."

And yet the reluctant 'musician' ALMOST made a record of his own – at the invitation of Ritz Records boss, Mick Clerkin. Since taking charge of the company in 1981, the astute Irishman had focussed attention on boosting the careers of established Irish artistes, in the process building an impressive roster of chart acts, among them the Fureys with Davey Arthur (*When You Were Sweet Sixteen* – No.14, 1981), Foster & Allen (*Bunch of Thyme* – No.18, 1982 and *Maggie* – No.27, 1983) and, of course, the supremely successful Daniel O'Donnell, who, although not established when signed to the label, soon became so.

Aware of his DJ friend's vocal limitations, Clerkin suggested a narration, the proposed title, *Old Paint*, coming from Bob himself, who knew of the song through a version by country comedy duo, Homer & Jethro (he would never undertake a sad or sentimental-type narration). Attempting to boost the performer's confidence, Clerkin promised the record would notch up one sale, at least: to Irish country star – and Ritz co-owner – Larry Cunningham. Whether he was serious or not will never be known, for, at this point, the project fizzled out. Not as a result of cold feet by any of the participants but rather a case of other things getting in the way – or perhaps it was just forgotten about. Whatever the reasons, it left the question of whether the presenter might make a good song interpreter unanswered. Still, one can't help but feel that, with his fine vocal projection and authentic Welsh roots, there must have been a great singing voice hidden in there somewhere ("If so, it's extremely well hidden," said Bob).

The Welsh connection leads to another celebrity from that part of the world, a man for whom our subject was occasionally mistaken, and who gained equal fame as a singer and comic: the late Sir Harry Secombe.[130] Born in Swansea on 8 September, 1921, the third of four children, Secombe managed to stay at the top of his profession throughout life, in the process developing considerably diverse talents: operatic singer, straight actor (*Sunstruck*, 1972), host of his own TV show, religious presenter – as well as a solo comedian. Awarded a knighthood in 1981, he died on 11 April, 2001.

So, might Robert Powel, if not as a singer, have earned his living as a comic? There are certainly enough amusing episodes from his childhood – and beyond – to support the notion, and, interestingly, he did not discount the idea, citing stints compering at the *Tramshed*, Woolwich, the *Grosvenor Ballroom*, London, and even in Dublin, Ireland, as examples of how he could cope in front of a 'live'

---

[130] British comedian, Max Bygraves, encountering Bob (then sporting long, bushy sideburns) at Radio London's front office, cried out, "Hello, it's Pickwick!" (Harry Secombe played lead role in the 1963 stage musical adaptation of Dickens' novel, *Pickwick!* plus a subsequent TV version). Later, in Thailand days, Bob was once greeted in the street with a shout of, "It's Russell Grant!" to which he fired back, "It used to be Harry Secombe!"

audience. Of these assignments, he told me, "I thought I was quite good, but my heart wasn't really in it." With his penchant for corny jokes, he might almost be described as a country version of fellow radio DJ, Tony Blackburn, and, ultimately, that is about as close as he came to fulfilling his comic potential.

On the journalistic side of things, quite separate from his work in the country field, he contributed articles to *Weekend* magazine, notably one (unlikely to ever resurface) extolling the virtues of American cooking, together with a photo of him consuming an oreo fruit! There were also Radio London news-reading assignments, which garnered critical acclaim, but insufficient financial reward to warrant taking up full-time.

Bob nurtured a secret desire to write, together with an undisguised admiration for songwriters, generally, especially country songwriters, and among his most cherished interviews was that with the late Harlan Howard. Born on 8 September, 1929 in Harlan County, Lexington, Kentucky, Howard notched up an impressive record of 147 hit country compositions up to 2005, including: *Pick Me Up On Your Way Down* (biggest early success, a No.2 country hit for Charlie Walker in 1958), *Heartaches by the Number* (a huge transatlantic pop hit for Guy Mitchell in 1959), *I Fall to Pieces* (a No.1 country hit for Patsy Cline in 1961, co-written by Hank Cochran), *The Blizzard* (No.4 country, 1961) and *I Won't Forget You* (No.3 UK pop, 1964), both by Jim Reeves, and many more familiar titles. Soul singers, in particular, seemed drawn to his heartfelt, lyrical style, notably Joe Simon (*The Chokin' Kind*) and Ray Charles (*Busted*), and it's telling that he cites Fats Domino and Chuck Berry as influences. Howard died in 2001, aged 74.

During the aforementioned interview (*CMP*, March, 1972), Bob, caught up with his guest's enthusiasm for the subject, declares his own 'mantra' on country music: "If you don't feel it, forget it," a sentiment obviously shared by Howard, for, some years later, while leafing through a copy of *Billboard* magazine dated 19 September, 1986, what should the amazed DJ come across but that very quote – uttered by Howard himself – with no due reference to its source. ("It's there in print," said Bob, incredulously). Needless to say, the prolific writer was sharply reminded of the phrase's origin on their next encounter, prompting him to hold up his hands in acknowledgment of blatant plagiarism – possibly for the only time in his life! The irony is that Howard had an oft-quoted 'mantra' of his own – his definition of what constitutes a great country song – "Three chords and the truth." Still, at least he refrained from putting chords and a tune to his 'plagiarised' title!

Being fond of catchphrases, it's probably inevitable Bob should discover one of his creations turn up as a fully-fledged song: *Do us a favour*, *You know what I'm like*, *Exactly*, *I wanna show you something*, *That's true*, *Leave it for now* – even *It does happen* or *You do get this* (all legitimate BP-isms) – any of these he might have expected, even accepted, being 'lifted.' But *Herman Schwartz*...?

For reasons unknown to anyone (including himself), this had been a 'nonsense-name' coined by him and indiscriminately dropped into casual conversation when and wherever the fancy took him. Doing so in London or Las Vegas is one thing. Doing so in Nashville – 'Music City USA' – is another, one that might be construed as an open invitation to song-muggers. So, perhaps he shouldn't have been surprised when a record called *Herman Schwartz* duly appeared on the country chart, written by Jerry Foster and Bill Rice and sung by Stonewall Jackson, the single reaching No. 41 in 1973. What hurt most of all was not the royalties missed, but the fact that no one believed the title was his. Well, now the world knows – although, of course, it might just be an amazing coincidence...

And what of his abilities as a talent-spotter? Did he have the perception to recognise special qualities in others?

The following quote is from his very first article for *Country & Western Roundabout* magazine in 1966, written shortly after observing a newcomer perform at Albuquerque, New Mexico the previous year:-

"(This) up-and-comer will undoubtedly be a big star soon."

The artiste's name? Merle Haggard. Meanwhile, to Don Ford (4 December, 1976), he laid claim to being first to spot Don Williams' talent:-

BP: "In spite of what Tom Whelan says, I was first into Don Williams in this country. I interviewed Don in the States in 1971 and we had to sit on the interview for six months because he only had one record out. I was playing his first single in 1971, which was not a great hit, but the second, which I think was *Come Early Morning*, was a big smash and started the Don Williams thing."

(Tom Whelan ran the *Four-On-The-Floor* Club, Hounslow, Middlesex, to which Don Ford's magazine is affiliated.)

A lady born Brenda Gail Webb nineteen years after sister Loretta Lynn earned the Powel vote of confidence in April, 1971's edition of *Country Music People*:-

"Also scheduled to be part of the Loretta Lynn show this year is yet another relation...a 16-year old beauty called Crystal Gail...I saw Crystal on the Decca show in Nashville last October and I'm convinced that she has a very big future ahead of her."

The spelling mistake is forgivable, as Ms. Gayle had not long changed her name and, obviously, had yet to achieve the super-stardom that came her way in the 1970s and beyond.

Of course, not all 'Powel's predictions' proved accurate – failures include: Linda Flanagan (whose recording of Dottie West's *There's Love All Around Me* he felt "inexplicably" 'bombed'), the Allen Reynolds-produced Mike Campbell, and Faron Young bass player, Dave Hall, who "discovered that establishing a solo career takes more than mere talent."

Bob's own success was due to a combination of hard work, talent and, most of all, sheer force of personality – with his enthusiasm always to the fore. Does he consider this a fair assessment?

BP: "I suppose so. I built up the 'larger-than-life' aspect a bit – it was a way of attracting people, generating interest, that sort of thing."

And, finally, would you like to summarise your career?

BP: "My determination was to have a radio programme, I had a radio programme. I met nearly every country star worth bothering about and I loved the music more than anything else. I think the thing I'm most proud of is that I made a job that didn't exist before, being one of the first to earn a living out of country music when very, very few people could, so it was good. All in all, I achieved what I wanted to achieve."

Chapter 16

Reflection

Adios Amigo ("Adios, my friend...")[131]

This chapter was to have featured a list of Bob's Top 100 country recordings, along with comments. However, as: a) at last count, the total stood at three hundred and something, and: b) I never saw the list, anyway, I shall instead focus on the final three and a half years of his life. (To compensate, an estimated list of 20 of his favourite recordings is included in the *Appendix*).

They say the only way to have a happy ending in a country song is to sing it backwards. And that certainly would seem to ring true in the case of Bob Powel. His childhood years (up to the age of 12, at least) were almost blissfully idyllic, the final ones, in Sidcup, considerably less so – except that he never viewed things in such black and white terms. To him, the whole of life was a journey, an adventure to be undertaken boldly, not a disjointed series of events, to be rated on a scale of one to ten for

---

[131] *Adios Amigo.* This Ralph Freed composition gave Jim Reeves a No.23 UK hit single in 1962 (but no US country chart placing).

enjoyment. In his own words, he "rolled with the flow," savouring the good along with the not so good. As one of the few people to share his latter-day experiences, I'm in a better position than most to assess his frame of mind during this period of his life and I shall now endeavour to convey as accurately and sensitively as possible the Bob Powel I knew.

I remember clearly the day I first met Bob: it was 22 November, 2010. The date remains firmly embedded in my mind because, apart from its being the anniversary of President John Kennedy's assassination, finally encountering this country "icon" (David Allan's words, not mine) whose radio show provided such a special musical backdrop to my growing up in the 70/80s was a big event for me. Well, he was one of the few DJs – country or otherwise – who affected me in any positive way and whose enthusiasm I admired and – to a degree – shared.

In fact, I shared many traits with Bob: a deep love of music, a similar birthdate: 16th of the month (he in January, me in March), each live(d) in two-bedroomed ground-floor maisonettes in Sidcup, both fascinated by Hollywood movies (even bearing famous actors' names), and, most importantly, both "Fans" – with a capital F – and obsessive record collectors.

On a personal level, neither of us married (although, as indicated, there are doubts about that as far as he is concerned), both teetotal, non-smokers, the youngest in our respective families, with one sister (I also have two brothers) and good, loving parents who stayed together into old age. In many other respects, we were total opposites – not least, physically – but, whatever the intricacies of our relationship, I sensed a 'chemistry' there, from the start.

Once, while conducting a spoof interview with me, Bob asked how I first heard of *London Country* and my earliest memory of it. Sadly, I could not recall either. I had not been a regular listener to Radio London, so assume it was on someone's recommendation, or perhaps it had been mentioned in *Country Music People*. As I replied at the time, it just seemed to be always *there*, throughout those two decades when country was at its most popular in the UK. Even so, I can't honestly claim to have tuned in religiously each week, and, as with so many of the best things in life, probably did not fully appreciate the show's worth until after it had gone (although I liked it sufficiently to tape several programmes, long since lost or deleted, unfortunately).

From speaking with other casual listeners, the general perception held (including by myself) was that, on the show's demise in 1988, its host had returned to Canada, and, in truth, I doubt that I gave either him or his programme much thought throughout the 90s. Well, life moves on, after all. However, around the turn of the millennium, with both country and pop growing increasingly bland and predictable, my thoughts began straying to those golden days of *London Country*. Where was its genial host now? Perhaps the resurgence of bluegrass also rekindled my interest – it seemed to be one of the few musical genres sounding – to my ears, at least – as good as, if not better than ever. Or maybe I was just indulging in morbid nostalgia...

Whatever the motivation, at odd intervals, I found myself 'Googling' Bob's name on the internet, once even phoning Dave Cash's Radio Kent country show for a clue to his whereabouts, Dave's brief 'on-air' response providing the first inkling that he was in Thailand. Well, that's that, I thought.

And so it might have remained, but for the fact that, in September, 2010, I came across a UK website (countrymusic.org.uk) whose forum contained comments not merely alluding to Bob but addressed directly to – and from – him, for he was back in this country, having recently undergone open heart surgery. Glad of the opportunity to post a comment of my own, I wished him a full recovery and thanked him for his part in furthering my country music education. I honestly did not expect a reply – however, a few weeks later, an email arrived from him, inviting me to phone. Being a mobile number, it provided no clue to his whereabouts, although of course, if I'd thought about it, with *CMP* having been printed in Sidcup during his editorship and the CMP Shop (which I visited a few times) being located in nearby St. Pauls Cray, I might at least have recognised his connections to the area.

Nevertheless, upon making the call and learning that he lived just down the road from me, I was amazed – and when, during our brief conversation, he extended an invitation to visit, I felt I must be dreaming. But the meeting did indeed take place…

Now, when visiting the Powel household, I soon learned there were 3 important rules to observe:-

1.   DON'T touch anything,
2.   DON'T criticise the state of the place or his lifestyle,
3.   NEVER interrupt when he's talking.

Of these, I found No.3 the hardest to abide by, he having a tendency to hesitate when speaking and I suffering from an irresistible urge to prompt. As a result, we sometimes resembled the Two Ronnies in 'Harry & Bert' mode, where Harry (Ronnie B.) offers endless amusing suggestions (all wrong, of course) as to what word comes next in Bert's (Ronnie C.) drawn out testimony! Only Bob didn't see the funny side. He claimed it put him off his stroke – also, I think he resented anyone trying to guess his thoughts, or worse, put words into his mouth. Eventually, I learned to refrain from doing this – peace was restored and a lesson learned.

But to return to my visit: once the initial shock at his living conditions subsided, we got on reasonably well. I found him lively, interesting company, with no airs or pretensions. Even so, at the end of three hours, I left with a splitting headache and the conviction that I ought not to return! But I did, of course. Why? Well, for one thing, genuine country fans are few and far between, especially in Sidcup, and it's refreshing to exchange views with someone so obviously knowledgeable and well-informed. Perhaps also, I detected a need…

Throughout my visits, Bob contributed around 80-90% of the conversational exchanges, which was fair enough – he'd led a more varied, interesting life than me, after all, and consequently had more to share. There was certainly never any shortage of anecdotes and recollections on offer, in spite of which, over two years elapsed before the idea of a book occurred to me. To my surprise, he accepted the challenge (if that's the right word) and so began the interviewing process, which lasted from February, 2013 to April, 2014. Before arriving at that position, however, our relationship went through several phases, including an 18-month spell of non-communication.

In truth, our encounters did not always run smoothly. I (for whom neatness *rules*) found it difficult relaxing in a small, cramped environment with cluttered surroundings, half-afraid to speak, while he, having landed back in England, "on his uppers" as Jon Philibert put it, and in increasingly poor health, was hardly likely to be at his jovial best. However, we learned to compromise.

The incident that triggered our 18-month 'hiatus' occurred in June, 2011 and it had been coming for a while. When finally doing so, it was something of nothing. Bob being on friendly terms with so very many country stars, it's only natural some of their names should crop up in his conversation. I just felt he overplayed this at times and hinted as much, provoking a rambling emailed reply to which there could be no answer, so I didn't venture to try. However...

Having welcomed him as one of several house-guests on Christmas Day, 2010, I repeated the gesture in 2011 (he declined, claiming to have another invitation, which, for some reason, failed to materialise), and again in 2012, which he duly accepted. The day passed successfully and we stayed in touch into the New Year. In retrospect, the six-week period that followed represented the high point of our relationship. Whether the break taught us to be more accommodating of each other, I don't know, but I sensed a deeper rapport than before. Then came my offer, and things seemed to slip back a bit – perhaps because we were now, in a sense, mixing business with pleasure.

Fortunately for me, Bob, with his vast experience, made the job of interviewing relatively easy, being endlessly patient, and ready and willing to respond to my haphazard questioning, something I appreciated very much. Yes, he suffered from a selective memory, and 'blank-recall' (don't we all?), which could be quite amusing at times, like the occasion when, perusing an old *CMP* article, he cried out, "This is really interesting, I'm learning something here!" Only to discover he'd written the piece himself! But honesty supersedes everything and it was always to the fore with him.

On certain sensitive subjects – like the Thai 'marriage' – he was not so forthcoming and I did not press him. Only once did our conversation become really heated, and this – perhaps predictably – concerned the merits or otherwise of British country music. At one point, when I suggested that British artistes lacked the confidence of their American counterparts, he growled, "How do *you* know, you've never spoken to a British artiste in your life!" Fair point (though not *quite* true). Later, when I took a different view – that they're less talented – it, illogically, provoked equal argument and seems to be one of those highly emotive subjects best avoided.

Gradually, we settled into a pattern whereby, having accumulated sufficient information, I would complete a chapter, then read it back to Bob for comments.[132] Here, in contrast to his unreliability in recalling specific events, he was exceedingly sharp, picking up immediately on the slightest inaccuracy or variation of details, all of which I took on board, eager to get things right. We'd then repeat the process, until arriving at a point where we were both satisfied. Although never objecting to my phrasing or structure, he considered the language to be 'over-flowery' (which I don't deny) but left it at that – fortunately, as I can't write any other way.

The arrangement worked well, until we came to one particular passage – the tale of a speeding incident that occurred when he and Tony Byworth were passing through Painesville, Ohio, on their way to the Nashville Convention in 1973. Tony's recollection of events, as conveyed by phone, differed radically from that of his colleague, who protested at my decision to print both accounts, side by side. But it seemed the fairest thing to do, and, at the end of the day, is just one person's word against another. So, there they are, as related to me, in Chapter 4. If I've erred, please forgive me, Bob.

As is well-known, Bob could be ruthlessly forthright and direct, which I took as an encouragement. When, for instance, I began doubting my suitability for the task of

---

[132] Bob eventually asked me to stop doing this, claiming it was adversely affecting our friendship. As he didn't elaborate, I could only guess at his objections. Upon returning to the book in March, 2015, quite unintentionally, I began to see it more from his perspective, which led to my making certain amendments, and, I'm sure, improvements. Now, while there's no doubt in my mind that Bob would not have approved of the book in its original form, hopefully, he would do the finished version – in fact, it's only the belief of this that kept me going.

writing the book, he shot back: "You've got to start somewhere!" I loved his blind faith! (If that's what it was).

When not working on the book, most of our time was spent indoors, often viewing – and/or listening to – YouTube clips, while expressing totally unbiased(!) opinions. Sometimes, we'd update his baseball or movie records – tedious work, yet with Bob, somehow fun. Another regular activity was furniture-moving. Rarely did I visit without being called upon to shift some item of furniture or piece of electrical equipment – not that it ever seemed to create more space! I remember one of my first tasks was helping to unpack and assemble a huge treadmill, which eventually took up the entire centre of his guest room. Did Bob ever use it? Yes, in fact, though admittedly with decreasing regularity. Then there were the wires and cables – dozens of them, criss-crossing wildly. Only *he* knew where they all led. How he didn't trip over them – or electrocute himself – I'll never know.

We also went out occasionally – either for a midday meal (usually just a local café) or further afield. One of our more adventurous trips was a Thames riverboat ride. The day went well, but the arduous walking involved, particularly from quay to vessel, dissuaded us from repeating the exercise. Outings closer to home were more easily achieved. We attended a couple of quiz nights at a local Church hall – and Bob particularly enjoyed the Saturday coffee-morning/bring & buy sales held at a (different) Baptist Church hall, 10 minutes' walk away (whose minister conducted his funeral service).

A special outing, for Bob only, occurred during our 18-month 'hiatus', when friend Robin Jones escorted him to the 2012 *Wembley Festival*. I think he relished this opportunity to meet up again with past acquaintances, though I'm not sure he was quite so taken with the actual music. Another country concert, at my suggestion this time, came the following year, 2013, when (driven by friend, Jill Bullman), we went to see local bluegrass outfit, the Biggin Hillbillies, perform at the General Wolfe pub (coincidental Quebec connections) in Westerham, Kent. During the course of the evening, Bob requested *Sweeter Than the Flowers*, which the group duly performed to his satisfaction.

Mostly, we ate indoors (or in the garden, in summer). I'd bring home a takeaway lunch. There was never any over-indulgence on these occasions[133] – in fact, Bob invariably gave me part of his meal. On the other hand, there were regular, almost weekly deliveries of food on trolleys piled head-high. These would be from whichever supermarket happened to have a special offer that particular week. He liked me to be present in the kitchen at such times, to assist in putting items away – a difficult situation, since, even while helping, I knew I was not really *helping*.

Bob was obviously in a fragile state of mind (overloading with all sorts of items, not just food), yet would accept help only on his terms. It's a fine line between intervention and interference and one he made me all too aware of. As for professional involvement, if I suggested anyone or anything at all (he needed a hand-rail at his outdoor steps, for instance), it would always end with, "Leave it for now."

Was he 'eccentric'? Only in so far as he was absolutely determined to do things his own way. In response to Neil Coppendale's enquiry re: his footwear – no, he did not "still wear odd socks," for the simple reason that he never wore any socks (unable to get on and off). As for Larry

---

[133] While researching this book, I heard odd rumours concerning Bob's eating habits, with no indication of how or where they originated. Well, having shared many meals with him, I can state that, in my presence, at least, his table manners were never less than perfect.

Adams' assertion that he was "difficult to get along with"
(*CMP*'s 500th edition, October, 2011), well, I can't deny he
seems to have fallen out with a lot of people over the years
– and at least a couple more in the time I knew him
(though not the neighbours). In truth, no one, including
myself, really knew what was going on inside his head –
only that a sharp, alert brain was constantly ticking away
there and one had to be careful not to upset the delicate
mechanism. Despite the assertion that he "mellowed" in
recent years, I think the combination of thriving mental
energy and declining physical capacity made matters worse
in many respects – but for himself more than others, as he
genuinely tried to keep his emotions in check, succeeding,
on the whole.

Still, the underlying tension was never far away. One
day, eager to help, I (with his permission) attempted to tidy
up his kitchen, which, as usual, had plates, saucepans and
utensils piled high on every available surface. This was a
tricky operation, since, if I cleared it too well, he'd
complain at not being able to find things. A good solution
seemed to be to hang items on hooks, where they would
still be within easy reach. There were already several of
these in place, but I needed another, so made a hole and
screwed it in. In retrospect, I suppose I should have first
checked with him, but the entire place was so overrun with
hooks, it's hard to believe he would have objected to just
one more – but object he did! In fact, he became so
enraged, he 'interrogated' me for a full 10 minutes on what
possessed me to commit such an act of wilful, wanton
vandalism, leaving me speechless. At times, I felt like I
couldn't win – he knew it and seemed to derive some sick
pleasure out of the situation.

I suppose no book could be written on Bob without
reference to his size. Yes, he was big – however, when in
close proximity, it was his more appealing features that
drew your attention: the pleasantly attractive face, intense

eyes, clear, confident speaking voice, and warm, genial manner. Only when venturing outside did his shape become somehow significant, but it didn't seem to concern him. Nor me, though the ugly, ill-fitting cardigan topped off with a bobble-hat-cum-tea-cosy hardly improved matters! (On this subject, Goff Greenwood's description of his friend as "no sartorial dresser" is one Bob would definitely have disputed – and, in fact, there is photographic evidence to support both viewpoints).

A day that stands out in my memory is 16 January, 2013, Bob's 70th birthday. I can see him now, as he opens the door to me, dressed only in one of the extra-long, flannelette shirt-cum-nightgowns he so loved, for their ease and comfort – they suited him, too, in a funny sort of way. His hair is dishevelled this day, and, although past noon, he has barely risen – not unusual, as he would regularly stay up until 3 or 4 in the morning. As I sit down, he reveals he's received half a dozen emailed birthday wishes, including two from Nashville friends, Vernon Oxford and ex-Faron Young guitarist, Richard Bass, which pleases him. We go out to a favourite local café, just 200 yards down the road. On returning home, I give him a 'Smartie' chocolate birthday cake, which he keeps for later. In a quiet moment, he confesses that the '70'milestone is a tough one, much worse than his 60th. I can't find words to comfort him and come away around 4, as usual.

The last winter of Bob's life, 2013/14, is one I'm unlikely to forget. I never felt happy leaving him, as, although he ate hardly anything during my visits (which could last up to ten hours), the huge amounts of food coming in had to be going somewhere. By now, the stress was starting to affect my own health – I had 6 colds in the space of 4 months. The following is a diary of events leading up to 8 May, 2014:-

Sunday, 20 April. Bob phones in the morning. He had a

win on the horses last night and is in buoyant mood –
almost unnaturally so. He says he has been thinking things
over and if I agree to care for him, he'll look into the
question of benefits. I say, having cared full-time for my
mother, I know about Attendance Allowance and am
willing to care for him, so he can go ahead and make the
necessary arrangements.

Tuesday, 22 April. My usual day and time for calling is
Thursdays at 10.30am, but every few weeks, he needed
help visiting the launderette, so I also call this day, at the
earlier time of 8am, helping him carry two large trolley-
loads of clothes. We catch the bus to the launderette,
several stops away, arriving as it opens at 9am. We return
home around 12 noon, shortly after which I bring in fish
(he pie) and chips, which we eat together and I stay until 4.
Bob never mentions the question of caring, so I remind
him I'm still happy to do so, but he says nothing.

Thursday, 24 April. I arrive at 10.30am for my weekly visit
to find Bob upset, having been expecting me at 9am. I say we
agreed any time between 9 and 10.30, but he is adamant and
becomes morose. I again go for fish and chips (he preferring
pie). One unusual thing he does this day is give me £20 for
future expenses, whereas previously, we'd always settled up
after I'd got any items, though I think nothing of this at the
time. I later find out from the newsagent that he cancelled the
papers by phone today, which seems to be the last anyone
saw or heard from him.

Friday, 25 April. Bob's note is dated this day.

Saturday, 26 April. I send an email suggesting we don't
see each other for a while. In retrospect, this seems crass –
and very unfortunate timing – but I honestly felt he didn't
want me there at that time. Anyway, it's unlikely he ever
read it, his note having been dated the previous day.

Thursday, 8 May. His upstairs neighbour, Liz,
concerned at not seeing or hearing him, knocks on the

door, and, receiving no reply, calls the police who enter flat, discovering body.

It's easy to look back on events and say we could and should have behaved differently. On the other hand, there's a school of thought that if a person is really determined to do something, they will. Both are true. I know I did things for Bob that no other person on earth would have done, but in the end, it wasn't – and probably never would have been – enough.

Were there ever hints of such action? No, although I heard subsequently that he had threatened to do this once before, in Thailand. Did I have any reason to suppose he might be susceptible? Not really – he was a 'glass half-full' person. The only relevant incident I recall (apart from his mentioning a grandfather or great grandfather who supposedly took this way out) is a show of interest when I happened to mention the case of Screaming Lord Sutch.[134] To be honest, I thought the most likely scenario would be that he'd eat himself into a state of ill-health and end up in hospital.

---

[134] Born David Edward Sutch in Hampstead, London, on 10 November, 1940, the stage name Screaming Lord Sutch, 3rd Earl of Harrow, having been inspired by American blues singer, Screamin' Jay Hawkins. Recorded some titles in 1960s for pioneering UK pop producer, Joe Meek (notably, *Jack the Ripper*, Decca, 1963), though none became hits. Continued recording intermittently without success, one album, *Lord Sutch & Heavy Friends* (Cotillion, 1970) being named as worst album of all time in a 1998 BBC poll (despite featuring Jimmy Page, Jeff Beck and Nicky Hopkins among credits). Began standing in parliamentary elections as early as 1963, forming the Official Monster Raving Loony Party 20 years later. Highest proportion of vote this ever received was 4%. A manic depressive, he committed suicide by hanging on 16 June 1999, following the death of his mother the previous year.

The official cause of death was given as 'aspiration pneumonia caused by multiple drug overdose.' Although his note was dated 25 April, the Coroner estimated the date of death as much nearer the day of discovery (8 May), possibly even on that day, owing to lack of body decomposition. If true, it could mean that Bob spent a full fortnight deliberating over his fate, which doesn't bear thinking about.

WHY? This one word was written at the top of the second note (the first contained a 'Will'). In it, the reasons given are exclusively health-related: decreased mobility, fear of falling and injuring himself, prospect of ending up wheelchair-bound, or, worse, in a home, and a burden on the state. He possibly had other reasons, the nature of which could be debated endlessly, but these were the only ones given.

Although Bob led a somewhat chaotic personal life, his finances, at least, were in good order. He left all relevant paperwork in a neat pile, enabling me to settle his affairs quickly – in under a month (sister Marylee being the main beneficiary), without incurring any expenses. His household possessions were another matter. To paraphrase Winston Churchill: never has so much been squeezed into so little! However, between five of us (Tony Byworth, Craig and Julie, Jill Bullman and myself), the flat was eventually cleared to the landlord's satisfaction, with as many items as possible being diverted to appropriately worthy causes.[135]

---

[135] Bob left the entire contents of his flat to me, meaning that, among other things, I now possess every issue of *Country Music People* produced during his tenure (February, 1970 to July, 1987 inclusive). One of his great wishes was that these be put online – however, as I have neither the time nor patience for such a task (which, at a rough estimate, would involve around 10,000 pages and several million words), this will have to remain one of the rare occasions he failed to get his way – unless someone else

It's probably insignificant yet oddly coincidental that Bob was in the process of reading Faron Young's (Diane Diekman) biography at the time of his death, especially since there were many similarities between the two men – spontaneous, outspoken characters who gave a lot of themselves yet felt rather forgotten and neglected by the industry towards the end of their lives (though Bob never said as much) and with serious, ongoing health problems, dealt with drastically.

Breaking the news of someone's – anyone's – death is obviously a delicate matter, to be handled carefully and, in retrospect, an emailed notification from me to a dozen or so of his friends (some of them quite distant) may not have been ideal. Nevertheless, it was disappointing to see the stark details reproduced boldly and coldly on a website immediately afterwards, for the whole world to see. The intention, at least, had been honourable: to avoid the spread of ill-founded rumours and speculation by being open and 'up-front' from the start.

Despite the brief, blunt funeral directions (Chapter 12), Bob was given a more formal send-off, courtesy of a cremation service conducted by local Baptist minister, Alan Mason, whom he had at least met a couple of times, and who carried out his duties with due reverence. It was heartening to see so many friends and colleagues turn out for the service – in particular, David Allan, who spoke both movingly and humorously. In no frame of mind to face a possible 'inquest', I declined to join the pub gathering afterwards – likewise, Tom Whelan's 70th birthday party, which Bob and I had been due to attend around the same time. One advantage in continuing with this book is the opportunity it affords to address unanswered questions and, hopefully, lay things to rest.

I was honoured to be invited to write an obituary for

feels so inclined...

Country Music People (June, 2014) and it seemed somehow fitting that Rosanne Cash's photo should grace the cover of that issue. As someone who never much cared for the blatantly commercial aspects of country music, nor the overly ambitious, career-manoeuvring of some stars, Bob "took a liking" to Johnny Cash's eldest daughter, for refusing to trade on her father's name and being "unworried about stardom."[136] Similarly, we fans (and I think I speak for most) took a liking to Bob for approaching his professional duties from our perspective, asking the sorts of questions we wanted to ask and responding how we would have done. He wasn't in it for the money, acclaim or kudos, but for the love of the music – and to try and get a bit closer to his heroes, like we all wanted to.

When reflecting on Bob, I recall someone who, more than anything, loved spontaneity – the 'magic of the moment'. If I planned to visit at a certain hour and day, I would, in all likelihood, receive a cordial welcome, but little more. If, on the other hand, I was delivering something without intending to disturb him, the chances are, he'd spot me, open the door, beaming, and greet me like a long-lost pal! I'm sure that's why *London Country* was so magical. Being totally unscripted, the show gave him the opportunity to be his normal, spontaneous self – someone who was as happy sharing banter with Vanessa, the launderette assistant, or Alex at the LIDL checkout as he was watching birds and squirrels feed in his garden or downloading clips of favourite songs and movies from YouTube. I can honestly claim never to have been bored in his company, however mundane the task we were engaged in – and some were VERY mundane – but then, he brought a unique, child-like enthusiasm to everything he did.

---

[136] These remarks were made to Bobby Bare and Ricky Skaggs in their *London Country* appearances of 12/9/81 and 19/5/85 respectively.

Someone said to me that what Bob did in ending his life was "wicked." Well, one had only to be with him to realise he was not a wicked person. Truer, I think, to say that wicked people drive the vulnerable to do such things – and, in the end, he was vulnerable, more than anyone realised. It's also sometimes portrayed as a selfish act, but I believe he, although pleased at my offer to care for him, may have wished to relieve me of the duty, and, in that context, it would be as difficult to condemn his action as to condone it.

Bob's greatest quality was that he remained true to himself throughout life, and, while no one could deny he had faults, I believe many of these stemmed from the fact that he remained at heart a wide-eyed kid, full of wonder and excitement at seeing and meeting his musical heroes. It probably never occurred to him that he represented a hero of sorts to his listeners – certainly to me, one reason why I began this book in the first place, and, despite discovering his flaws along the way, proceeded with it. Then, from banishing the enterprise to a drawer in my spare room for 10 months from the date of his death, finally coming round to accept that he would have wanted it completed. Whether his spirit guided me, I don't know. I just hope and pray I've done him justice – it's the least he deserves. Adios, Amigo.

Photos and Illustrations

Lamorbey House, Sidcup, c.1930. Converted into a long-stay hotel around 1910, Mr. Powel, senior, stayed here from arrival in England (c.1937) until marrying in 1939.

Lamorbey House, 2013. Known as Rose Bruford College, it now houses – and trains – drama students.

Laurison House, Bickley, c.1985. A flat here served as the
Powel family home throughout the war years.

Lauriston House. As it looks today – a private nursing home.

317

Lauriston House. As it looks today – a private nursing home.

7th birthday party of Marylee, extreme right, with brother Bob on extreme left.

Fletcher Cottage, April 2012. Built in the 1870s, it served as the Powel family holiday home from the 1950s to 1970s. Now a playwright's residence.

CRUISE SHIP QUEBEC BURNING AT DOCK IN CANADA

New York Times (1857-Current file); Aug 16, 1950; ProQuest Historical Newspapers The New York Times
pg. 43

CRUISE SHIP QUEBEC BURNING AT DOCK IN CANADA

The luxury liner of the Canadian Steamship Lines smouldering at Tadoussac after damaging fire on Monday night. The passengers and crew members were landed safely.

Associated Press Wirephoto

How the *SS Quebec* disaster was reported in the *New York Times*, August 16, 1950.

Bob's beloved Tadoussac, as it looks today.

The Journal of Country Music   3 6 Monthly
Vol. 1 No. 5 – Nov.

Opry magazine, November 1968, issue no.5, containing
Bob's first article.

the bob powel
column

Welcome to the first of what is intended to be a regular series. I would like first to introduce myself. I am 25 years old, single and I live in South London. My parents are Canadian; I lived ten years in Quebec City, leaving there in 1955. I have loved Country Music since I was very young, and in Quebec I used to listen to the whole of The Grand Ole Opry every Saturday night. In 1965, my dreams were fulfilled: I made a six month trip to the USA and Canada, seeing many shows including The Grand Ole Opry.

In the last few years great progress has been made in the fight for acceptance of Country Music, moreover it has been steady progress, which is far better than a sudden craze, because crazes never last, and frequently things become worse after it has all died down. USA labels (MCA), Mercury, Pickwick and RCA have all suddenly realised that there is a market over here, and are beginning to release material accordingly. Some are the class forever, I hope, when there were two or three album releases per year. MCA's policy of issuing LP's which are recent releases in the USA is an enlightened one. It is most frustrating for the collector to import an LP at great expense, and then three months later find it released over here. During the last 18 months the prices of imports have risen considerably. Previously LP's cost $3.98 7/4d a dollar, with import duty chargeable at 33%, now LP's cost $4.98 8.4d. a dollar, with import duty chargeable at 50%. This means that if you import records yourself and pay the full retail price and duty, you can pay over £3 per album. For this reason prices in import shops have risen steeply. At The World of Country Music shop in London for instance charges vary between 45/- and 55/6 for full price LP's. The latter price is necessary for the newer LP's as they have to be air freighted in.

The argument of old versus modern still rages, and will continue in the air until a balance is met. I'm in the happy position of liking anything from Charlie Poole to Waylon Jennings, providing it's well done. Therefore I consider myself a liberal in the matter, but I was astonished when Wally Whyton, who plays the record review on Country Meets Folk, told me that he prefers the Hank Williams with strings and churches to the original recordings. How can a person who pretends to like Country Music say that? If he doesn't like Country Music then he should not air his views to over two million listeners. The remixed recordings are unforgivable. If Williams was alive today and wanted to record with the Royal Philharmonic Orchestra then that would be his privilege, but for MGM to completely alter his recordings

(twenty two)

16 years after his death is quite a different matter. The butchered recordings are said to be selling like hot cakes. Who would buy them? Surely not the real Country Collector.

With Welsh Summer Time now in force all the year round country fans should find it easier to obtain AFN on 344 metres at 6 p.m. on Saturdays for an hour of the Grand Ole Opry. The show of course is recorded and a hastily edited, with all advertising deleted, and there is a great deal of chopping and changing. In spite of this faults, it is worth listening to as all the big names appear such as Porter Wagoner, Flatt & Scruggs, Roy Acuff etc.

Richard Day's interesting article last month Country Music at the Movies contained I believe a slight error. The Hank Williams Story was actually called Your Cheatin' Heart. The star was George Hamilton the Hollywood actor, not George Hamilton IV the singer. Richard also states that the USA version of the film contained an insert of the real Hank Williams singing a song. I saw the film in Canada, USA and England and can say that this was not the case. The confusion occurred, I believe, because in the USA the film was often reamed with Country Music on Broadway, which did show Hank Williams singing a song.

Another Greenwood last month asked readers to write to him regarding deleted material which they wished to see reissued. If enough people write in the record companies will take notice. I agree fully with his two suggestions - Frankie Miller on Columbia and Lost Butler on Capitol, and how about Grandpa Jones on RCA and Leon Payne on RCA, Capitol and Mercury. Send in your suggestions. There are thousands of great recordings gathering dust. Some of the greatest authentic material presently available is on the tiny Rural Rhythm Label. They have five fantastic albums out by Hylo Brown plus others by Jim Eanes, Red Smiley, Mac Wiseman, Les Moore and J. E. Mainer. They are not sold in shops in the USA, but are advertised on the Radio. There are about 20 songs per album lasting an average of about 1½ minutes per track. The Hylo Brown's in particular are outstanding, with dobro, fiddle etc. they contain some of the best material he has ever recorded. It is good to see small companies producing such high quality material, as the large companies are no longer interested in this fine music. The Rural Rhythm Label is available from Charles Newton (whose ad can be found on Small Ads page).

See you again next month.

Powel's Point of View

This photo was used to illustrate either *Powel's Point of View* or *From the Editor's Desk* in *CMP*s from March 1970 (issue no.2) to June 1971 inclusive.

B.C.M.A. - NASHVILLE 1970

BUSES: Please keep to the bus allocated to you, otherwise confusion will occur, and someone could be left behind! Please remember that the seat immediately behind the driver is reserved for the tour leader. Please remove all belongings each evening from the bus. Apart from the transfers between the airport and the Royal Manhattan Hotel in New York the buses will be numbered, 1 to 4 with a large label near the front of the bus. At Kennedy airport you can get on any bus, but make sure your baggage is loaded before boarding.

BUS ONE:	BUS TWO:	BUS THREE:	BUS FOUR:
Mr. E. Alder	Miss Birchall	Mr. R.M. Allen	Mr. W. Almond
Mr. R. Arnold	Mr. W.G. Brealey	Mr. R. Atkinson	Mr. Bansher
Mr. J. Atkinson	Mr. R.A. Butterfield	Mr. Atkinson	Miss D. Brown
Mr. D.A. Baker	Mr. H. Carvalho	Mrs. Atkinson	Mr. Baxton
Mr. H. Baker	Mr. A. Dovey	Mr. R. Arsonis	Mr. A. Byworth
Mr. P. Bayliss	Mr. Davies	Mr. Boden	Mr. K.P. Conroy
Mr. H. Brindley	Mr. A. Dolbey	Mrs. Boden	Mr. L.R. Darby
Mr. R. Bristow	Mr. G. Greenwood	Mr. R. Boswell	Mr. H.R. Dewbery
Mr. J.G. Clausen	Mr. E. Gregory	Mr. A. Cook	Mr. H. Davies
Mr. F.E. Deathar	Mr. C. Gilbert	Mr. A. Cooper	Mrs. H. Davies
Mrs. J. Deatker	Mr. W.D. Hogue	Mrs. Cooper	Mr. J. Davies
Mr. J. Ellis	Mr. B. Haskell	Mr. G. Croft	Mr. B. Davies
Mr. M. Grinham	Mrs. F.W. Hatherley	Mr. M. Dawson	Miss A. Davies
Mr. Jackson	Mr. J. Hughes	Mr. B. Hall	Mr. M. Firbager
Mr. P.F. James	Mr. L. Jenkins	Mr. Hutton	Mr. J. Fearn
Mr. J. Kramer	Mr. C.D. Kennard	Mrs. Hutton	Mr. D. Hartlin
Mrs. Kramer	Mr. F.C. King	Mr. L. Jones	Mr. M. Hodges
Mr. C. Mailey	Mr. E. King	Mr. J. Kilpatrick	Mr. W. Jolley
Mr. D. Mapen	Mrs. J. Leonard	Mr. J. Lemon	Mr. Kavanagh
Mr. Grantrex	Mr. A.P. Lukey	Mr. J. Lenz	Mrs. Kavanagh
Mr. A. Pagano	Mr. L. McLaughlin	Miss L. Lodge	Miss A. Lambert
Mr. L.G. Payne	Mr. D.J. McLoughlin	Mr. L. Lundgren	Mr. J. Lambert
Mr. J. Pettifer	Mr. A. McNicholas	Mr. G. Marshall	Mr. G.J. Lane
Mr. Read	Mr. Matthews	Mr. Maxwell	Mr. R.J. Lyon
Mr. T. Ramsden	Mrs. Matthews	Mrs. Maxwell	Mr. J. McLaughlin
Mr. R. Richardson	Mr. J. Shiel	Mr. F. Weller	Mr. P.J. Miller
Mr. Roberts	Mrs. S. Pomfrett	Mr. F. Owen	Mr. A. Parsons
Mr. Spain	Mr. Rice	Mr. D.L. Perry	Mr. G. Porter
Mrs. Spain	Mrs. F. Smith	Mr. H.L. Powell	Mr. E. Powell
Mr. L. Squelch	Miss E. Smith	Mr. L.W. Getchell	[illegible]
Mr. M. A. Storey	Mr. J. Taylor	Mr. Stevens	Mr. R. Scothern
Mrs. M.M. Storey	Mr. D. Toombs	Mrs. Stevens	Miss A. Sudworth
Mr. Taylor	Mr. B. Timmins	Miss G. Talbot	Mr. Upton
Mr. D. Vulpus	Mrs. B. Timmins	Mr. G. White	Mrs. Upton
Mr. J. Warner	Mr. I. Tracey	Mr. F. Wainwright	Miss Y. Ventris
Mr. D.J. Witts	Miss Whitehouse	Mr. Weatherhead	Mr. R. Weaver
Mr. W. Wragg	Mr. E. Woodward	Mr. A. White	Mr. A. Wiseman
Mr. J. Barker	Mr. P.W. Wormleighton	Mr. F. White	Mr. B. Wiseman

IMPORTANT: If anyone wishes to "swop" buses he must arrange this himself whilst we are in the U.S.A. and at the same time he must advise the tour leaders so that they are aware of the "swop". We cannot undertake to alter names around prior to departure as the amount of work involved precludes it.

List of participants for *BCMA*'s 2nd Convention Trip, 1970.

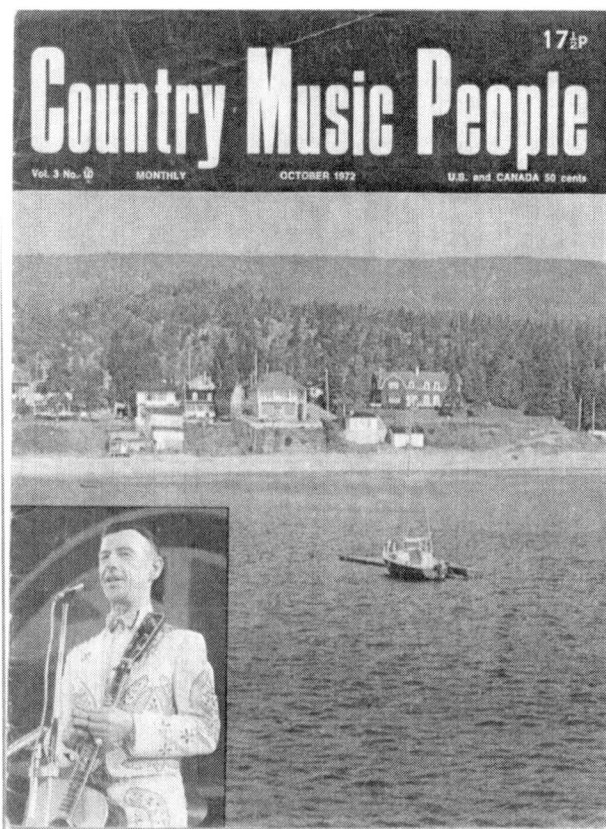

CMP, October 1972. The Canadian issue, featuring a
Bob-taken photo of Tadoussac (*Fletcher Cottage* is the dark
building, centre-right). Plus, Hank Snow, inset.

(Courtesy Doug McKenzie Photography)

With Joe 'Red' Hayes during the singer's fateful UK
visit, February 1973.

(Courtesy Doug McKenzie Photography)

With next-door neighbours, Dolly Waterton and
husband, outside their Broomwood Road bungalow.

(Courtesy Doug McKenzie Photography)

With the *Singing Troubadour*, Ernest Tubb, 1973.
(Courtesy Doug McKenzie Photography)

With 3 members of Jonny Young Four (Luce Langridge, Dave Crane and Jonny Young), plus Craig Baguley (extreme left). Award is for *Billboard* Top UK Country Group, 1973.

(Courtesy Doug McKenzie Photography)

With Marty Robbins during singer's 1975 UK trip.
(Courtesy Doug McKenzie Photography)

Presenting 'All-Time favourite Country Record' award to Don Williams for *You're My Best Friend* in 1977.

(Courtesy Doug McKenzie Photography)

An example of Jean Earle's sketch work.

FOUR

ON THE FLOOR

price 10p

Cover of January 1977 issue of *Four-On-The-Floor*
magazine, produced by Don Ford in conjunction with
Tom Whelan's club of same name. Sketches again courtesy
of Jean Earle.

COUNTRY MUSIC PEOPLE MAGAZINE
PRESENTER LONDON COUNTRY ON BBC
RADIO LONDON

BOB POWELL
BROADCASTER & JOURNALIST

23, Brookwood Road
St. Paul's Cray,
Orpington,
Kent BR5 2AL,
England

Orpington 70433
29/11/..

Dear Tom,

I have not as yet had the opportunity to get hold of a copy of your book,however my friend Tony Byworth has lent me the remarks you have made about me in it. I feel a reply is in order,I became a fan of yours from the date your first album appeared,and as one of my trips to the States I made a point of meeting you and interviewing you(this was a couple of years before Jonley),there you stated we first met). I also gave your albums good reviews in the magazine I then edited, as well as printing interviews etc to such an extent that I was accused of favouritism both in print and on my programme.

As you say I went out to know you and your delightful wife Dixie,and visited your house on two occasions and took a memorable three day bus trip to Florida with you and the Storytellers. However basically I felt that some of your later albums lacked the sparkle that made me rush a fan of yours in the first place. I am a reviewer ,and no matter how well I get to know a person this will never influence me. In my opinion of the quality of his product,I just felt that the records were not of the high quality that I knew you were capable of.

What annoyed me most your remarks is you appear to imply that as we became ,what I term as your friends,that I can no longer have a balanced judgement of your work,the reason I have been to your house I was only made flattering reviews about you,that is not being a critic you, that is being a yes man,and you're too great a talent to need that ,I tried to be constructive ,and I'm sorry if I failed.

I have nothing but contempt for you,I consider you one of the greatest talents in Country music ,and for what it's worth I feel some of your later product is among the best you've done,but if you again do what I consider a poor album,and I'm called upon to review I'm damn well going to say it.

Your faithful Reader

Letter written in response to criticism in Tom T. Hall's book.

333

In Singapore during one of the early Thailand/Far East
trips.

Interviewing Bobby Bare for *London Country*,

12 September 1981.

(Courtesy Doug McKenzie Photography)

NEWS SHOPPER, 13th September, 1984

DIARY DATES

Stagestruck

Summer Memories

What is Marquetry?

Autumn Show

Ripley Recitals

Olde Tyme Music Hall

Social Benefits

Cutting from local *News Shopper* paper, 13 September 1984.

The Opening of the C.M.P. Shop

How *CMP* reported shop opening – November 1984.

(Courtesy Doug McKenzie Photography)

Outside Tudor Café flat, c.2002.

Outside 31 Amberley Court, shortly after moving there,
February 2007.

(Courtesy Doug McKenzie Photography)

In a serious mood, October 2007.
(Courtesy Doug McKenzie Photography)

Bar Phoenix (July 2008), previously *The Roebuck* pub,
Rennell St., London, SE13.

North side of Rennell St., SE13 as it looks today (south
side adjoins Riverside Shopping Centre).

With Tony Byworth in St. Thomas's hospital, shortly after April 2009 heart op.

(Courtesy Doug McKenzie Photography)

The Four Musketeers: Tony Byworth, George Hamilton IV, Bob, and David Allan, pictured at the Byworth-organised Knebworth Festival, 2010.

(Courtesy Doug McKenzie Photography)

The last photo, taken in front of Amberley Court flat, Christmas 2013.

(The gap in curtain was intentional: to spot callers. You couldn't sneak up on Bob!)

Appendix

1970	
February	Faron Young
March	Chet Atkins
April	George Hamilton IV
May	Don Gibson
	Skeeter Davis
	Loretta Lynn
June	Buck Owens
	Roy Acuff (pt.1)
July	Roy Acuff (pt.2)
	Owen Bradley
August	Conway Twitty
September	Bill Anderson
October	Buck Owens
November	Tex Ritter (pt.1)
December	Tex Ritter (pt.2)
	Hank Snow
1971	
January	Jerry Reed
February	Ray Price
March	Charley Pride (pt.1)
April	Charley Pride (pt.2)
May	Lynn Anderson
June	Hank Williams, Jr.
July	Waylon Jennings
August	Mac Wiseman
September	Willie Nelson
	Connie Smith
	Shot Jackson (pt.1)
October	Glenn Sutton (pt.1)
	Benny Martin
November	Shot Jackson (pt.2)
December	Glenn Sutton (pt.2)

1972	
January	Tom T. Hall
February	Carl Perkins
March	Bobby Bare
	Harlan Howard
May	Don Helms (pt.1)
	Buddy Emmons
	Ralph Mooney
June	Don Helms (pt.2)
July	Charlie Louvin
September	Del Reeves
November	Pete Drake
1973	
January	Marty Robbins
February	Faron Young
May	Curley Putman
July	Bob Luman
September	Bob Neal
December	Roger Miller
1974	
January	Jethro Burns
February	Dave Dudley
	Red Simpson
April	Charlie Rich
May	Susan Raye
July	Bill & Cliff Carlisle (pt.1)
August	Bill & Cliff Carlisle (pt.2)
	Grandpa Jones
October	Diana Trask
December	Johnny Bond
1975	
January	Ernest Tubb
April	Tammy Wynette
June	Gary Stewart
July	Tom T. Hall
August	Curley Chalker

	Hal Rugg
	Lloyd Green
September	Narvel Felts
October	Guy Willis
November	Hank Locklin
December	Marvin Rainwater
1976	
January	Ronnie Milsap
February	Ben Peters
March	Tanya Tucker
April	Don Williams
May	Faron Young
June	Hank Snow
July	Grant Turner
August	Ray Griff
September	Shelby Singleton
October	Tillman Franks
	Webb Pierce
November	James O'Gwynn
December	Vassar Clements
	Johnny Rodriguez
January 1977 – October 1983	
NIL (though plenty of articles)	
1983	
November	Boxcar Willie
1984	
March	Charley Pride
April	Billy Walker
May	Hank Snow
June	Conway Twitty
August	Ricky Skaggs
September	George Hamilton IV
October	T. G. Sheppard
1985	

January	Duffy Bros.
March	Harlan Howard
April	Moe Bandy
June	Bill Monroe
July	Vince Gill
August	Jimmy C. Newman
_1986_	
February	Merle Haggard
March	Rex Allen Jr.
April	Johnny Russell
May	Tommy Collins
June	Rosanne Cash
July	Lee Greenwood
August	Kathy Mattea
October	Wilf Carter
December	Cal Smith
_1987_	
February	Bob McDill
March	Slim Whitman
June	George Strait
July	Sonny Throckmorton
August	Dan Seals
September	Holly Dunn
October	Jean Shepard
November	Tompall Glaser
December	Red Steagall
_1988_	
January	Grant Turner
February	Craig Bickhardt
March	Charlie McCoy
April	Marty Robbins
May	Don Williams
June	Billy Joe Royal
August	Jack Clement

London Country Guests - Year-by-Year

I've tried to make this as comprehensive as possible by researching available material, but gaps are inevitable. Bob once had a complete list, which unfortunately got lost during his Thailand sojourn. The list excludes British country singers, journalists, musicians and personalities who sometimes acted as co-presenters at regular intervals, among them David Allan, Tony Byworth, Bryan Chalker, Bill Clifton, Chris Comber, Brian Golbey, Ian Grant, Shaun Greenfield, Goff Greenwood, Brian Maxine, Malcolm Price, Pete Sayers, Dave Travis.

1971

Roy Acuff/Shot Jackson/'Bashful' Brother Oswald/Benny Martin (these four-named appearing together), Stompin' Tom Connors, George Hamilton IV (first of many appearances), Slim Whitman, Albert Lee, Tex Ritter, Lorene Mann.

1972

George Hamilton IV/Loretta Lynn/Conway Twitty/Tom T. Hall/Bill Anderson (all five from *Wembley Festival*), Anne Murray, Johnny Paycheck, John Denver, Pete Drake, Patsy Montana, Bobby Bare, Charley Pride, Ray Lynam/Cotton Mill Boys/Noel Andrews (all three from Dublin's St. Patrick's Day Show).

1973

Onie Wheeler/Eddie Noack/Dave Hall/Dolly Parton/Dickey Lee/Allen Reynolds/Don Williams (all from Nashville), Hank Snow, Red Hayes, Faron Young, Connie Smith, Carl Belew, Tex Ritter, Buddy Emmons, Mac Wiseman, Skeeter Davis, Tompall Glaser, Statler Brothers, Bill Anderson, Country Gazette, Redd Harper, Roy Warhurst.

1974

Cliffie Stone/Buck Owens/Susan Raye/Buddy Allan/David Frizzell (all five from Bakersfield), Jimmy Payne/Johnny Rodriguez/Narvel Felts (all three from Nashville), Vernon Oxford, Slim Whitman, John Stewart, Diana Trask, Chris Darrow, Lynn Jones, Gus Thomas.

1975

Melba Montgomery/George Jones/Johnny Carver/Red Sovine/Barbara Mandrell (all five from *Wembley Festival*), Charley Pride, Vernon Oxford, Bill Anderson, John D. Loudermilk, Mac Wiseman, Marijohn Wilkin, Gary Stewart, Hank Locklin, Marvin Rainwater, Barbi Benton, Ronnie Milsap, Crystal Gayle, Gregg Gailbraith, Jimmy Payne, Arthur 'Guitar Boogie' Smith (from Charlotte, North Carolina), Jimmy Gateley, Mary Lou Turner, Don Drumm, Country Gazette.

1976

Freddie Fender, Lloyd Green, Tanya Tucker, Carlene Carter, Rosanne Cash, Johnny Bond, TexWilliams, Harlan Howard, Slim Whitman, Jack Routh, Dick Damron, Tommy Jennings, Billy Walker, Tom McBride (of Big Tom & Mainliners), Eddie Noack, Jo Ann Steele, Emmylou

Harris (by telephone link), Philip Strick, Billy Armstrong, Jimmy Lawton.

1977

Dennis Weaver, Jeanne Pruett, Melba Montgomery, Faron Young, Gene Cotton, Lloyd Green, Dermot O'Brien, Huey Meaux, Bob McKenzie (Nashville gospel record producer), Lloyd Perryman, Jimmy Wakely, Eddie Dean (these three from Hollywood, Ca.), Buddy Knox/Warren Smith/Charlie Feathers (these three-named appearing together), Original Drifting Cowboys (Jerry Rivers, Don Helms, Bob McNett, Hillous Butrum), via telephone link.

1978

Jerry Naylor, Boxcar Willie, Carl Perkins, Roy Clark, Ralph Emery, Stella Parton, Ronnie Prophet, Kenny Seratt, Freddie Hart, Merle Haggard, Larry Gatlin, Bud Tutmarc, Hank Locklin, Ray Lynam, Tony Frost, Hank Farr, Dave & Sugar.

1979

Jay Lee Webb, Laura Lee McBride, Carroll Baker, Cathie Stewart, Mack Allen Smith, Barbara Mandrell, Don Gibson, Commander Cody, Jim Glaser, Duane Allen (of Oakridge Boys), Jack Clement, Patsy Montana, Rusty Douch, Carroll Baker, Cathie Stewart.

1980

Kendalls, Boxcar Willie, Joe Sun, Tompall & Glasers, Janie Fricke, Emmylou Harris, Reg Lindsay, Wanda Jackson.

1981

Roy Drusky, Billie Jo Spears, Vern Gosdin, Bobby Bare, Leon Everett, Kenny Roberts, Felice & Boudleaux Bryant, Billy Armstrong, McPeake Bros., Jean Shepard.

1982

Roy Drusky, David Allan Coe, T. G. Sheppard, Rattlesnake Annie, Hoyt Axton, Jimmy C. Newman, Hank Williams, Jr., Eddie Bond, Merle Kilgore, Billy Armstrong.

1983

Lee Greenwood, Billy Walker, Chet Atkins, Merv Shiner, Ed Bruce, Jack Clement, Don Williams, LeGarde Twins, Steve Young, Gary P. Nunn, Peter Rowan, Buddy Knox.

1984

David Houston, Roy Drusky, Ray Pillow, George Hamilton IV, Warner Mack, Sleepy Labeef, Maurice Gibb, Jim Glaser, Wesley Parker, Joe Sun, J.J. Barrie.

1985

Ricky Skaggs, Herb Remington, Sonny Curtis, Riders In The Sky, Conway Twitty, Billy Walker, Eddie Bond, Boxcar Willie, Whites, Jerry Douglas, Gail Davies.

1986

Barbara Fairchild, Jean Shepard, Rusty Adams, Billy Walker, Chris Martin, McDonald Craig, Daniel O'Donnell, Eileen King, Brendan Quinn, Jimmy Payne.

1987

Guy Clark, Nanci Griffiths, Rose Maddox, Carroll Baker, Tompall Glaser, Carlton Moody & Moody Brothers, Townes VanZandt, Paul Richey, T. Graham Brown, Dwight Yoakam, Johnny Russell (by telephone link).

1988

Patty Loveless, Randy Travis, Sweethearts of The Rodeo, New Grass Revival, Steve Wariner.

'London Country Shows on CD'

<u>GUEST/THEME (Date) Tracks(Remnants) Time</u>

1. L. ROADHOG MORAN (16/3/73) 6(0)   28min
2. RED HAYES/2 (6/7/73) (16(0)/7(0)   77/ 31min
3. HANK LOCKLIN (-/-/75 part)   8(0)   34min*
4. PHILIP STRICK/2 (-/-/76) 14(0)/9(0)   56/36min
5. Faron Young (7/2/77)   16(5)   80min
6. WESTERN SHOW (L.PERRIMAN, E.DEAN,
  J.WAKELY)/2 (17/12/77) 15(0)/9(0)   74/50min
7. Hank Williams/2(31/12/77) 24(4)/26(4)   80/80min
8. E. Noack/Yodelling (18/2/78)   21(0)   60min
9. Ralph Emery (23/3/78)   16(5)   80min
10. Tony Frost (6/5/78) 18(0)/20(0)   60/60min
11. H.Locklin/R.Lynam (24/6/78)   20(4)   80min
12. Bud Tutmarc (1/7/78)   20(0)   80min
13. Ronnie Prophet (30/12/78)   15(3)   80min
14. B.Wills/L.McBride/2 (20/1/79) 17(4)/4(0)   80min
15. Jim Glaser (24/3/79) 19(4)   80min
16. P.Montana/R.Douch/2(-/9/79) 18(0)/15(0)   80min
17. D.Allan/Oak Ridge Boys(10/11/79)12(0)   80min
18. Reg Lindsay (12/4/80)   15(0)   60min
19. Wanda Jackson (13/12/80)   14(0)   60min

20. Kenny Roberts (24/1/81)   15(0)   60min

21. Miscellaneous (-/5/81)   19(0)   61min

22. F. & B. Bryant 1. (27/6/81)   21(0)   78min

23. Bobby Bare (12/9/81)   16(4)   80min

24. McPeake Bros. (1/11/81)   20(3)   80min

25. F. & B. Bryant 2. (5/12/81)   20(5)   80min

26. Xmas Show/G. Stoker (-/12/81) 25(5)   80min

27. Roy Drusky (7/2/82)   18(4)   80min

28. Billy Armstrong (28/3/82)   19(3)   80min

29. Eddie Bond (4/4/82)   7(0)   30min

30. Hoyt Axton (14/11/82)   1(0)   37min

31. Leon Payne feature (28/11/82) 25(5)   80min

32. 78's feature (26/12/82)   26(4)   80min

33. LE GARDE TWINS/2 (24/4/83) 11(0)/3(0) 80/10min^P

34. Don Williams (8/5/83)   12(0)   60min

35. Jimmie Rodgers feature (29/5/83)   21(2)   80min

36. Merv Shiner (28/8/83)   16(0)   60min

37. C. Atkins(Motor Show) (30/10/83) 6(0)   30min

38. Ed Bruce (13/11/83)   19(3)   80min

39. 1950's feature (11/12/83)   27(4)   80min

40. Old Songs (1/1/84 part)   18(0)   47min

41. Ray Pillow (22/4/84)   13(0)   60min

42. JOE SUN/J.J. BARRIE (29/4/84) 15(2)   80min^R

43. WESLEY PARKER (6/5/84) 19(4)   80min^R

44. MISCELLANEOUS (5/8/84) 27(1)   80min^R

45. Warner Mack (14/10/84)   21(3)   80min

46. No.1 Hits of Year (30/12/84)   22(3)   80min

47. Requests Show (17/2/85)   23(3)   80min

48. 1950's feature (23/3/85)   30(2)   80min

49. RIDERS IN THE SKY (-/5/85) 11(0)   70min

50. Ricky Skaggs (19/5/85)   15(3)   80min

51. Billy Walker (14/7/85)   22(3)   80min

52. Current Top 40 (22/9/85)   22(3)   80min

53. Herb Remington (-/-/85)   26(0)   80min

54. Bluegrass feature (8/12/85)   25(3)   80min

55. RUSTY ADAMS/2 (12/1/86) 19(0)/3(0)   80/10min

56. 1950's FEATURE (23/2/86)   23(4)   80min

57. Irish Stars (Daniel O'Donnell, Eileen King,

 Brendan Quinn) (16/3/86)   20(3)   80min

58. Jimmy Payne (-/5/86 part)   16(0)   58min

59. Requests Show (10/8/86)   24(4)   80min

60. B.Walker, J.Shepard, R.Adams(14/9/86) 20(3) 80min

61. C.MARTIN/McD.CRAIG(16/11/86)18(2)   80min

62. Rose Maddox (24/5/87)   11(0)   60min

63. DWIGHT YOAKAM (26/7/87)   2(0)   80min

64. MISCELLANEOUS. (28/2/88 part) 20(0)   61min[R]

65. 50's/60's Mono feature (7/5/88) 27(7)   80min

66. LAST-EVER SHOW (1/10/88) 18(0)   80min

'Country Sounds Shows on CD'

1. Mono Feature (7/4/90) 26(5)   80min
2. Last-Ever Show (11/8/90) 19(0) 60min

Non Block Capitals = Originally on cassette tape

[R] – Orig. on CD-ROM (4)

[P] - Poor Recording

* On PHILIP STRICK, PT. 2

/2 - 2 CD's

No. "Live" appearances (46)

20 OF BOB'S FAVOURITES

Obviously, no one can guess another individual's musical (or other) preferences, which are liable to change from day to day, anyway, but here, for what they're worth, are 20 country (+ 1 non-country) tracks I know Bob liked and which would have figured highly on any list of his personal favourites. (In artiste alphabetical order).

1. ROY ACUFF - Sweeter Than The Flowers

2. HYLO BROWN - The Great Historical Bum

3. BROWNS - Rusty Old Halo

4. BILL CARLISLE - Getting' Younger

5. WILF CARTER - Bouquet of Memories

6. ROSANNE CASH & BOBBY BARE - No Memories Hangin' Round

7. JACK CLEMENT - When I Dream

8. JIMMIE DAVIS - The Last Few Miles I've Travelled on my Knees

9. LITTLE JIMMY DICKENS - Life Turned Her That Way or Out Behind the Barn

10. MERLE HAGGARD - Time Changes everything

11. G. HAMILTON IV - Where Did the Sunshine Go? (or almost anything)

12. CHARLIE MONROE - I'm Gonna Sing, Sing, Sing

13. GEORGE MORGAN - No One Knows It Better

Than Me (or almost anything)

14. ALLEN REYNOLDS - Wrong Road Again

15. HANK SNOW - Gloryland March or My Nova Scotia Home

16. LUCILLE STARR - Crazy Arms (possibly all-time No.1)

17. HANK THOMPSON - New Green Light

18. WILBURN BROS. - Making Plans

19. MARIJOHN WILKIN - Barnstorming

20. HANK WILLIAMS - The Old Log Train

NON-COUNTRY TITLE: FRANKIE FORD - Sea Cruise

12 OF THE MOST PLAYED ARTISTES
ON *London Country*

This list is taken from a small sample (representing 7%) of all *London Country* shows aired (around 900). It excludes tracks by artistes appearing specially. So, for instance, the total no. of songs included in the sample by Hank Williams is 18, but as 8 of these were featured in two special shows commemorating the 25th anniversary of his death, the total shown is 10.

1. Merle Haggard	21	different tracks
1. George Jones	21	
3. Marty Robbins	19	
4. Hank Snow	15	
5. Jim Reeves	13	
5. Slim Whitman	13	
7. Johnny Cash	12	
7. Little Jimmy Dickens	12	
9. Willie Nelson	11	
9. Webb Pierce	11	
9. Kitty Wells	11	
12. Hank Williams	10	

10 OF THE MOST 'WAY OUT' RECORDS
ON *London Country*

Bob was renowned for playing off-the-wall tracks – invariably country-flavoured, of course. Here is a list of some that feature in the same, above-mentioned sample.

1. Hello DJ (bleeped version) - DON BOWMAN (23/3/78)

2. That's Good, That's Bad - ARCHIE CAMPBELL (23/3/78)

3. Toho-waha-waho - SPIKE JONES (1/7/78)

4. Golfing Prophet - RONNIE PROPHET (30/12/78)

5. Help Me Make It Through Night - RONNIE PROPHET (in Donald duck mode) (30/12/78)

6. My Mama Was a Grizzly Bear - RED BLANCHARD (-/9/79)

7. Hard to be a Rock & Roll Star - GARY PAXTON (13/12/80)

8. Poor Old, Ugly Gladys Jones - WILLIE, WAYLON, BOBBY BARE, DON BOWMAN (12/9/81)

9. Rudolph, the Red-necked Reindeer - BARRY KAY (-12/81)

10. I'll Take the Dog - RAY PILLOW & JEAN SHEPARD (22/4/84)

IMPORTANT DATES

1896 - 6 March - Harcourt Powel born in Philadelphia

1900 - 3 May - Betty Sharpe born in Montreal

1923 - 17 September - Hiram Hank Williams born in Mount Olive, Alabama

1925 - 28 November - *Grand Ole Opry* founded as one hour radio (station WSM) 'Barn Dance'

1927 - 10 December - Phrase *Grand Ole Opry* first uttered 'on air'

c.1936 - Harcourt & Betty meet in Grand-Mere, Canada

c.1937 - Harcourt transferred to London

1939 - June - Harcourt & Betty marry in Bromley, Kent

- 1 September - Commencement of World War II

1941 - 26 July - Marylee Powel born in Southport, Lancashire

1943 - 16 January - Bob born in Bickley, Kent

1945 - 8 May - End of World War II

- May - Powel family returns to Sillery (Quebec), Canada

1947 - May - Hank Williams' first recording session for MGM label at Nashville's WSM studio

363

1950 - 14 August - *SS Quebec* disaster

1953 - 1 January - Hank Williams dies aged 29, in the back seat of a Cadillac, suffering a severe heart attack with haemorrhage

1955 - February - First *Quebec Winter Carnival*

 - September - Powel family re-locates to Sevenoaks, Kent, England

1958 - Formation of Nashville's *Country Music Association* – first-ever trade association for a single genre of music

1961 - *CMA* establishes *Country Music Hall of Fame* (first inductees: Jimmie Rodgers, Fred Rose and Hank Williams)

1963 - June - *Music City News* magazine founded by Faron Young

1964 - *Country Music Foundation* chartered in Nashville

1965 - 5 May - Departure for Nashville

 - 12 October - Return to UK from Nashville

1967 - July - Launch of BBC Radio 1's *Country Meets Folk* (simulcast on Radio 2)

 - Opening of *Country Music Hall of Fame & Museum* in Nashville

 - October - Nashville's *DJ Convention* tied in with *Grand Ole Opry* birthday celebration and *CMA Awards Show* for first time

1968 - 4 March - Launch of BBC Radio 2's *Country Style*

 - July - Issue No.1 of *Opry* magazine

 - September - *BCMA (British Country Music Association)* founded by Goff Greenwood, Jim Marshall & Mike Storey

 - November - First article for *Opry*

1969 - 5 March - Opening of *Nashville Room* (W. London)

- March - Opening of *Ponderosa* (near Portsmouth, Hampshire)

- 5 April - First *Wembley International Festival of Country & Western Music* (one-day event)

- c. May - Pat Campbell replaces David Allan on *Country Style*

- July - Hired as agent for *Ponderosa*

- c. August - *Country Meets Folk* shifted to Radio 2 (simulcast on Radio 1)

- 12-24 October - First *BCMA*-organised trip to Nashville

- December - Final issue of *Opry* magazine

1970 - February - First issue of *Country Music People*

- April - Radio debut, as guest record reviewer on BBC Radio 2's *Country Style*

- September - Leave Smithfield Market employment

- 6 October - BBC Radio London launched on 1458kHz/206metres/94.9VHF frequency

- December - First *CMP* issue as Editor (Initial Term)

1971 - 10-11 April - 3rd *Wembley Festival* (first to be a two-day event)

- 21 May - Launch of *London Country* on BBC Radio London

- 27 August - Commence hosting *London Country* (via recording)

1972 - 20 March - Harcourt Powel dies

- 12-15 April - First *Country Music Fan Fair* held at Nashville's *Municipal Auditorium*

- May - Margaret Tschirren replaces Irvine Brookes as *LC* producer

- September - Final broadcast of *Country Meets Folk*

- September - Formation of *Saguenay Music* publishing company

- 30 September - Launch of *Up Country*, weekly one-hour show on BBC Radio 2, recorded at *Nashville Room* & featuring (initially) British talent

- Oct.- Dec. - 6-week trip to US & Canada, including 3-week stay in Nashville with Tex Ritter & visit to Florida (w. Tom T. Hall, etc.)

1973 - June - Last edition of *Country Style*

- July - Launch of *Country Club* on BBC Radio 2

1974 - January - Opening of *Tennessee Club* (Wimbledon, S.W. London)

- April - Opening of *Four-On-The-Floor* Country Music Club (Hounslow, Middlesex)

- November - Departure for 5-week trip to USA and Canada

- December - Appearance on Hairl Hensley WSM all-night radio show

1975 - May - *CMP* article: *London Country* 'Four Years Not Out' interview with David Redshaw

1976 - 17-19 April - 8th *Wembley Festival* (first to be a three-day event)

- 4 December - Interview with Don Ford for *Four On The Floor* magazine

- December - Final *CMP* issue as Editor (Initial Term)

1977 - January - Thailand holiday with Dave Travis

- August - First of two *CMP Powel's Point Of View* articles, commemorating *London Country*'s 6th Anniversary

1978 - May - 100th edition of *CMP*

- July - First All-British Country Music Festival held at Brighton

1979 - 10 March - *London Country* broadcasts from *Ideal Home Exhibition*

1980 - 4-7 April - 12th *Wembley Festival*, first under name of sponsors, *Marlborough*, also, first to be spread over 4 days, attracting 37,700

 - August - First *Peterborough Festival of Country Music* organised by Jed Ford

1981 - 17-20 April - 13th *Wembley Festival*, first under title *Silk Cut* (new sponsors)

1982 - 9-12 April - *Silk Cut Festival* attracts 30,000 people (2,000 down on last year)

 - 10 December - Opening of *Mean Fiddler Club* (Harlesden, North London)

1983 - September - First *CMP* issue as editor (Second Term)

 - 30 October - *London Country* broadcasts from *Motor Show*

1984 - March - Opening of Bill Monroe's *Bluegrass Hall of Fame* in Nashville

 - September - Reg Field retires as publisher of *Country Music People*, Bob takes over

 - 15 September - Grand Opening of *CMP* Shop

1986 - July - First ever article (on 1965 Nashville trip) reproduced in full in *CMP*

 - September - 200th edition of *CMP*

 - Betty Powel dies

1987 - July - Sale of *CMP* to Craig Baguley & Jon Philibert

 - August - Craig Baguley listed as *CMP* Managing Editor, Bob as Editor (remaining this way up to and including June, 1988)

1988 - July - Craig Baguley *CMP* Editor, Bob Editorial Consultant

- 1 October - Last ever *London Country* show

- 7 October - Radio London closes down

- 25 October - GLR (Greater London Radio) commences broadcasting on same wavelength as Radio London

 - December - Final *CMP* issue as Editorial Consultant

1989 - 4 February - First *Country Sounds* show, Radio Sussex

 - July - CMP Record Shop bought by Shaun Greenfield

1990 - 14-16 April - 22nd *Wembley Festival* renamed *International Music Festival*

 - 11 August - Last ever *Country Sounds* show

 - August - Move to Thailand

1991 - 30-31 March - 23rd *Wembley International Festival of Country Music* (last until 2012)

2001 - 30 December - Return to UK from Thailand

2002 - February - Move to flat above Tudor Café, Maidstone Rd., Sidcup

2007 - February - Move to 31 Amberley Court, Sidcup Hill

2008 - 18 Sep. - 3 Oct. - Final *BCMA*-organised trip to USA

2009 - 10 April - Aortic heart valve replacement operation at St. Thomas' hospital, London

- April-May - Stay at convalescent home, Herne Bay, Kent

2011 - October - 500th edition of *CMP*

2012 - 26 February - 24th *Wembley International Festival of Country Music* (1-day event)

RECORD OF WEMBLEY FESTIVALS

There is probably more comprehensive data available elsewhere but I've managed to glean the following information from back issues of *Country Music People* magazine, plus other sources, especially the Stan Laundon website: www.stanlaundon.com. For a brief overview of the event's history, see page 6 of *Country Music People*'s September, 1991 issue.

Year	No. days (Att.)	Date(s)	Title
1969	1	5/4 (Sa)	International Festival of C. & W. Music
1970	1	28/3(Sa)	" " " " "
1971	2	10-11/4(Sa-Su)	" " " " "
1972	2	1-2/4(Sa-Su)	" " " " "
1973	2	21-22/4(Sa-Su)	" " " " "
1974	2	13-14/4(Sa-Su)	" " " " "
1975	2	29-30/3(Sa-Su)	" " " " "
1976	3	17-19/4(Sa-M)	" " " " "
1977	3	9-11/4(Sa-M)	" " " " "
1978	3	25-27/3(Sa-M)	" " " " "
1979	3	14-16/4(Sa-M)	International Festival of Country Music
1980	4 (37,700)	4-7/4(F-M)	Marlborough Int'l Festival of Country Music
1981	4 (32,000)	17-20/4(F-M)	Silk Cut Festival
1982	4 (30,000)	9-12/4(F-M)	" " "
1983	3	2-4/4(Sa-M)	" " "
1984	3	21-23/4(Sa-M)	" " "
1985	3	6-8/4(Sa-M)	" " "
1986	3	29-31/3(Sa-M)	" " "
1987	3	18-20/4(Sa-M)	" " "
1988	3	2-4/4(Sa-M)	International Festival of Country Music
1989	3	25-27/3(Sa-M)	" " " " "
1990	3	14-16/4(Sa-M)	International Music Festival
1991	2	30-31/3(Sa-Su)	" " "
1 9 9 2 – 2 0 1 1			N O F E S T I V A L
2012	1	26/2(Su)	International Festival of Country Music

BOB POWEL TRIBUTES

ALAN POTTER (Radio Presenter)

So sorry to hear of Bobs death. A massive influence in country music & respected writer, broadcaster with a real knowledge & love of the music.

ALBERT LEE (musician)

Gerry Hogan has just passed on the sad news about Bob Powel. He was always very keen on whatever I was involved with and, of course, was a great promoter of country music in the UK, I do hope there are some obits to confirm the fact.

BOB TUBERT (Nashville Exec)

Very sad news....but it was people like him, Pat Campbell and Tony Byworth who did so much to help music city become music city...after all, all of our music started over there and we sometimes forget that. Peace in the valley.

BRIAN CLOUTH (Radio Presenter)

Sad news indeed. He was a larger than life character in the greatest sense and one of the most knowledgeable in the business.

CARROLL BAKER (Canadian country music artist)

I was very sorry to hear the sad news about my friend and friend to all of Country Music, Bob Powell. Although it has been several years since I last had any contact with Bob, he has always remained in my heart as a fine decent man. He once came to Canada and surprised me with a visit to one of my concerts. He was that sort of man.

DAVID BUSSEY (former UK Jim Reeves Fan Club organiser)

I had not been in touch with him since his days at CMP. He was not a big fan of Reeves but always gave support as & when he could. Bob was a big character and will be sadly missed by all his friends.

DAVID CALLISTER (Radio Presenter)

Sad news. He was a great champion of both American and British country music artists and a personal memory I have is appearing live on his London show in the 70s when he played a recording of mine called the TT Hall of Fame. (A tribute to the Isle of Man TT Races). His most lasting contribution to country in UK will certainly be his years editing CMP.

ERIC GUNN (Country music fan)

Although I never met Bob, I do remember all he did for Country Music. He was in there right at the beginning.

ERNIE REED

What a great gentleman.

FRANK JENNINGS (UK country performer)

I knew Bob a long time and had great respect for his detailed knowledge of country music. We always got along pretty good and I think that's because we had similar likes in artists and their music.

GEORGE HAMILTON V (artist)

Very sad news. Bob was a GREAT Guy!!! I remember doing his Radio Show once back around 1987 or 1988 when I was there for Wembley with George IV. We had a FUN time!!!

GILBERT ROUIT (French promoter)

Sad news, Bob still in my mémorial as a Country Music builder in Europe.

GLORIA BRISTOW (UK music publisher)

Very sad news indeed. Bob was certainly *one of the good guys* and the world in general and Country Music in particular was privileged to have him pass this way.

GRAHAM BARKER (photographer)

It is so sad to learn of the circumstances of his death. I had only seen him once since his return from Thailand, but used to spend quite a bit of time with him in the 1980's when I lived in Orpington. Sometimes at his bungalow, sometimes at the shop and sometimes up at the radio studio. He was truly eccentric, and as you will recall his "home" reflected his character! I am sure we could all tell stories about him which would add up to a very entertaining book. He did a lot to establish Country music in the UK.

HELEN MacPHERSON (Radio presenter)

Sad news about Bob Powel, I always remember him about at the Wembley Fests etc but only knew him to say hello! And of course reading his articles.

HOWARD DEE (Irish manager)

This is sad news. Bob was a massive asset to me personally during my early days and would always give me time when I was checking on some information and was never impatient with a greenhorn like me. May he rest in Peace.

JO WALKER-MEADOR (former Execetive Director, CMA)

I am sorry to learn of his death. I have some good memories of Bob and how he loved Country Music and its people.

JOE SUN (US artist)

When I classify folks they go into two categories. Regular folks and then... Characters. Bob fit (albeit a tight one) well into the latter. Characters are those who've, down through the years, made our business of Country Music like a sparkling bottle of fizzy top dollar Champagne. Characters are what make the entertainment business what it is...and Bob marched right along to the tune.

JOHN DAINES (Charley Pride's manager)

Sad indeed. Spent many a good time with Bob. He was there when Gordon Smith and I were working the Opry Mag.

JOHN LOMAX III (Nashville journalist/music exec)

Can't say I can add a lot to what others may be saying but can describe him as a jolly teddy bear of a fellow with vast knowledge of country music. Wonder what he'd make of scene now and this rap-rock infused crap that passes for country!

JOHN McKENZIE (son of photographer, Doug)

My father has asked me to reply to your email as he is in hospital at the moment. He was very sad to hear this news (as were we all, the whole family remembers Bob very fondly).

JON PHILIBERT (UK songwriter/journalist)

I can imagine the response from Nashville. Bob was especially well regarded and remembered there. When Craig (Baguley) and I used to visit on a regular basis and it was known that we were from Country Music People, the next question would invariably be "how's Bob?" even though Bob had long ceased to be owner/editor.

MARIE O'CONNELL (Professional photographer)

A big man, in every sense of the word, both in stature and personality.

PAT McINERNEY (Nashville musician)

I remember him well – he was very kind to me.

PAT TYNAN (UK record promoter)

Sad news. I will never forget Peterborough! Do you recall when he got up in the morning and came down to breakfast and we were still in the bar?

ROGER RYAN (Irish CMA)

Sad news indeed. I think the Wembley Fest in 1969 was the first time I met Bob. He contacted me recently and we exchanged some messages, so I was shocked to hear the sad news of his passing. Last time I actually met him was at the George IV celebrations at the US Ambassador's residence in London.

ROGER WHEATLEY (Record seller)

How very sad. He was a lovely man and my chief regret is that I never managed to see him in the last few years. He will be sorely missed by many people. Many memories of him come flooding back – memories of a friend, a DJ and a writer.

SHAUN GREENFIELD

Very sad to hear of Bob's passing. Even though he was a cantankerous old so and so I still had a soft spot for him.

STACY HARRIS (Nashville journalist)

I didn't know Bob, but was certainly known of him. I'm sorry for our industry's loss.

SUSAN FULLER (Peterborough Festival co-ordinator)

Sad loss. Great man.

TOM GILMORE (Irish journalist)

He was a real gentleman and gave great service to

Country music this side of the Atlantic. With Country Music People, in particular, he helped so many Country artists. Good memories of a good man – may he rest in peace.

TONY BYWORTH – RECOLLECTIONS OF A GOOD FRIEND

Bob Powel was one of the best friends that country music ever had, his knowledge of the music seemed beyond extensive, enabling him to bring incomparable insight into radio programmes and articles alike. As he said, he grew up with country music which provided him with information that was second-to-none, although he did acknowledge, as the years past, I was more familiar with the contemporary scene. Then we both became unenthusiastic with the music as it changed in recent years.

Bob and I were very good friends, although – like everyone – we had our differences of opinion, especially during the early days when we'd meet up pretty regularly. Since Bob's return from Thailand, we didn't see that much of each other although we kept in contact by phone or exchanged snippets of news by email. One of the last times our paths crossed was in 2012, when he and photographer Doug McKenzie came to Knebworth where I staged a concert with George Hamilton IV. Afterwards we went to my house for a couple of hours of pleasant reminiscences. A particularly poignant evening, as all three of these good friends have now passed on.

Our last communication was in April 12, 2014: I was in Florida and emailed him, asking if he'd like me to pick a certain baseball annual that he collected every year. He cheerfully responded: *"what a nice thought, but I happened to get it via the internet this year, but just for you I am about to play 'She broke my heart at Walgreen's and I cried all the way to Sears'."* So, right until the end, his country music knowledge never failed him, this being a reference to a pretty obscure recording by his favourite country comedians, Homer & Jethro. Less than a month later I received the tragic that he had died. Bob Powel was one of a kind. R.I.P.

TREVOR CAIJIO (Editor: "Now Dig This" magazine)

Very sad news. Bob was very helpful to me back in the 1980s when I was launching NDT. Often saw him at Wembley and Radio London. Nice fella.

TRISHA WALKER-CUNNINGHAM (UK born, Nashville based promoter)

Very, very sad to hear the news about Bob. He was one of a kind and I remember the days we all spent together at Wembley. He was a pioneer in his day and I can see his face as if it were yesterday.

VERNELL HACKETT (Nashville journalist)

I am so sorry to hear this. Bob was always very nice to me. I wrote for him for several years and he was a great person to work with.

WILLIE MORGAN (Radio presenter)

Thanks for passing on this sad news. During my time as an RCA plugger, alongside Tommy Loftus, back in the 70s, Bob was always a useful contact, given the Country product our London office was promoting. I always found him a most courteous and good chap to know.

GEORGE HAMILTON IV – Funeral message:

I was shocked and saddened to hear that my good friend Bob had died – he had always been part of my life in Britain, ever since I first met him when I first came here, about 45 years in the 1960s – and then almost every visit afterwards as well as many times in Nashville. He was not only a true friend but also helped my career in so many ways with albums and sleeve notes, interviews and radio broadcasts... he even wrote a book about my early days!

But I was just one of the many of the country music artists he knew and helped. I reckon he must have known everyone back when he was editing Country Music People and had that wonderful programme on Radio London. They were great interviews, just chatting with Bob and never knowing what he'd say next or surprise with some little known fact. He was greatly respected for his great knowledge and helping people.

Bob was not only a great friend to me but also to country music. He will be very sadly missed by many folks. He is in my thoughts and my prayers – I'll be saying a very special one today. Rest in peace, Bob.

BIBLIOGRAPHY

Country Music People magazine. Publ. Country Music Press Ltd. (1970-87), Music Farm Ltd. (1987-2009) and Kickin' Cuts Ltd. (2009-2015).

Opry magazine. Publ. Country Music Enterprises, 98 Courtfield Avenue, Walderslade, nr. Chatham, Kent.

hankwilliamsdiscography.com

Tadoussac: The Sands of Summer - Benny Beattie (Publ. Price-Patterson Ltd., Montreal, Quebec, Canada. ©1994).

Joel Whitburn's Top Country Songs, 1944-2005. (Publ. Record Research Inc., Wisconsin. ©2005).

US National Archives & Records Administration, 8601 Adelphi Rd., College Park, MD 20740-6001.

www.pricefamily.ca/family_tree.php

Billboard magazine (20 September, 1986).

Live fast, love hard: The Faron Young Story – Diane Diekman (Publ. University of Illinois Press. ©2007). www.press.uillinois.edu.

Rough Guide to Thailand. Written & researched by Paul Gray & Lucy Ridout. (8th ed. Publ. 2012). www.roughguides.com.

Tides of Tadoussac – Lewis Evans (Publ. Perry Printing Ltd., Canada, 1982).

The Majestic Stream, the Saguenay: New York Times (1857 – Current File); Aug. 31, 1930; Pro Quest Historical

Newspapers, New York Times (pg.BR5).

Guinness British Hit Singles & Albums (18th ed. publ. 2005).

Four-on-the-Floor magazine, edited by Don Ford (January, 1977).

Are you ready for the Country? – Peter Doggett (Penguin, 2000).

www.mountvernon.org/research-collections/.../elizabeth-willing-powel/

The Storyteller's Nashville – Tom T. Hall (Publ. Doubleday, 1979).

Mr. Music Man – My life in Showbiz – Mervyn Conn with Andrew Crofts (Publ. Tonto Books Ltd., 2010). ©Mervyn Conn & Andrew Crofts.

BCMA Yearbook & Directory (1970).

BMI Country Hits 1944-75. (Publ. Broadcast Music, Inc. ©1976).

Country & Western Roundabout (Ed. C.R.F. Benson, 21 Roseacres, Takeley, nr. Dunmow, Essex, 1964-68).

Country Radio Seminar. www.theboot.com/country-radio-seminar-2013.

www.abbotsholme.co.uk/Abbotsholmes-History

http://en.wikipedia.org/wiki/Rex_Allen

http://en.wikipedia.org/wiki/Baseball

http://en.wikipedia.org/wiki/CMA_Music_Festival

www.hotngold.co.uk/Otr/nashvillecmahistory.html

http://en.wikipedia.org/wiki/Canada_Steamship_Lines

www.shipspotting.com/gallery/photo.php?lid=66828

http://en.wikipedia.org/wiki/Tommy_Collins_(country_music)

https://en.wikipedia.org/wiki/Concorde

http://en.wikipedia.org/wiki/Country_Music_Hall_of_Fame

http://en.wikipedia.org/wiki/The_Establishment_(club)_
and_Museum

www.lizlyle.lofgrens.org/RmOlSngs/RTOS-
FadedCoat.html

http://en.wikipedia.org/wiki/October_Crisis

http://en.wikipedia.org/wiki/Jack_Good_(producer)

http://en.wikipedia.org/wiki/Grand_Ole_Opry

http://en.wikipedia.org/wiki/Homer_and_Jethro

http://en.wikipedia.org/wiki/Harlan_Howard

http://en.wikipedia.org/wiki/Ideal_Home_Show

www.stanlaundon.com/bio.html

www.ideal-
homes.org.uk/bromley/assets/galleries/bickley/lauriston-
house

http://en.wikipedia.org/wiki/Bill_Mack

http://en.wikipedia.org/wiki/McGee_Brothers

http://en.wikipedia.org/wiki/Montreal_Expos

https://en.wikipedia.org/wiki/British_International_Moto
r_Show

http://en.wikipedia.org/wiki/Pattaya

http://en.wikipedia.org/wiki/Players'_Theatre

http://en.wikipedia.org/wiki/Powel_House

http://en.wikipedia.org/wiki/Samuel_Powel

http://en.wikipedia.org/wiki/Powell_(surname)

http://en.wikipedia.org/wiki/Quebec_Winter_Carnival

http://en.wikipedia.org/wiki/BBC_London_94.9

www.bbc.co.uk/london/content/articles/2007/02/08/bb
clondonradio_history_fea...

http://en.wikipedia.org/wiki/Tex_Ritter

http://en.wikipedia.org/wiki/Harry_Secombe

http://en.wikipedia.org/wiki/Sevenoaks

http://en.wikipedia.org/wiki/Sidcup

http://en.wikipedia.org/wiki/Sillery,_Quebec_City

http://en.wikipedia.org/wiki/Lucille_Starr

http://en.wikipedia.org/wiki/BBC_Sussex

http://en.wikipedia.org/wiki/Screaming_Lord_Sutch

http://en.wikipedia.org/wiki/Tadoussac,_Quebec

http://en.wikipedia.org/wiki/Thailand

http://en.wikipedia.org/wiki/Tupolev_Tu-144

http://en.wikipedia.org/wiki/1973_Paris_Air_Show_Crash

http://en.wikipedia.org/wiki/List_of_songs_written_by_
Hank_Williams

http://en.wikipedia.org/wiki/MS_The_World

http://en.wikipedia.org/wiki/Steve_Young_(musician)

PHOTO ACKNOWLEDGMENTS

www.dougmckenziephotography.co.uk

www.boroughphotos.org/bexley/pcd_1840/

www.flickr.com/photos/mynameismisty/!

www.ideal-homes.org.uk/bromley/assets/galleries/bickley/lauriston-house

https://plus.google.com/105022822559785679267/photos2hl=en&.socfid=web;lu;kp;p

http://commons.wikimedia.org/wiki/File:Tadoussac_-_Maison_Fletcher(

Pro Quest Historical Newspapers – New York Times (1857-Current File) August 16, 1950 (pg 53)

www.beauxvillages.qc.ca/villages_fr_tadoussac

News Shopper, Mega House, Crest View Drive, Petts Wood, Orpington, Kent, BR5 1BT.

www.flickr.com/photos/55935853@NOO/2664012482

About The Author

Tom Baker, the youngest of four children, was born and brought up in Dulwich, South-East London and educated at Salesian College, Battersea, by an order of Catholic priests and brothers.

Among a wide range of occupations, he has, at various times, been an Insurance Clerk, Civil Servant and landscape gardener. Then, in 1989, he gave up employment altogether to care full-time for his mother.

A lifelong country music fan (first two records bought: Battle of New Orleans by Lonnie Donegan and Rawhide by Frankie Laine), pop historian and occasional singer/songwriter/musician, he has lived in Sidcup for the past 37 of his 64 years. *Heart of a Fan* is his first published work.

Index

INDEX – Song Titles

INDEX

Bushell, Gary   251
Bussey, David   55, 86
Butler, Carl & Pearl   52
Butler, Tom   63-4
Butlin, Billy   41
Byrd, Jerry   113
Byrds   136
Byworth, Tony   4, 33, 57, 72, 77-80, 91-3, 102, 105-6, 108,
110-13, 116, 119, 126, 128, 170, 185-93, 195, 201, 209, 212,
261, 271, 278, 301, 308, 336 (Illustr.), 341 (Illustr.), 342
(Illustr.)
'Byworth-Wootton International'   92, 191-3, 197
Cackett, Alan   55, 87,89, 102, 106, 188
Calgary Stampede   *51*
Camden, Roger   128, 281
Campbell, Archie   50, 104
Campbell, Glen   107, 194
Campbell, Mike   294
Campbell, Pat   170, 57-9, 117, 130, 165
Canadian Steamship Lines   7
Carmania ship   52
Carter, David   119, 121
Carter, Maybelle   156
Carter, Wilf   224
Casey   22, 162-4
Cash, Dave   102, 297
Cash, Johnny   57, 85, 93, 101, 107, 123, 187, 195, 199,
202, 205, 310
Cash, Rosanne   310
Cash, Tommy   195
Chalker, Bryan   4, 33, 54-5, 57, 153
Chandler, Colin   105

CPSIA information can be obtained at www.ICGtesting.com
Printed in the USA
LVOW07s1954131015

458083LV00030B/971/P

9 781514 303474